Quiet All Along

A Skeptic's Journey into the Unexplained

Julia Pax

Contents

Dedication

I dedicate these pages to The Quiet Ones, who, despite their silence, know that there is more to life than what meets the eye.

To The Quiet Ones

There are chapters of our lives that the world never sees—realities we mask with humor and knowledge we hide with ignorance. This book is my attempt to come clean and share the parts of myself I have always kept sealed.

Before we proceed, I'd like to address the elephant in the room: I am not a writer. I'm a marketing manager with a psychology degree who grew up in the shadow of a dictatorship in Eastern Europe and now lives a quiet life in a big city in America. I've been a good student and a troublemaker. I've been married and divorced, loved and betrayed. I've known joy, despair, and everything in between. Through it all, I have been an ordinary person trying to make sense of extraordinary things.

This is not the story of my whole life, but of my interactions with the unexplained. For as long as I can remember, I have had unexplained encounters that left me with more questions than answers. After losing my father, those questions became urgent. Where do we go? Do we simply fade to black, or is there something more?

Everything you are about to read is precisely as it happened. I am not here to be right; I am here to share my story and let you be the judge of what it all means.

My hope is to reach others like me—those who have been called an old soul or told they don't quite seem to be from here. People who see the root of the matter a little too clearly, who understand things a little too quickly, and who have learned to play a part, wear a mask, and keep their true thoughts to themselves.

I know—I've been there. Sometimes I still am, as this insidious feeling doesn't go away easily.

I see you on the subreddits and in the chat rooms, where you find a space to whisper the things you have seen. Just like you, I have found myself in a world that makes no sense—a world quick to label what it doesn't understand. This book is a mirror I am holding up for you. Look into it and see how beautiful you are—how unique and special.

You do not need to be enlightened or carry all the secrets of the world. You don't need a degree in metaphysics or a glowing aura. You only need the courage to ask questions and share what you know.

Tell your story, even if it doesn't make sense to you. It might make sense to others. Your experiences are important. Learn to listen to them. In breaking your silence, you can help others find and follow their own inner voices, too.

So here I am, terrified but determined. Letting the fear of stigma silence you is a coward's game. I have been called many things, and most of them were true. The irony is that no one ever called me a coward, even when I was one for the longest time.

The moment I chose to share my story, the mask I'd worn for a lifetime began to crumble. The fear gave way to a profound sense of release. I see now it was never about the judgment of others. The real battle was won when I changed the story I told myself in the mirror.

Seekers, travelers, experiencers, and all other kindred spirits—I am here, too. And with this book, I am saying, "Yes, me too." If it helps even one person feel brave enough to share their own truth, then my purpose is fulfilled.

Chapter 1: Arms

That's what you're all supposed to be. Vessels of Truth. All of you. Try to help others find themselves by showing yourself as you are. Make life better for them, for others. You can! You do! Keep doing it! Do it boldly! Bravely!

—Message from The Unseen

I have always been a collector of "firsts"—not of stamps or Barbie dolls, but of the earliest events people can recall from their lives. It's a habit that often raises eyebrows. When asked about the earliest thing they can remember, most people just don't have much to say. And I can't hold it against them. According to numerous studies on infantile amnesia, the majority of adults cannot recall specific moments from their lives before the age of three.

It isn't the blank look that I find odd, but the lack of curiosity behind it.

Don't you want to remember the first moment you were alive in this world? Most people reply with a perplexed "No," and the academic world has offered a well-documented explanation for this reaction, which will be discussed shortly.

I suppose what gives me pause is not wanting to know—not caring. I'd often sit for hours, delving into the archives of my mind, tracing the threads of my earliest moment of awareness. In that sense, I am lucky. For me, the answer was always there, presented to me as a gift.

What is your oldest memory? I can tell you mine. It's not just the first time I remember opening my eyes to the world. In all honesty, it is the first time I witnessed the veil between the seen and the unseen shimmer and part. It's a memory as old as I am, yet it feels as if it happened yesterday. When I close my eyes, I'm right there, at the exact moment it happened.

I remember the feeling of arms holding me—bony and not as comfortable as my mother's. The grasp stirs a nascent irritation, a desire to awaken and escape the strange grip. Slowly, my eyelids flutter open. I see my mother's robe: a navy blue with scattered light pink and turquoise flowers. The singular, comforting scent of home drifts from the fabric, a scent I know better than anything.

For a second, a vivid scene of my mother's presence flashes through my mind. Her arms are soft, and she smells like the best thing in the world. I almost cozy up just at the thought, but these foreign arms and this smell are still bothering me. Beneath the scent of the robe, another smell exists—a smoky, sweet aroma that is pleasant but foreign. It lacks the resonance of my mother's embrace, and the irritation I feel amplifies.

This is not her. This is obviously not her. I might be a baby, but I am not so easily fooled. I'd never mistake this impostor for my mother.

As the person holding me turns, I see my mother and another person. They are standing before me, ready to leave. I am unsure how I know they are leaving, but they are. At first, it doesn't bother me. Nothing really does. But then, a cold flash of realization hits me: *I'm being deceived.* They have purposefully dressed this imposter in my mother's robe. This person is holding me as if she is my mother, but it is all nothing but a lie.

A rush of insult, followed by a surge of pure, infant rage, engulfs me, culminating in one question: *Do they think so little of me that they believe such a shallow trick would work?* I am offended, I am furious, and I will show them. My revenge will be a scream—a mighty, earth-shattering sound that will surely teach them never to try to fool me again. They will see.

As I prepare to unleash my vengeful concerto, an abrupt thought, clear and calm, almost amused, speaks to me: *They are trying to make you comfortable. It is for your own good—or what they think was your good—that they have deceived you. Are you not comfortable?* I don't question where the message comes from. I simply accept it as a given. Whoever is communicating to me makes sense, and somehow, in that instant, I know the arms holding me are my grandmother's. I have met her before, though I couldn't recall when or where. Somehow, I instinctually knew her. And with that conviction, the solace returns.

I am safe. This deception is out of love. She is holding me. My anger, I decide, was premature, and my plans for vengeance were a little too hasty. I suppose I was a bit of a hothead from the get-go.

I cozy into the new scent, accepting the reality of the situation: Some arms are better than no arms at all. Stillness returns. I slip back into the wholeness of the night sky in my mind—a well-known, boundless place where I remember I have come from. A place of tranquility and safety. A sense of home.

This was the first hint of a type of truth that would later lead me on a lifelong quest for answers.

My mother later confirmed this was the first time she left me with someone else. I was about two months old. At that moment, I was in this body, but I was also somewhere else. I was in an infinite place, and I had already experienced anger, reason, and ego. I knew ego.

The Paradox of Early Consciousness

Over the years, this memory has stayed with me. I brought it up first as a small child, then as a teenager, and then later in life. It was a thread I never let go of, and my stubbornness was rewarded. When I was grown, I mentioned it to my mother again, and this time, she was more comfortable speaking.

She opened up about her own experiences, her own glimpses behind the veil. Much later, she told me about a house she visits in her dreams and a family she has somewhere else. These "confessions," however, only came after I had grown up and found the courage to "confess" my connection to something more.

My mother's story is a fascinating one. She grew up in the countryside with no television or books. Her father was a farm vet, and her mother had what she called "witchy tendencies." As the only girl in a family with four brothers, she was often overlooked. Boys were considered more valuable. She used to draw girls in big puffy dresses—dresses she had never seen in real life, on TV, or in books.

When asked what she was drawing, she would simply say, "This is from when I was older." To a busy farmer and his wife, this was nothing more than child's nonsense. But what if it wasn't? What if she was remembering?

Her story was one of the catalysts for this book. I cannot and will not hide anymore. Confessing my authentic self to my mother unlocked hers. This is what happens when we are authentic. We inspire others. All of a sudden, we are not alone. There are a lot of people like us, and speaking is no longer scary.

It feels as though we are told to get educated, get jobs, pay taxes, and reproduce in service of a larger structure. We are told we are free, but freedom only exists as long as we don't question the system too much. The truth of God, Source, and the Universe often seems to have no place between deadlines, KPIs, and profit margins.

Scientists who research these topics are mocked, spiritualists are called frauds, and experiencers are given medicine prescriptions. That's the end of the conversation. But what about those of us who are healthy and sane, and yet have these unusual experiences? Society seems silent about us because, according to its rules, we do not exist.

We come into this world, and before we can even open our mouths to scream, we are given a name, a nationality, and a gender role. We are taught that babies are just babies, and that they do not have complex cognitive processes. This is taught in schools and universities, becoming a widely-accepted fact we mistake for truth. But how do we know? Has a baby ever said, "I don't have complex cognitive processes" right after being born? No.

In fact, there are countless tales of children remembering past lives, pre-birth memories, and imaginary friends who turned out to be real people from another time. The documented accounts are all there; all you have to do is look.

My memory from when I was two months old, with its complex emotions and self-awareness, seems to be in full contrast with the mainstream theories that a baby can't have a notion of identity or complex thought at such a young age. In fact, according to these theories, my account simply shouldn't be possible. While psychology acknowledges that babies have procedural memory, my experience was a conscious, self-aware, and self-referential one.

This creates a compelling paradox: How can a two-month-old have such a complex recollection when the cognitive structures for autobiographical memory are undeveloped? It suggests that the mental frameworks of initial autobiographical recollection are incomplete. Alternatively, it points to a form of sentience and remembrance in early infancy that operates outside the understood neural and linguistic frameworks.

Psychology and Infantile Amnesia

The impression of my grandmother's embrace was so clear that I found myself compelled to find out why I could hold onto it, even though, according to all conventional reason, I shouldn't have been able to. This propelled me on a journey to the same field I had studied in college: psychology. I hoped to find a definitive account, but what I found instead were theories that dismissed my story before I was even able to explain it.

I learned that psychology explains away early childhood memories. This curtain of forgetfulness is called infantile amnesia. It's a well-documented aspect of human development where most adults cannot retrieve information of specific situations or experiences from before the age of three or four. What is recalled from ages three to six tends to be scarce or fragmented. The formation of a life narrative—which involves a sense of time passing and a sense of self—typically stabilizes around five to six years of age[1] .

Traditional theories of the mind offer two main categories of understanding for this amnesia.

The first psychological model emphasizes the late development of recollection capacity. It suggests the neural structures or mental faculties needed for forming and retaining autobiographical remembrances are completely absent in early life. Think of it as a house under construction. The very capacity for retaining the past simply isn't built yet in early life. For instance, Jean Piaget[2] proposed that infants under eighteen to twenty-four months lack symbolic representation, making it impossible to access past information.

---

1. Hayne, H. (2004). "Infant memory development: A guide to graphs, queries, and conclusions." *Journal of Experimental Child Psychology.*

2. Piaget, J. (1952). *The Origins of Intelligence in Children.*

He also suggested that children up to five to seven years old lack the cognitive structures required to organize events chronologically, which is crucial for coherent life recollections. Similarly, other theories point to the later development of a "self-concept" or "autonoetic consciousness"—the ability to mentally time travel and recognize a recollection as a past occurrence—as prerequisites for autobiographical memory.

The second category of theories focuses on the functional disappearance of initial recollections. It indicates that these remembrances are formed, but then become inaccessible—in other words, they are there, but we can't get to them. Sigmund Freud suggested they might be repressed due to their disturbing content. More contemporary mental and linguistic accounts propose that the non-verbal encoding in infancy becomes inaccessible as language skills develop and the mind's architecture becomes "saturated with language." Changes in an individual's identity or worldview over time can also render older records of reality inaccessible.

To hear it, you'd think my two-month-old self was a blank slate, not a vessel of pure, nascent rage. And this view is supported by a large body of academic work on child development.

As I delved deeper, I found emerging evidence that was already beginning to complicate these traditional views. It turns out infants are more capable than those old theories give them credit for.

For example, pioneering research by Carolyn Rovee-Collier[3] showed that infants as young as two months old can learn procedural tasks, such as kicking their legs to make a mobile move. They can even retain that information for several days. This indicates that the capacity for learning is present, even if the type of memory (procedural versus autobiographical) differs.

More recent findings further suggest that recollections can be encoded in the brain during the first years of life, with activity in the hippocampus correlating with retention strength even in infants. While this correlation is strongest in infants older than twelve months, it appears that the recording of past events occurs earlier than we thought.

---

3. Rovee-Collier, C. (1999). "The development of infant memory." *Current Directions in Psychological Science.*

The question then shifts from "Are memories formed at all?" to "What happens to them over time?"—whether they are not converted to long-term storage or simply become inaccessible. Some studies even indicate that very young infants can retain that cognitive content over the entire infantile-amnesia period if they are reminded.

The "complementary processes account" attempts to integrate these findings with a single idea: Infantile amnesia is a result of a combination of two things. First, early recollections are of lower quality, and second, our later retrieval processes diminish in efficiency. This theory explains why young infants can retain that mental content if reminded.

Beyond the Brain

My research transformed into a personal mission to understand if my encounter was unique, or if it was part of a larger, unseen world. I began to explore the ideas of prenatal consciousness and memory, finding out that the academic world was catching up to what some have known for centuries. Prenatal retention is increasingly recognized as a crucial aspect of human development, fostering mother-infant attachment and ensuring survival.

I found that substantial evidence for fetal learning has been identified at around thirty weeks after conception. The study employs various techniques to measure this, primarily focusing on implicit or procedural learning rather than explicit recollection of memories, as an adult might have. These include a number of techniques.

Classical Conditioning: Studies[4] show that fetuses as early as thirty-two weeks of gestation can demonstrate conditioning, responding to stimuli after repeated pairings. For example, in one experiment, researchers played a tone followed by a gentle vibration on the mothers' abdomens. After several repetitions, the fetuses began to respond with a change in heart rate to the tone alone, demonstrating they had learned to associate the sound with the vibration.

---

4. Hepper, P. G. (1996). "Fetal memory: An update." *The "aware" fetus: A consequence of first trimester complexity.*

Habituation: This involves repetitively stimulating the fetus and observing a gradual decrease in response, indicating that the fetus has become accustomed to the stimulus. For example, if a researcher shines a light on the mother's belly, the fetus might startle or increase its heart rate. With each repetition, the fetus's response lessens, showing that it has "habituated" to the light and is now "remembering" it.

Exposure Learning: This technique involves presenting a stimulus, such as a television theme tune, to the fetus in the womb. After birth, newborns exposed to the tune in utero show physiological changes, like a decrease in heart rate, upon hearing it again—a reaction not observed in unexposed newborns. This recognition is strong for a few days, but diminishes without continued exposure.

These findings collectively demonstrate that the unborn child is an "aware, reacting human being"[5] from the sixth month onward (and even earlier), capable of living an active emotional life. The fetus can see, hear, taste, and learn in utero, and can also feel. For instance, the mother's voice is clearly heard from inside the womb, and the fetus can differentiate between speech sounds, showing a preference for the mother's native language after birth. Infants also prefer their mothers' smell, having memorized their scents as fetuses. This points directly at my recollection of my mother's smell and ability to immediately identify the distinction between my mother and grandmother.

While science focuses on the "how," I was drawn to the "why"—the deeper meaning. From this point on, I decided to explore these ideas independently from the traditional paradigm.

From a philosophical and transpersonal psychology perspective, a human being is considered a "stream of consciousness." This stream expresses itself through a physical body that forms around its own nonphysical matrix or astral model-body. Within this framework, the unborn child is the expression of a preexisting non-physical entity.

This is a human being who is trying to re-embody after having been born many previous times on this planet. This perspective aligns with concepts of reincarnation and suggests that consciousness exists prior to and independent of birth.

---

5. DeCasper, A. J., & Spence, M. J. (1986). "Prenatal maternal speech influences newborns' perception of speech sounds."

Consciousness is understood as a fundamental resonance with the Truth, the Source, the great I Am, or the experience of unconditional love. This bond exists from the very beginning of life, and even prior to being born on Earth.

Proponents of this view suggest that babies, as embryos, are closest to pure consciousness. They also propose that memory resides in the metaphysical portion of us. This record of the soul endures from life to life, implying an extraneurological system that stores information beyond the cerebral confines.

The scientific evidence for fetal learning and retention establishes a foundation for initial sensory input, even if primarily implicit. The transpersonal and philosophical views then provide a conceptual structure to interpret my explicit, conscious two-month-old awareness as a continuation of a pre-existing consciousness. The idea of an "extraneurological record-keeping system" offers a potential mechanism for remembrances that precede the developed hippocampus or language.

This indicates that human consciousness is not just a product of our brains. Instead, it might be an enduring part of our life, interacting with our developing physical bodies. My recollection of anger and reason at two months old seems to suggest this pre-existing consciousness brings with it not just awareness, but also nascent cognitive and emotional capacities. Can it be that these are far more developed than conventional psychology currently acknowledges for the age?

Innate Knowledge and A Priori Concepts

My recollection of the night sky as home resonates with philosophical concepts of "innate knowledge" and "eternal being." This is not a vague notion, but a known place, suggesting a pre-intellectual or a priori grasp of reality. When considering this, I am drawn to several philosophical foundations.

Plato's Theory of Recollection (Anamnesis[6]): Plato posits the pre-existence of the human essence, which he believed to be immortal. This essence knows the "truth" before entering the body. Learning, therefore, is not the acquisition of new knowledge, but the

6. Plato's dialogues *Meno* and *Phaedo.*

retrieval of what this essence already holds from the "world of ideas." This innate knowing can be awakened by sensory experience or Socratic inquiry.

Descartes' Innate Ideas[7] **:** René Descartes is traditionally associated with the doctrine that certain ideas, such as those of God, eternal truths, and true and immutable natures, are innate. On some occasions, he even argued for a more radical view: that all ideas, including sensory ones, are innate in the mind, formed by the mind on the occasion of sensory stimulation.

Gottfried Wilhelm Leibniz[8] **:** Leibniz proposed a universe composed of non-composite, immaterial, soul-like entities called "monads." These monads are "windowless," meaning they do not interact with each other in a causal sense, but they mirror the entire universe. As part of his philosophical system, Leibniz also discussed innate ideas, suggesting that knowledge is inherent within the monad itself, unfolding according to a pre-established harmony ordained by God.

Immanuel Kant[9] **:** Kant introduced the crucial distinction between a priori knowledge (independent of sensory input) and a posteriori knowledge (based on observation). He explored "synthetic a priori" judgments, which are less trivial truths known independently of direct experience. Kant wrestled with similar issues as earlier rationalists regarding the origins of fundamental concepts, even as he placed boundaries on human knowledge in the sphere of empirical data.

Aside from philosophical speculation, there is growing evidence from psychology and transpersonal studies that children possess a rich and remarkable inner life. They have an inborn and fully present capacity to connect with the divine. This natural spirituality is seen as integral to the human constitution, linking brain, mind, and body, and is considered a biologically based, identifiable, and measurable aspect of development. Children

---

7. Descartes, R. (1641). *Meditations on First Philosophy.*

8. Leibniz, G. W. (1714) *Monadology* and (1704) *New Essays on Human Understanding.*

9. Kant, I. (1781). *Critique of Pure Reason.*

are described as hardwired to relate with the divine, and are ready to dialogue with God and perceive His guidance.

Observations suggest that young children often express extremely wise or insightful things. Some pose profound philosophical challenges that get to the heart of life and death and demonstrate an ability to see beneath the surface of the material world. These moments are considered similar to those described by mystics and can serve as touchstones for lasting personal growth.

One documented case describes a three- to four-year-old boy who, during a moment of altered consciousness, recalled his "self as nameless, formless, and infinite." He said he "transcended all recollections," perceiving "blankness or emptiness as an immensity extending to infinity." This momentous revelation of an ethereal, boundless self at a very young age resonates with my "night sky" remembrance.

Transpersonal psychology explores children's capacity for genuine occurrences of the supernatural, oneness, and interrelatedness. This can include a sense of energy pulsating in all objects (whether animate or not), a self that is incorporeal, and a sense of continuity between life and death. My sense that the vastness of the cosmos is the ancestral home from which I came finds resonance in philosophical concepts of innate knowledge and prior being. This is not just a vague notion, but a place imprinted within me, suggesting a pre-cognitive or a priori understanding of the nature of being.

The three- to four-year-old boy's description of a "nameless, formless, and infinite self" strengthens this resonance. It indicates how my own "vastness" moment is not unique, but rather an archetypal descent into a deeper, transcendent realm.

Children, being closer to "pure consciousness," might simply access it more readily. This implies that the core of my exploration might be an inherent, remembered fundamental knowing rather than learned knowledge.

Reincarnation, Pre-Existence, and Precognition

My assertion that there are many children who remember past lives and exhibit other unusual abilities is strongly supported by systematic inquiry and anecdotal confirmation from various fields.

I was drawn to Dr. Ian Stevenson's work on past life recollections[10] . Dr. Stevenson is a psychiatrist who dedicated decades to investigating cases of young children who claimed to remember previous lives, beginning his investigation in 1961. These children started recounting previous lives at between two and three years of age, and typically ceased to do so by six to seven years of age. They made their statements spontaneously, without hypnotic regression. Their reports often included verifiable details about a deceased individual, such as names, locations, and habits.

Stevenson's rigorous methodology involved verifying these details against public records or eyewitness testimony. A notable finding was that over 70 percent of the previous personalities in these cases had died by unnatural or violent means, often suddenly.

Aside from verbal memories, many children exhibited physical manifestations such as birthmarks or birth defects. These matched wounds from their previous lives and provided "tangible evidence of carryover" from one life to another. Furthermore, these children often displayed behavioral correlates linked to their purported past lives, including emotional longing for the previous family, phobias related to the mode of death, and repetitive play that reenacted the previous occupation or death scene.

Stevenson's investigation found these cases occurring worldwide, not exclusively in cultures believing in reincarnation. His inquiries also challenged the "faulty recollection" explanation, showing reports tended to weaken over time rather than strengthen.

Physical Evidence[11]

The Boy with the Birthmark Wounds: One well-documented case involved an Indian boy who had a set of birthmarks on his chest. He claimed to remember being a soldier, killed by a shotgun blast. They were able to find accounts of the man the child was identifying as. An investigation of the deceased individual's autopsy report stated that the birthmarks on the boy's chest precisely matched the entry and exit wounds from the shotgun blast.

---

10. Stevenson, I. (1974). *Twenty Cases Suggestive of Reincarnation.*

11. Stevenson, I. (1997). *Where Reincarnation and Biology Intersect.*

The Child with Missing Fingers: Another case was of a boy born in India with stubs for fingers on his right hand. He had very early childhood memories of a life where he had his fingers cut off by a fodder-chopping machine.

Behavioral Correlates

The Girl with a Phobia of Buses: A girl in Sri Lanka screamed whenever she was carried near a bus. When she was old enough to speak, she recalled a past life where she was a young girl who drowned after a bus knocked her into a flooded rice paddy. An investigation found a family that had lost a girl in a similar way.

The Child Who Reenacted His Death: In a case from Burma, a child had a birthmark that corresponded to a wound from a sword. The child later reenacted his death in play.

Stevenson's work emphasizes these cases weren't isolated. He often found a combination of tangible and behavioral data, plus details they described that he could verify and quantify. He also noted that the birthmarks corresponding to fatal wounds were often bizarre and irregular, like entry and exit wounds from a bullet. About 20 percent of the children also reported "interval memories"—recollections of the period between the previous personality's death and their own birth—which presented striking similarities to near-death experiences.

Stevenson's systematic exploration moves the discussion from mere anecdotal "nonsense" to a field of serious, though controversial academic investigation. The existence of physical correlates like birthmarks adds a layer of objective evidence, challenging explanations based on theories of the mind or culture. This suggests a deeper mechanism for memory transfer or the continuity of consciousness. This kind of proof points to something more than a remembered story. And it implies that my own vivid recollection, while unique, might be part of a broader, more common—but often suppressed—reservoir of information.

Aside from my own personal story and the academic findings, I was also able to find examples of other children, some of whom remembered entire past lives.

James Leininger, the Reincarnated Pilot[12] **:** At the age of two, James began having intense, vivid nightmares of a plane crash. He would shout phrases like "airplane crash on fire" and "little man can't get out!" while slamming his toy airplanes into a coffee table. When his parents asked him the name of the boat he had flown off of, he responded with "Natoma." An online search conducted by his father, Bruce Leininger, later revealed the USS Natoma Bay, a WWII escort carrier. Over time, James provided more specific details, including the name of his friend, Jack Larsen, and the location of his death, which he said resulted from being shot down by the Japanese over Iwo Jima. James's parents were able to identify the pilot whose life and death matched their son's statements: a young man named Lt. James M. Huston, Jr., who was killed on March 3, 1945, when his plane crashed during the Battle of Iwo Jima. A crucial aspect of this case is the documented presence of statements made by James's parents before they identified James Huston, Jr., which provides a measure of insulation against accusations of retroactive fabrication or embellishment.

Ryan Hammons, the Hollywood Agent[13] **:** At the age of three, Ryan began recounting a life as a Hollywood agent who had died four decades before his birth. He expressed a longing to return to his "other family" in Hollywood, and recounted details about his life, including his occupation, his home, his love of tap dancing, and his multiple wives. The process of verification was particularly rigorous. Ryan's mother, Cyndi, brought home a book about Hollywood, and Ryan pointed to a man in a photograph, stating, "That's me." A film archivist was later able to identify the man in the photograph as a relatively obscure figure named Marty Martyn, a dancer, actor, and agent who died in 1964. A total of fifty-five of Ryan's statements about Martyn's life were later corroborated through public records and by speaking to Martyn's surviving daughter. The sheer number of accurate, obscure details found in this case is considered to be suggestive of an anomalous recollection. It is also worth mentioning that Ryan's account was not perfect. He was incorrect about certain details, such as the cause of Martyn's death, and his cremation.

---

12. Leininger, B., & Leininger, A. (2009). *Soul Survivor: The Reincarnation of a World War II Fighter Pilot.*

13. Tucker, J. B. (2013). *Return to Life: Extraordinary Cases of Children Who Remember Past Lives.*

Cameron Macaulay, the Boy from Barra[14]**:** The case of Cameron Macaulay from Glasgow, Scotland, highlights the intense emotional distress that can accompany these accounts of a previous life. From a young age, Cameron began to narrate vivid tales of a previous life in which he claimed to have resided on the remote Isle of Barra in the Outer Hebrides. He described a white house with a commanding view of the street, a black-and-white dog, and a father named Shane Robertson. Cameron's emotional longing for his "Barra mother" and family escalated so severely that his current mother, Norma, decided to take him to the island in an effort to ease his distress. Accompanied by a documentary crew and Dr. Jim Tucker, the family's trip provided significant corroboration. Cameron was able to recognize landmarks and the white house he had described and drawn countless times, despite never having been to the island. The airport on Barra is famous for its unique feature of planes landing directly on the beach, a detail Cameron had recalled. The family also discovered a Robertson family who had indeed lived in the house at the time Cameron's memories suggested. However, there were also discrepancies. For instance, while a Robertson family was confirmed, no record of a father named Shane was found.

The investigation conducted by Stevenson and Tucker has faced a number of critiques from the academic community. Their main concern is the reliance on anecdotal accounts rather than controlled experimental work. Critics argue the conclusions drawn may be undermined by confirmation bias (the tendency to search for, interpret, or recall data in a way confirming or supporting one's pre-existing beliefs) and motivated reasoning (a type of reasoning in which a person uses a desired conclusion to influence the reasoning process, leading to a biased evaluation of evidence).

The issue with this approach is that these experiences can't be easily measured or reproduced in a laboratory setting. This is a primary criticism from the scientific community. Glimpses will happen when they happen, if they happen at all, making it nearly impossible to monitor in a controlled environment—unless, of course, you want to monitor the child 24/7.

These children were able to remember, for the most part, entire lives. Some details were incorrect. However, we have to remember that these children got glimpses into a past they

---

14. British television documentary: *The Boy Who Lived Before* (Channel 5, 2006).

shouldn't have been able to see at all. Can we really disregard their entire stories, based on a few discrepancies? Perhaps not. But it is important to acknowledge these discrepancies, as they are a key point of contention for skeptics.

I also found that the things that happened to my mother, alongside my own instantaneous knowledge, aligned with broader observations of children exhibiting unusual abilities that transcend the ordinary or are psychic in nature.

Invisible Friends and Spirit Visitations: Many children interact with "invisible friends" who sometimes provide accurate information not otherwise revealed to the children or their parents. Some children also report visits from deceased relatives, often in dreams, accompanied by visual clues, as if they are on a passage to the afterlife.

Precognition and Telepathy: Psychic children may demonstrate precognition (ability to foresee future events) by telling things in advance, such as the arrival of a new baby and its gender, or even predicting accidents. Telepathy, or apparent mind-to-mind communication, is also reported, especially among young children.

Innate Wisdom and Spiritual Connection: These children often appear exceptionally wise and knowledgeable for their age, possessing an amazing understanding of the universe and its workings that they have not been taught. They may describe a direct linkage to angels, guides, or even God.

Unusual Sensory Abilities: Some children have reportedly demonstrated talents outside of the typical five senses, such as seeing perceptual content with their fingertips while blindfolded or using mind force to influence objects, like opening flower buds.

These anomalies of behavior and conscious reality, including non-sensory experiences like telepathy and psychokinesis (moving objects with the mind), fall under the domain of parapsychology.

The consensus on psi phenomena (anomalous processes of information transfer not explained by known physical mechanisms) is that there is insufficient evidence to support their existence. Scientists argue that many of these claims can be explained by fraud, wishful thinking, or mental biases like confirmation bias, where people see what they want to see. However, the persistence of these claims and continued exploration highlights a consistent thread in the human psyche.

My mother's remembering of dresses from a different era and a soul family—and my own knowledge at two months—align with the broader category of psychic children. These children exhibit precognition, telepathy, and innate wisdom.

This suggests that memory in the context of childhood and unexplained phenomena extends above conventional autobiographical recall. It encompasses a broader spectrum of intuitive insight that may include future events, telepathic content from others' minds, or inherent devotional insights. This implies that the "complex cognitive processes" dismissed by society are not just about logical thought, but a more holistic, intuitive, and interconnected way of perceiving reality.

My recollection of the sky as a place of origin resonates with a notion of pre-existence that has endured for millennia. This belief posits an individual human essence existed prior to incarnation. While some variations suggest this essence is eternal, others propose it came into being at some point before conception and then entered the body before birth. I have studied a number of different perspectives.

The Doctrine of Pre-Existence in Early Thought: The Greek philosopher Plato posited the pre-existence of human consciousness, linking it to his theory of innatism. For Plato, knowing was not acquired, but recollected from a pre-mortal state, suggesting that this consciousness possessed truth before embodiment. Similarly, the prominent third century Christian father, Origen[15], championed the doctrine, suggesting God created each human entity prior to conception. However, this view was later condemned as heresy by the Second Council of Constantinople (AD 553), which famously declared its advocates anathema[16]. Mainstream Christianity, adhering to the council's decree, interprets scriptural references as God's foreknowledge, believing that the soul comes into being at conception or later, as "it is appointed for men to die once and after this comes judgment" (Hebrews 9:27).

---

15. Origen. (c. 220–230). *On First Principles* (Latin: *De Principiis*).

16. The Anathemas of the Second Council of Constantinople (553 AD).

Reincarnation in World Religions: Reincarnation, or saṃsāra[17] (the continuous cycle of death and rebirth), where souls are continually reborn into new bodies, is a central tenet in many major world religions. Hinduism, Buddhism, Jainism, and Sikhism all embrace the concept of reincarnation. In these traditions, souls are reborn based on accumulated actions (karma), with the ultimate goal of achieving liberation (Nirvana)[18] from the cycle of birth and death. Reincarnation also appears as an esoteric belief in various streams of Judaism[19] (such as Kabbalah, a branch of Judaism concerned with the deepest, hidden secrets of the universe, and Hasidic Judaism), certain pagan religions (including Wicca), and among the Druze[20] . Meanwhile, in Chinese mythology, the Naihe Bridge and the deity Meng Po (Lady of Forgetfulness)[21] explains why souls do not remember their past lives before reincarnation. Meng Po serves a "soul-beguiling soup" that erases all remembering, allowing souls to enter their next lives without past burdens.

While mainstream Abrahamic traditions largely reject pre-existence, some specialized groups hold different views. For instance, the cornerstone doctrine of premortal life in Latter-Day Saints[22] (Mormonism) teaches that souls are co-eternal with God, existing in incorporeal form in a pre-mortal plane, learning and progressing before mortal birth. Islam[23] holds a similar belief, namely that all souls were created in adult form concurrent with God's creation of Adam. This pre-existence is forgotten, leaving only an innate awareness of God and oneness (Fitra).

---

17. The Bhagavad Gita.

18. Rahula, Walpola. (1959). *What the Buddha Taught.*

19. Scholem, Gershom. (1941). *Major Trends in Jewish Mysticism.*

20. Abu Izzeddin, Nejla M. (1984). *The Druze: A New Study of Their History, Faith and Society.*

21. Birrell, Anne M. (1993). *Chinese Mythology: An Introduction.*

22. The Pearl of Great Price.

23. The Qur'an.

I also found the idea of a "pool of souls"[24] or "locus of universal memories" theorized in some philosophical and esoteric traditions, such as Kabbalah. A soul preparing for incarnation can access the information from this pool. This doesn't subtract from the pool, meaning multiple individuals are able to access or remember aspects of the same past lives. This theory potentially explains communal or seemingly borrowed recollections. This idea provides a framework for interpreting how my sense of home and vastness might be a connection to a collective, pre-existing consciousness rather than an individual, brain-bound one.

My remembering of a vast night sky where I come from directly taps into the long-standing and ongoing debate about the pre-existence of the soul. A vast array of global traditions, including major Eastern religions and specific Abrahamic branches, embrace it, while mainstream Western thought, in particular post-553 AD Christian doctrine, largely rejects it. This highlights a fundamental divergence in worldviews regarding the nature of human identity and consciousness. The societal dismissal of "babies are just babies" can be seen as a reflection of this dominant Western theological stance rejecting pre-existence.

My mother's narratives, alongside my own instantaneous knowing, illustrate experiences that challenge linear concepts of time and memory, aligning with precognitive and intuitive abilities. Her recollections at a young age of drawing girls with big puffy dresses she had never seen suggest a clear instance of recognition. This is like accessing details about states or events she was never present to. Her perceptions of dresses from a different era and another family challenge the linear concept of time and conventional memory. This aligns with parapsychological concepts of precognition and the idea that consciousness might operate outside of the boundaries of space and time.

My own case of inner certainty of who my grandmother was, despite not remembering meeting her, can be interpreted as a notable instance of intuitive insight. This was accompanied by a rush of thoughts that somehow made sense despite my ability for verbal communication and comprehension being undeveloped. This bypasses the brain's typical way of retrieving the past, suggesting a direct, albeit non-linear, access to information. I was not supposed to remember—not at that age, and not with such clarity. According to science, the voice speaking to me shouldn't have been able to do so, because I had no

24. The Zohar

verbal communication abilities yet. And yet, the message arrived fully formed, like a fully understood code in my every fiber.

They say the brain cannot hold such things—but what if the history of who we were lives elsewhere—in the soul's architecture, or in the breath before birth? You may not have conscious access to your own first glimpse, but perhaps something in you stirs now. A flicker. A pulse. A pull. Do you feel it? If you do, give it heed. Surrender to it. Let it lead you. Follow it, and you will find...something. And when you do, be smarter than I was and give it a voice.

What is your oldest memory? Mine is that I don't like being lied to, which is funny, because once you see through the social construct, you realize that deception has been the norm. It is as common as the air you breathe. You might see how you've been lied to—by everyone and everything. I sure did. It didn't feel good. And for that reason, I decided to stop lying. Now, I ask you: What is the truth you are ready to unveil?

Chapter 2: In Hushed Whispers

You need Power, only when you want to do something harmful. Otherwise Love is enough to get everything done.

—Charlie Chaplin

To be three years old is to be a citizen of a world of pure, unfiltered fun—a world full of vibrant colors, the scent of rain on concrete, sour cherry jam, and collectible trinkets. This was my world, a small universe contained within the walls of a fifth-floor apartment in Communist Romania. I had little knowledge of the world outside, only that it was a place of endless possibility—a place I perceived as a little too odd for me, even then.

Even in my small, sunlit bubble, the outside world pressed in with a persistent weight. It came in the sudden chill of a cold room after the heat was cut off right after dinner, a daily occurrence that plunged our home into a kind of frozen twilight. It came in the thin, watery soup that filled our bowls, and in the silent tension I could see tightening my parents' faces when they spoke of...well, anything. We had money, they said, but it sat uselessly in a drawer, because the stores were like a row of forgotten tombs: empty, silent, and poorly lit. We had money, but you can't eat money. And you can't complain—not when the patriotic thing to do is to be grateful for your hunger.

For a child, a lack of heat and a half-empty plate were not things to be feared; they were simply the way things were. My parents were magicians. They would find a single apple when the markets were bare, or produce a tiny piece of candy from a pocket as if it were a rare and brilliant gem. I didn't know the risks they took, the way they bartered with the forces that held them captive, exchanging their dignity for the small necessities that filled our lives with light.

Information, too, was a scarce commodity. Our little black-and-white television hummed with an unrelenting stream of Communist propaganda—a droning lullaby designed to keep us all asleep. The five minutes of Russian cartoons were a privilege in our drab existence, a brief window into another world. But even at such a young age, with no news or international TV to guide me, a whisper of a different future had already settled inside me, like an undeniable truth.

"I am going to America and I will be an American!" I announced one afternoon, my voice echoing a little too loudly in the silence of our living room.

My parents froze. The air, which moments before had been still and warm, suddenly turned brittle and thin. My father's hand, which had been resting on a book, went slack. My mother's face, a second before flushed with the warmth of the day, drained of all color until it was a pale, frightened mask. They stared at me as if I had spoken in a foreign tongue or conjured a forbidden ghost. My three-year-old self didn't understand why their faces had gone so pale. I did not grasp that a word, a single notion of "America," would bring such serious repercussions in our oppressive world—a regime where the right to free speech was a luxury we had never had, and where even the friendliest neighbor might be an informant to The Security.

"Where did you hear this word? It's a bad word, don't say it again!" my mother admonished in a whisper, as if the walls themselves had ears.

I had no answer for her. I didn't know where the thought had come from, only that it had bloomed inside me, fully formed and certain. I was aware that America was a place, and I was certain it was where I was going. *They will see*, I thought with the stubborn confidence of a child.

For years, the audacious pronouncement of a three-year-old was lost to the currents of a young life and unfolding realities. I had merely a vague memory of that whispered certainty and the fear it instilled in my parents. Life, as it always does, moved forward, a winding trajectory through unexpected turns until, twenty-four years later, in a different, free world, albeit still recovering from oppression, I married. Three years after that, after a few life-altering changes, I landed in America. Five years after I arrived, I stood with a crowd of other hopefuls and swore an oath. I was no longer a guest; I was a citizen. The childhood premonition had become my reality, even if its origin was, for a time, almost forgotten.

It was on a video call, many years later, that my mother brought it up. We were talking about something mundane, and then she paused, tilting her head to the left, as she always does when she remembers something she deems important.

"Do you remember when you were shouting in the living room, at three years old, that you were going to America?" she asked. A smile touched my lips. I remembered.

"We were so worried someone would hear you," she confessed, her voice thick with the lingering feeling of that fear. "We had been so careful never to say anything dangerous around you. We had no idea where you heard the notion."

I still don't have an answer for her, and perhaps I never will. The source of the thought remains a mystery to me, a truth kept safe in the vault of my childhood mind. It certainly was not the news—the single government-run TV station only ran during the day, a never-ending loop of propaganda designed to convince us of our prosperity even in the face of the lack of heat, food, or electricity.

Dictatorships do this. They try to take away our very humanity, gaslighting us into believing we should be grateful for our servitude. And for those who did not behave, there were serious consequences: long, hard years spent in horrible jails, and even torture and murder.

My parents were right to be concerned. But through the eyes of a three-year-old, the world is a wonderful ball of fun, ready to be explored. I had no idea of fear, only of wonder.

Fear is a puzzling thing, isn't it? It makes us forget how loving we are. It makes us speak in hushed whispers, reprimand our children for asking questions, and keep to ourselves when we have so much to say. It is a cage keeping us in jobs we hate, relationships that stifle us, and roles we never chose. But that single, unfiltered thought, spoken in the living room of a small apartment decades ago, was proof that the human spirit, even when surrounded by the walls of scary things, can still find a way to whisper its deepest, most impossible truths.

The Architecture of Scarcity: How We Lived

It's funny what a three-year-old takes for normal. For me, life in Romania during the 1980s was just life. What I didn't know then was that our struggles were part of a deliberate and brutal plan.

Our dictator, Nicolae Ceauşescu, was obsessed with paying off a huge foreign debt. He decided the best way to do it was to starve his own people and sell everything the country had abroad.

It wasn't merely a tough time; it was a constant, draining state that defined my early life and the lives of everyone around me.

The food shortages were the worst part, and they weren't an accident. The government even had a "Rational Eating Programme," which was a fancy way of saying they wanted us to eat less. I was too young to understand what it was like, but I could hear my parents talk about the scarcity, and could clearly see the empty shelves and long lines for food.

We were on a rationing system for the basics, like bread, cooking oil, milk, and sugar. My mom has told me how we would sometimes get only a kilogram of sugar or a liter and a half of cooking oil for an entire month. People would get in line at 5:00 a.m. for a loaf of bread or a single chicken.

It's hard to imagine, but fruit and meat were basically no more than stories you told to your kids. Our food was almost all soy-based, and I remember the margarine tasted like plastic. It was a daily battle, a permanent reminder that the government didn't care about us—as if we needed to be reminded. We knew.

It was not just the hunger we struggled with. The cold and the darkness were just as bad. Ceauşescu's government would cut electricity and heating to save energy for factories and exports. Winters were unbearable. We would lose electricity, heat, and hot water, which was often only available one day a week. My parents told me a story about how dozens of babies died in a hospital one winter because the lights went out and their incubators stopped working.

The streets were dark at night because they turned off the lights. This was our reality, even as the government was watching it all from the People's House in Bucharest. This enormous, crazy building was a slap in the face to everyone who was suffering, but its purpose was to satiate the ego of a madman.

As bad as the physical struggle was, the scariest thing was the terror. The state's secret police, marketed as "The Security" ("Securitate" in Romanian), had spies everywhere. The name ironically suggested that its job was to keep citizens safe, but it was a pervasive and brutal instrument of control, designed to instill fear and crush dissent. The rumor was that one in four Romanians was an informant. Even though the real number was closer to one in forty-three, it was still enough to make you feel like someone was always listening.

They planted microphones in homes, tapped phones, and read our mail. My parents were right to be worried someone would hear my little voice shouting about America.

The Security manufactured conflicts and spread rumors to make people suspicious of each other. I came to know that an American anthropologist who came to Romania had a file more than 2,700 pages long, filled with reports from seventy informants, including her own friends and acquaintances.

It was a horrible scheme they played, forcing normal people to make terrible choices about betraying their neighbors to keep their jobs or small privileges. The struggles and the unrelenting dread worked together, leaving us too tired to fight and too paranoid to trust anyone enough to organize a protest. They had us exactly where they wanted us.

But the question remains: If they were so careful, where did the word "America" come from? The simplest answer lies in the nonverbal world. What the mouth could not say, the atmosphere of fear spoke constantly, and my young mind, unburdened by adult rationalization, was tuned to hear it.

Survival Sense vs. Prophecy

The unexplainable certainty I had as a three-year-old begs a question. Where did the thought truly come from? When I look back with the perspective of an adult, it's easy to see how my mind—even at that young age—may have been a sponge, soaking up everything around me. This is where I started to explore the connection between what I experienced and what psychology has to say about it.

Research suggests a child's mind between the ages of three and seven relies on "intuitive thought,"[1] making quick judgments based on their own senses and observation rather than what they are told. It's as if my three-year-old brain, with its intuitive thought and lack of fear, was operating in a different way. It was constructing its own little map of how the world worked by observing everything.

My brain functioned like a computer running a silent, continuous background check on my world. My mind was picking up on all the nonconscious cues in my surroundings, from my parents' whispered conversations to the tension in their faces. I did not need to be consciously aware of the content for my brain to process it; it was a form of intuitive, nonverbal analysis.

My parents might have been trying to hide their concern, but I was still able to see it, clear as day. I sensed it in their whispered conversations, in the way they held their breath when I talked too loud, and in the way they looked at the empty stores. The world was a lie, so my brain had to find the truth in the unspoken, in the feelings, and in the atmosphere around me. It had to develop a survival instinct.

When I look at what happened through this lens, it makes a little more sense. What I experienced was not so much a supernatural gift as it was a sensitive part of my brain supercharged by the oppressive environment. It learned to see the world beyond appearances.

My foresight was a natural extension of my humanity, not some magical, one-off event. It was a result of the extreme pressure of living in a country that had all but relinquished its own soul. The more I read, the more it made sense. What appeared like a prophecy born of awe and wonder might have been an expression of human intuition, a survival mechanism born out of a very real anguish. This perspective allows me to see both the mystery and the human condition in my story.

While science may struggle to define or explain my lived reality, my story exists in a space between what can be proven and what can only be felt. This isn't just a personal dilemma; it's a modern expression of a timeless archetype, an echo that has resonated across different

---

1. Piaget, J., & Inhelder, B. (1969). *The Psychology of the Child*. Basic Books.

cultures and religions. It turns out the story of a young person being able to speak a hidden truth is a pattern, one which often appears when the adult world has lost its way.

Exploring this as an adult, I've learned that scientists find precognition difficult to investigate. It cannot really be recreated and, in my experience, it happens randomly. It's not a given. I reasoned it was worth looking into it and seeing how my experience, combined with the details of my environment, would have impacted me and caused me to have this certainty.

Throughout history, people have believed in precognition and prophecy, and you can find a thread of these beliefs woven through cultures all over the world. The modern world, with its cold light of objectivity, isn't so sure about these things.

The Aberfan Landslide[2] : In 1966, a coal mine waste tip collapsed and engulfed a school in Wales. A British psychiatrist collected more than sixty cases of people who had premonitions about the disaster. One notable account was from a ten-year-old girl who was killed in the landslide. She told her mother the day before the event that she'd dreamed that "something black" had covered her school.

Katie the Psychic Girl[3] : A mother reported that her young daughter, Katie, displayed precognitive abilities, knowing who was at the door or on the phone before anyone answered. In one instance, Katie told her confused mother that a family friend had a "baby in her tummy" even before the mother found out she was pregnant, and correctly disclosed the sex of the baby.

Mainstream studies say there's no known way for precognition to work because it breaks the rule of cause and effect. On a logical level, this makes sense. They also point out how a lot of the old investigations on these topics had serious problems, like flawed methods and manipulated data. What people think is precognition, they argue, can often be explained

---

2. Barker, J. C. (1967). Premonitions of the Aberfan disaster. *Journal of the Society for Psychical Research*, *44*(734), 169–181.

3. Tucker, J. B. (2013). *Return to Life: Extraordinary Cases of Children Who Remember Past Lives*. St. Martin's Press.

by simpler things like coincidence or mental bias, where you only remember the dreams or visions that happen to come true.

These are fair, critical points, and it would be dishonest to ignore them. But these pages aren't intended to be a scientific paper. My story isn't designed to prove anything. The story of a little kid in Communist Romania seeing a forbidden future isn't about objective proof. It's about a subjective, unshakeable conviction that came to me when the world around me was a lie. This reality is the very fabric of my being, and nothing can take it away.

It was a modern expression of a timeless story, an echo that has reverberated through millennia and resonated across different cultures and religions. The story of a young person being able to speak hidden knowledge—when the adult world has become blind to it—is a powerful and recurring archetype across human history.

You can see this pattern repeated everywhere. In the Bible, God chose the young boy Samuel—a child prophet—to deliver a message of judgment, a sign that the innocence of youth can perceive a truth that had been lost to the adults. Likewise, the prophet Jeremiah was told, "Before I formed you in the womb I knew you, before you were born I set you apart; I appointed you as a prophet to the nations." This speaks to a calling that predated even his birth.

The question guiding me is this: Was it the universe telling me I was part of something much bigger than myself? I did not even know what America was, if I'm honest. But my little voice shouting about America was not a kid's random outburst.

Finding the Voice in the Quiet

The thing about being afraid is that it doesn't only keep one subdued; it also makes one an active participant in their own shrinking. It told me to stay in my lane, to not give my opinions a voice, and to never have a say. And so I did. I stayed silent and amiable, a ghost in my own life, until one day the dam broke.

I had been hurt so much—cheated, betrayed, beaten down, and abused—that the pain became a familiar landscape. That's when fear ended. I had already dealt with the worst; what else could they do to me? It was nothing more than pain, and I almost didn't feel anything at all anymore. The things I was scared of had already happened. I knew pain intimately, to the point where death looked like a kinder, gentler prospect.

That is when I began an honest conversation with Death. I realized there was nothing to be scared of—a truth I had carried all along, but simply forgot. After a lifetime spent searching for answers that were already within me, I remembered that it's all a choice. Suddenly, what had once been so terrifying lost its power. And in that moment of surrender, I was truly free.

It is in confronting this ultimate unknown that a shift occurs—that's the ultimate paradox.

As this shift happened, I began finding it harder and harder to stay silent. The things that screamed at me from within wouldn't let me be. Because those things I'd seen as wrong all that time? They were wrong. They had always been wrong.

Our ancestors understood it, too. They lived and died and passed down wisdom that still rings true. The old texts are riddled with the same message: Fear is a false god. Love and kindness are all that matter. No matter how loud greed and power get, that is all they are—loud. Not right.

This truth echoes through all of history. All you have to do is look. The conviction that love and kindness are the true powers, and fear is the false god, is woven into the wisdom passed down through the ages.

Christianity: I can see it in the Bible. "Blessed are the meek, for they will inherit the Earth"[4] is a monumental statement about the power of humility, taken from Jesus's Sermon on the Mount. It's a promise that those who possess gentleness and kindness will, at last, receive a lasting inheritance—not of land or gold, but of a world restored to balance. This virtue, often misunderstood as weakness, is affirmed as the path to spiritual elevation.

---

4. The Gospel of Matthew, 5:5.

Buddhism: In Buddhism, the practice of "loving kindness" (Metta)[5] is a fundamental value, one of the four sublime states of the mind. It is a cultivated state of wishing for the happiness and well-being of all sentient beings, without exception, and is systematically practiced through meditation to dissolve feelings of hatred or aversion. It's a recognition of our collective humanity and shared desire for peace.

Islam: The same type of insight is woven into the teachings of Islam. The Prophet Muhammad's saying, "Whoever is humble for God He will raise them up,"[6] teaches that true elevation comes not from pride or worldly status, but from internal humility. This principle is tied directly to ihsaan (perfection or excellence), the awareness that one is always in the presence of the Divine, which inspires constant sincerity and kindness in one's actions toward others.

Greek and Roman Mythology: We also find it in Greek and Roman mythology, in the story of Baucis and Philemon[7], a poor, elderly couple who welcomed two weary travelers—who were really Zeus and Hermes in disguise—into their humble home. They were the only villagers to show hospitality, and they were rewarded by being saved from a flood that consumed the rest of the land, becoming intertwined trees after their deaths. Their story is an enduring symbol of the importance of genuine humility and unconditional love for the stranger.

Ancient Greek Culture: And it goes even deeper. The Greek concept of "xenia,"[8] a social custom of guest-friendship, was considered inviolable in the eyes of the gods, and was so important it was overseen by Zeus himself. It was a profound moral code that demanded kindness and protection for all travelers, regardless of their status. This sacred bond is the very reason the cruel Cyclops was punished in Homer's *Odyssey*—not just for his violence, but for his complete violation of this sacred, loving code.

---

5. The Metta Sutta (Karaniya Metta Sutta).

6. Sahih Muslim.

7. Ovid's *Metamorphoses*, Book VIII.

8. Homer's *Odyssey*.

Hinduism: Hinduism also holds countless narratives that speak to the virtue of generosity and selfless service (seva). The story of Krishna and Sudama[9] is a classic example. Sudama, a poor childhood friend of the great lord Krishna, arrives with only a meager gift of flattened rice. Krishna, valuing the purity of the gesture over its monetary worth, elevates Sudama's poverty to immense wealth, teaching that a small gift from a pure heart is more valuable than any lavish offering.

Ancient Egypt: And in ancient Egypt, the principle of ma'at[10], or cosmic balance, truth, and harmony, was at the very core of their beliefs. After death, a person's heart was weighed against the Feather of Ma'at. To withstand judgment and secure a favorable afterlife, they had to be able to sincerely declare, "I have not denied food to the hungry." The entire path to eternity was paved with acts of kindness and the maintenance of moral equilibrium, proving that compassion was the ultimate currency.

And so it is confirmed. What so many believe deep down is true. The notion that money and power matter most is just an illusion. The good news is that we are not alone. Others before us saw through this façade, their words echoing through the ages. Many who are alive right now see it, too, yet have been silenced—often, as I once was, by their own thoughts. But it is time for us to give a voice to our authentic selves, because words have power. The more we bring love, kindness, unity, and compassion to the forefront, the more real they become.

In the end, it's all for love, isn't it?

After the storm ends, after the dust settles, when I look back, I only remember the kindness shown to me. The lessons. The strength I gained. And, above all, the people who stood by me—the ones who cared.

And in that moment, I realize that love is all that matters. It comes in so many forms: in the kindness of strangers, in the unconditional affection of animals, in a foreign thought that sounds like truth, in a song or a smile. All of those things that have made me feel a little bit safer, a little bit better, were all love, reminding me that I am not alone.

---

9. Bhāgavata Purāṇa.

10. The Book of the Dead.

And then I realize that I, too, have done so much for love. Because in the end, giving love is what brings us joy. We've always been astute observers because we could see that love was the only thing that mattered all along.

Just like you, I understood that kindness had the power to make this world the heaven it was destined to be. I kept my silence because it didn't seem to be what others believed in—because greed and violence are so much louder. I was quiet, often only whispering to that voice inside.

But just because I was silent doesn't mean I was asleep. I saw the exploitation and cruelty, and I understood there was a better way. My intuition—my divine guidance—told me so. I saw what was truly happening all along.

In the end, every single one of us matters; every single one of us is made of the same stuff. We are all love, aren't we? So, in that love, are we not one?

We are in The Great Game. Make no mistake, friends—we are playing on Insanity Level. It's a chaotic, unpredictable journey filled with unexpected turns and moments that defy all logic. And yet, there's a certain beauty in it, a wild dance with the unknown that pushes the boundaries of what we thought possible.

Each challenge, each obstacle overcome, stands as a testament to the boundless resilience of the human spirit. This is the relentless pursuit of purpose against a world that perpetually attempts to stifle it. It is in these very struggles that we uncover the true primordial depth of our strength.

I step outside for a bit, needing a moment to absorb the vastness of the world beyond the four walls of my bedroom. I look up and meet the sun, its warm embrace a comforting balm. The sheer size of the sky, the endless expanse of blue, reminds me of the infinite possibilities that exist, even when life feels confined.

I feel so much love and peace, such a sense of serenity that settles inside my heart. And I am so grateful for finally learning to listen to my heart. It's a pull that transcends logic, an inner voice telling me that everything is exactly as it should be, even in its imperfections. I giggle and wave at the sun, just in case it's God watching—a silly gesture, perhaps, but one that feels fully natural in this moment of blissful connection.

It's all for love, right? Every challenge, every triumph, every breath we take—it all comes back to that truth. Love is the true currency of life, the ultimate motivator, and the guiding force that binds us all. It's the answer to every question, the balm for every wound, and the light that illuminates even the darkest paths. And the best part about it? It doesn't cost a penny. It's free!

Chapter 3: The Me Too That Gave Me Wings

Because you are alive, everything is possible.

—Thich Nhat Hanh

When you are a child, the world is not yet bound by the same hard edges and heavy rules. It is a place of infinite possibility, where every surface holds a secret and every moment is ripe with wonder.

When you are a child, everything is possible. There are those who might argue that this is mere fantasy, the fleeting product of a mind not yet able to distinguish between what is real and what is not. But I believe it is something else entirely.

I believe that children are the truest philosophers, the wisest of sages. They have not yet been tainted by the subtle, insidious fears that the world instills. They remember what came before—before this life, before this role, before the weighty cloak of adulthood settled on their shoulders. They still feel the echo of a place we can only later, as adults, long for.

One of my most cherished memories is of gliding—a wellspring of pure, unadulterated joy that has never run dry. I was only around five years old when I first realized it was a private grace.

Until that moment, I had simply assumed everyone was capable of what I could do; why they chose not to remained a mystery. Why would anyone ever want to walk when they could fly? It was a puzzle I never bothered to solve, a question I never truly had to ask. I kept my ability to myself, not out of a need for secrecy, but from the simple conviction that it was as trivial as breathing. The act itself was effortless—all I had to do was want it to happen, and it would. Surely, if it were anything noteworthy, it would have been much harder to accomplish.

Besides, a part of me worried it might get me in trouble. The thought of asking my mother if flying was permissible did cross my mind, but I couldn't predict her answer. If there was even the slightest chance she would say "no," why risk it? Better to just keep this secret blessing to myself and enjoy the fun of it. And what fun it was!

I was flying! Well, not flying in a fantastical, superhuman way, but a soft, effortless glide from one place to another—a whisper of movement more than a grand gesture.

Our old apartment building in Constanţa, Romania, was the stage for this hidden trick. Our apartment was on the fifth floor, and the concrete stairway right outside our door, with its cool, smooth railing, was my rollercoaster. I would slip past my mother when she was caught in the timeless rhythm of a neighbor's conversation—the one from across the hall or the woman from the fourth floor whose door was visible from ours. They would stand there, lost in their own small world of adult concerns, while I was about to embark on an adventure into another.

I would take to the stairway railing, a smooth, cool metal that served as a slide to nowhere and everywhere all at once. The first plunge down was followed by an impossible, weightless ascent, a soundless rising before I would glide down again. It was a dance between gravity and grace, a fun park right outside our front door.

I found it funny how neither my overprotective mother nor the neighbor ever reacted to my shenanigans. Why would I say something that would likely cause my mother to tell me to stop? The joy was too immense, the sentiment too consuming.

I reasoned that if my little games were forbidden, my mother would surely have said something. She always did. But since she never acknowledged it, I was clearly doing nothing wrong. My flights must have been so mundane that they weren't even worthy of her notice. It never crossed my mind that she simply couldn't see me. That realization would not dawn until a lifetime later, when I looked back on this memory as an adult.

Gliding was as simple and natural to me as walking. I did it so often that I stopped thinking of it as anything special, moving through our home with an unconscious ease. Then, one day, something shifted. The memory is as clear as a photograph: my mother opening the front door, the familiar murmur of her voice as she spoke with our neighbor. I followed her, drifting silently behind her.

For some reason, for the very first time, I felt an urge to look back into the apartment. There, cast in the soft light of the hallway, I saw her—a small, five-year-old girl who looked just like me. She was not standing at my vantage point behind my mother. In fact, she had never moved at all. She sat right where I had left her, on the floor, playing quietly with a stuffed animal.

She had shoulder-length dark brown hair, wispy bangs framing her face, and was dressed in a vibrant pink sweatshirt with glittery text sparkling on the front. She was utterly absorbed in a different kind of play, gently petting the soft, pink stuffed bunny that nestled in her lap.

She was me, alright. My face, my hair, my sweatshirt...my bunny. There I was, sitting inside the doorway, petting the plush pink stuffed bunny my father had brought me from one of his trips. For a moment, I wondered, "If I never left my spot, how am I standing right behind my mom, too?" I wasn't able to find an explanation for it then, and that was okay. I figured I'd find a solution to the puzzle later. For the time being, I knew I could glide, and I knew there were two of me. With that new information, I decided to go back to what I was doing—specifically, spying on my mom to see what she and the neighbor were talking about. The me on the floor would be fine sitting right there with the stuffed bunny while the other me, the gliding me, went off to play.

I left without a second thought, without a flicker of concern that there were two of me. It is a fascinating, almost comical thing, the truths a child can accept without question. In that moment, I had the certainty, the knowledge that the other me, the one sitting with the pink bunny, couldn't glide. But the one who was gliding, who was me, was doing it.

And in that same breath, I understood that we were often one, and then we would separate, and then we would merge again. "We" had the power to float, and it was "our" little secret. I didn't care which one of us was which, or why. The point was, I could fly!

This was no illusion, no fleeting dream. It was a state I entered nearly every day, and it felt as tangible as the act of walking. It was as certain as the feeling of the carpet beneath my feet. This experience became so routine that I eventually concluded, with the limitless logic of a child, that there were simply two of me, and we both could do it. But then, the world intervened....

My big brother was standing outside our apartment, caught up in conversation with a neighbor. My brother was, and is, to this day, my role model. He was the embodiment of the sturdy bedrock of the world. What better way to one up your sibling than to reveal an impossible, wonderful skill? So, as he stood there, I decided to unveil our little discovery. I would float right in front of him! Both of us, the one with the bunny and the one on the railing, would show him what we were capable of. Finally, I was going to win the proverbial sibling competition!

I stepped onto the railing, preparing to begin my effortless descent, when his hand shot out and gripped my arm. He stared at me with an expression I had never seen before: not amusement, not playfulness, but concern. His eyes were shadowed with a warning that wasn't for himself, but for me. He asked me what I was doing. I explained, with a simple innocence, that I would just glide down the railing. With not a trace of amusement in his eyes, he pointed at the space between the metal bars and the distance to the ground. "You would die if you tried that, so don't try it," he replied matter-of-factly.

I stared at him as if he had grown three heads.

Die? That did not sound right, not one bit. I had been gliding for as long as I could remember. Granted, my entire life had only spanned five years, but it was all I had ever known. To me, it was a completely safe and natural act. The genuine fear in his eyes was a language I couldn't comprehend; the danger he spoke of felt utterly alien to my reality.

I offered only silence in return. Arguing was pointless—he was the older brother, and he always knew best. That was the perk of being older, I supposed. So, when he made me promise that I would never, ever do it again, I accepted that he always knows best and made a promise.

And so I promised. And I have never glided again. Not once. It was not a physical act of will, but a silent, immediate overwrite. It was as if the ability was magically deleted from my mind. The words of my brother, spoken out of love and concern, had become a new law of nature, a new unyielding principle I was forced to accept.

It is a curious thing, the way it was so easy to do something until I was told that I couldn't. Once the knowledge of impossibility was introduced, the ability vanished. Knowing is an interesting thing, isn't it? What is it, really? Is it what liberates us, or is it a cage? Is it a truth to be trusted, or is it nothing but a collection of other people's "don'ts" and "won'ts?" The wisdom of the world, delivered by a loving hand, had taken away my own.

Years later, when I was a teenager, I found a piece of myself echoed in a poem by Shel Silverstein. I wish I had read it when I was a child. It would have been the incantation I needed to hear. Perhaps you will like it, too.

"Listen to the MUSTN'TS, child. Listen to the DON'TS. Listen to the SHOULDN'TS, the IMPOSSIBLES, the WONT'S. Listen to the NEVER HAVES, then listen close to me: Anything can happen, child, ANYTHING can be." – Shel Silverstein, "Listen to the MUSTN'TS."[1]

The memory has never ceased to amaze me with its vividness. It is more real than anything—more real, even, than what I did yesterday. I can still feel the exhilarating rush of freedom, the lightness of my body, the boundless joy. It has never diminished. It is one of my most treasured memories, and for that reason, I have had to come to terms with the loss. I was able to glide once—a truth no subsequent law of physics can erase.

Life went on. I grew up, and I mastered the art of being different without showing it. I crafted the mask. I assumed the role. I tucked the magic away inside. It didn't matter; that inner knowing was more than enough for me. It was a hidden blueprint of a forgotten self, a beacon in the back of my mind reminding me that I had once defied the laws of this world.

---

1. Silverstein, Shel. (1974). "Listen to the MUSTN'TS" from *Where the Sidewalk Ends*. Harper & Row.

Until one day, when I was reminded. During an involuntary out-of-body experience, I glided again. Only once, for a fleeting moment. It was a perfect reminder that, yes, we can fly. We've merely forgotten how.

But even then, I spoke nothing of it. The same old fears remained—the fear of stigma, of being written off as ill, of ridicule, and of alienation. I could see that there was so much more to the world than the mundane reality it presented, but I also was able to clearly see that the world was not crafted for magic, but for deadlines and spreadsheets. So I stayed silent. After all, keeping my mouth shut had never stopped me from playing detective.

When the World Still Had Wings: The Reality of Duality

The past is alive in my mind, visceral and detailed as a photograph. The cool, hard linoleum floor of the apartment building in Romania. The constant hum of a mundane afternoon, punctuated by the soft, rhythmic cadence of my mother's conversation with a neighbor. And, nestled within this ordinary scene, a private universe of extraordinary sensation: the exhilarating thrill of using the stairway railing not only as a slide, but as a launchpad—a slide that, somehow, went up as well as down.

The central question that arose from this recollection was important to me: Was this a child's game, a moment of unbridled imagination, or a glimpse into a way of being that I, as an adult, had long since let slip away?

Seeking to chart this question, I turned to the psychology of childhood consciousness. Illuminating the process, Maria Montessori's work[2] unveiled a paradigm: She proposed the young mind is a "spongy mind," uniquely primed to absorb and adapt to its environment.

Montessori drew a key distinction between imagination and fantasy. Imagination, she argued, is a creative process based on real experiences or a person's interactions with their own world. In contrast, fantasy is the introduction of impossible scenarios that can never come true, such as having superpowers, fighting dragons, or being able to fly. She contended that fantasy is often a byproduct of external sources, like television, and can be

---

2. Montessori, Maria. (*The Absorbent Mind* or *The Discovery of the Child*).

confusing to children under the age of six, as they have a limited capacity to differentiate it from the real world.

Gliding on the apartment building stairway presented a compelling paradox for me in light of this research. My memory is not of a fantasy, where I imagined an out-of-body episode, but of a perceived reality. I felt it, I saw it, and I witnessed it the same as everything else. A child doesn't know about the laws of physics. They only know what they experience. And in my experience, I could fly. It wasn't a miracle or a secret power; it was simply a fact of my life, as normal as breathing or walking. When something happens to you every single day, you don't question it. The experience itself becomes the only proof you need. It creates its own rules.

Looking back, I understand that I was living in two different worlds. There was the reality everyone else shared, and then there was my own, built around this one impossible thing that, for me, was perfectly ordinary.

The Mirror of the Self: Multiplicity Without Trauma

For me, the most striking moment in the memory is the one that introduces an element of duality. I glided behind my mother, only to look back and see myself playing with the pink stuffed bunny. (I still have that bunny, by the way!) There was no concern, no alarm, only a pure, childlike acceptance that it was ok that there were two of me. This state of being, where two selves can exist and operate simultaneously, was accepted as a given fact, a little mystery that would be lost to the adult world.

I found that psychology offers a number of frameworks for making sense of the mirroring of the spirit in a second self. The closest I ever came to an explanation was learning about imaginary friends. Psychologists say these companions are really just a piece of the child's own mind, brought to life. It made me wonder. Maybe that's what my other self was: not an imaginary friend, but an imaginary me, created to hold the part of my life that knew how to fly.

I also found a more clinical interpretation: dissociation[3], a coping mechanism for severe emotional trauma. Dissociation is a survival tool of the mind that children use when they feel helpless or unable to escape a dangerous situation. Evidence suggests that childhood trauma can interfere with the development of the brain's frontal cortex, leading to a structural impairment that manifests as numbing, avoidance, and other dissociative behaviors.

My experience, however, defied the clinical profile of dissociation. True, we still lived in Romania, but the political climate was drastically altered. Communism had dissolved; the dictator was gone. My inner landscape held no residue of anxiety, helplessness, or fragmentation. Instead, my truth was benign acceptance, a cohesive oneness found even within multiplicity: "until we separate only to merge again." This account presented a compelling counter-narrative to the standard clinical model.

I found that my story had parallels in the parapsychological and religious phenomenon of bilocation, an alleged psychic or miraculous ability wherein an individual is located in two distinct places at the same time. This ability has a long history, appearing as a *siddhi*[4] in Hinduism and Buddhism and as a miraculous gift among Christian figures like Padre Pio.

In conclusion, self-limiting beliefs are negative self-perceptions rooted in societal input. The loving warning from my brother, rooted in social conditioning[5], imposed a new, limiting reality that deleted a formerly accepted ability. This highlighted how the prevailing storyline of the world, while protective, can also become a cage that stifles individual potential.

When the World Taught Me to Walk: The Brain as Filter

For me, the pivotal moment of the story occurred with the introduction of my older brother. He was the older sibling, a provider of guidance and safety. When he saw me preparing to climb the railing, his intervention was not an act of malice, but of brotherly

---

3. Van der Kolk, Bessel. (Key work on trauma, *The Body Keeps the Score.*)

4. Yogasūtras of Patañjali (Siddhis).

5. Bandura, Albert. (Social Learning Theory or work on self-efficacy.)

care. He pointed at the space between the stairs and the big distance to the first floor. Then, with a voice filled with gravity, he explained that I would die.

This simple, common-sense warning, delivered from a place of genuine care, was the instrument of change for me. This pivotal moment illustrated to me the power of self-limiting beliefs, which are negative self-perceptions that live in our conscious and subconscious. My brother's warning, "You would die," became an unconscious anchor point—a piece of external input I accepted as absolute truth. The capacity for gliding was not physically removed; rather, my internal belief system was overwritten by a new, socially conditioned rule.

The discipline of social conditioning provided a broader context for my transformation. The force that keeps us safe and creates a functioning society is also the force that restricts our individual, "magical" potential. The question I pose in these pages—"Is knowledge really what empowers us, or is it not knowing?"—is the unresolvable tension at the heart of this trade-off. The ability was lost in a gesture of love.

Despite the loss of my ability, the echo of gliding persists with remarkable clarity. The feeling of real freedom. The lightness. The joy. They remain an active testament to a moment when I and the world were in a different, more harmonious relationship.

Much later, I stumbled upon a concept that offered an explanation: "flashbulb memo ries."[6] The idea is that our brains take a perfect snapshot of moments tied to powerful emotions. The sheer impossibility of seeing myself sitting on the floor, of being in two places at once, burned that image into my mind forever. It wasn't a memory I chose to keep; it was one my brain refused to let go of. This was a moment of unadulterated bliss, one that defied the ordinary rules of our world.

The Return of the Soul: The Science of Ascension

Years later, a familiar sensation returned to me during a spontaneous out-of-body episode. The ability, which appeared to have been erased from my programming, was briefly re-

6. Brown, R., & Kulik, J. (1977). "Flashbulb Memories." *Journal of Experimental Psychology: General*, *106*(1), 73–97.

stored. This later-in-life phenomenon invited a multidisciplinary analysis of out-of-body experiences (OBEs).

From a neurological standpoint, investigation has linked OBEs to a failure of integration of proprioceptive, tactile, and visual information. Electrical stimulation of a precise brain region, the temporo-parietal junction (TPJ), can evoke feelings of elevation, flying, and lightness, and the impression of seeing one's body from above. This provides a materialistic approach, suggesting that OBEs are an illusion generated by a specific neural malfunction.

However, my involuntary OBE, in this context, did not feel like a hallucination to me, but a brief return to unconditioned being. It suggested that the brain may not be the generator of consciousness, but rather a filter or transceiver. The ability was never lost; the brain's filter was permanently tuned to a different frequency.

My involuntary OBE was a temporary recalibration, suggesting that my self is larger than my physical body and its socially-conditioned programming. This concept of a non-local consciousness is supported by documented anecdotal and clinical accounts.

Dr. Jeffrey Long's Research and Dr. Melvin Morse's Work: These researchers have specialized in collecting and analyzing near-death experiences (NDEs) and OBEs, including a significant number from children.

Dr. Morse's[7] key findings, derived from interviewing children who survived critical illnesses (like cardiac arrest), suggested that children's NDEs follow the same pattern as adults', often including OBEs where they float above their bodies. This consistency across a population that lacks the cultural baggage or theological training of adults argues against the experiences being mere fantasy.

Dr. Long's[8] comprehensive work, based on thousands of narratives, highlights the consistent and unique nature of these experiences—such as verifiable perceptions during

---

7. Morse, Melvin, et al. (1986). "Near-Death Experiences: A Neurophysiological Explanatory Model." *Journal of Near-Death Studies.*

8. Long, Jeffrey. (*e.g., Evidence of the Afterlife: The Science of Near-Death Experiences*).

OBEs—which are difficult to explain by simple psychological or neurological means. Both studies find patterns that strongly suggest the experiences are real, objective events, and not just products of a dying or traumatized brain.

The Pam Reynolds Case[9] : This is one of the most compelling and detailed cases on record, often cited as strong evidence for consciousness outside the body. During her 1991 brain surgery, Pam Reynolds was placed in a state of clinical death for a procedure known as hypothermic cardiac arrest. Her body temperature was lowered to 60° F, her blood was drained, and her brain showed zero electrical activity (flat EEG and absent brainstem response). Yet, she later recalled specific, verifiable details from a disembodied perspective, including the distinct, odd sound of the surgical saw and a conversation between surgeons about her condition, which occurred while her brain was supposedly inactive.

General Scientific Research by Dr. Olaf Blanke[10] : Dr. Blanke's research at the Swiss Federal Institute of Technology has shown that stimulating the TPJ can trigger OBE-like sensations, such as the impression of seeing one's body from above. While this provides a strong materialistic approach, suggesting the experience may be an illusion generated by a neural malfunction, it also introduces the central tension of our narrative: Why does a localized manipulation of the brain create a universal experience described in spiritual texts?

A Sky Full of Ascensions: Mythology and Meaning

I've come to realize that my obsession with the OBE is part of a collective, long-standing narrative that transcends cultures and eras. It is a reflection of a deeper yearning, a desire to transcend corporeal limitations and commune with the sacred.

It is vital to draw a distinction here. In my experience, I was not *truly* flying. I knew, without a doubt, that my body remained seated in the hallway. My personal ascension was

---

9. The Pam Reynolds Case (documented in publications by Michael Sabom, such as *Light and Death*).

10. Blanke, Olaf, et al. (Research published in *Nature* or *Brain* on the Temporo-Parietal Junction (TPJ)).

purely one of consciousness—a weightless gliding of my awareness that separated from and moved around my physical form.

Religious and transcendent traditions are filled with stories of flight and levitation. St. Joseph of Cupertino was observed levitating more than seventy times. In other traditions, flight is linked to shamanic abilities and journeys to other realms. The Māori people used large kites called *manu tangata*, or "bird people," reflecting the ancient connection between humans and aerial ascension.

Perhaps the most famous of these is the myth of Daedalus and Icarus, a tale that feels particularly poignant to me.

The tale recounts how Daedalus, a master craftsman, fashioned wings of feathers and wax so he and his son, Icarus, could escape imprisonment. Daedalus gave his son a strict, two-part warning: do not fly too high, lest the sun melt the wax binding the feathers, and do not fly too low, lest the damp sea weigh down the wings. Despite this instruction, Icarus, filled with the hubris and sheer joy of flight, soared too close to the sun. The wax melted, and he fell to his death.

My brother's warning, "You would die," mirrors the core theme of the Icarus story: a loving protector cautions against a transgression that would lead to death. I've come to see my story as the myth of Icarus, told in reverse. His tragedy was one of ambition; mine was one of obedience. It's strange how the very stories meant to keep us safe can sometimes be the same things that clip our wings.

Looking back, I understand that whether I ever physically floated above the carpet isn't what matters. What matters is that the experience—the pure, weightless joy of gliding—was undeniably real. That part is the truth.

When Quiet Ones Speak: The Power of the Shared Truth

I didn't discuss these topics because that inner knowing was precious—a fragile thing I had learned to protect from the harsh glare of a world that would have either judged it or dismissed it entirely. I feared the stigma, the label, the whispers of "crazy" that might follow me for the rest of my life.

One day, while scrolling on some social media platform, a headline caught my eye: "Does anyone else remember being able to fly?"

My heart stopped. It was a question so simple, so aligned with my deepest secrets, that I was met with a jolt of recognition coursing through my body. Another person remembered this very same thing. I devoured the post, then read the comments. One after another, the voices rose from the anonymity of the internet, each one a mirror of my own unspoken truth. I read of one person who remembered hearing a "tonal noise," a sound that preceded the detaching, and of others who described a "thunderous hurricane rushing noise." My own sensations were validated by a collective, unspoken language.

I commented too, my fingers trembling as I typed the words: "I used to glide, too."

And in that moment, the isolation of a lifetime began to dissolve. Others jumped in, their statements echoing mine with astonishing detail. We were no longer alone. It was a revelation.

That person, the one who made that post, the one who asked first—I am forever grateful to them. In my eyes, they were a torchbearer in the dark. Their innocent question broke a silence I had thought was unbreakable.

My story has been a journey: from a child's simple, unquestioning knowledge, through a period of forced disbelief, and finally toward a new kind of acceptance. For most of my life, silence was my shield. But that kind of protection can eventually become its own kind of cage.

The goal now is to bring the hidden parts of myself back into the light, embracing a reality that is made of both what can be seen and what can only be felt. I know that I must speak my truth. I wrote this book as an act of faith in my own experience, in the hope that I can shine one of those lights and be a voice that gives courage to others.

By sharing my story, I embrace the belief that what I felt was more real than what the world told me was possible. This journey is a collective pilgrimage, and by giving my story a body and a voice, I hope to find others.

Chapter 4: When Grownups Come Out to Play

Christ Consciousness is loving life. All life. Even a bug. Even a flower. Even things you judge as "bad." Loving everything is the way to Oneness, to collective consciousness. So stop worrying. You are safe and protected. Just keep seeking and finding the best in everyone, in everything. You are not alone.

—Messages from the Unseen

When I look back on my life's tapestry, the threads reveal an intricate pattern—a design woven by a hand beyond my sight. Every veiling and unveiling of my being, every fleeting moment, was a destined stitch leading me inevitably to the person I was always supposed to become. My immersion in the metaphysical began the moment I opened my eyes, but the conscious pursuit of the seeker?

The journey of the seeker only became possible after meeting someone. This true transformation began, as many profound events do, not with a violent shift, but with the subtle resonance of a kindred presence.

I was only a child of nine—a small, curious thing in a world that often felt too big and too loud—when I met Mirela. To this day, she remains one of the most remarkable human beings I have ever had the privilege to know. There was an undeniable resonance between us, a shared way of seeing what rippled beneath the surface of everyday life. She saw the world with the same eyes that I did. For the first time, I was seen.

Mirela was a friend of my family—an accomplished attorney by day, but a traveler of worlds and a connoisseur of the spiritual by night. She had a certain openness to the hidden realms that I'd never encountered in an adult before. I was only a child, but I recognized in her the first grown-up who had a curiosity for similar things that I did.

Her acknowledgment of a deeper essence was a confirmation, a validation that what I was experiencing was not a figment of a child's imagination. It was real. And so, I began to beg my mother to visit her, to sit at her kitchen table with a cup of hot cocoa between my hands and absorb every word that came from her mouth.

She was one of those rare people who, without ever knowing it, held my hand and guided me onto this path.

In the 1990s, when New Age philosophies were still whispered secrets rather than mainstream trends, Mirela was a quiet pioneer. She was delving into the mysteries of astral projection and had a knowledge that seemed boundless. Her cosmology was a beautiful, seamless blend of Christian, Buddhist, and esoteric knowledge. For Mirela, there were no contradictions between the teachings of Jesus and Buddha, the practical power of manifestation, or the long-standing art of divination. It was all a single, flowing river of interconnected universal knowledge that somehow worked together.

It was from her that I learned the sacred act of building a shield of light around myself. This was a practice I did before embarking on what I, in my youthful innocence, believed was a simple visit into dreamland. "When you decide to step into the dreamworld," she would say, "make sure you first protect yourself." She taught me to imagine a protective bubble of pure, white light, a sanctuary for my spirit to venture out in. And I was content with it being a dreamland, because as long as the magic was allowed to exist there, it was real to me. It existed. It was just somewhere else.

I would sit there for hours, a torrent of questions spilling from my lips. Mirela, ever patient and kind, indulged every single one. It was like a game with a grown-up who was willing to play with me. I was having the time of my life, and in that play, I gained knowledge that would one day save my life.

She was my first guide to the art of self-protection, offering a skill I would one day rely upon. She taught me how to connect with the earth's rhythm, how to replenish my core essence by drawing energy from the sun or walking barefoot on the grass. Most remarkably, she taught me how to see people's auras, which she described as invisible, luminous energy fields that surround a person or living being. This was a gift she gave me that remains with me to this day, a vibrant, ethereal language that speaks louder than words.

Mirela did not have the academic jargon for these things, but years later I understood that she had been teaching me about astral travel, remote viewing, and divination. She was living proof that you do not need a word for something to have a direct understanding of it.

It was also through her that I was taught an esoteric principle: the Law of Three. "Say something three times," she would say, "and someone up there will listen." Whether she was alluding to the Holy Trinity or some other law of hidden workings, this rule became a core belief for me. It is a cosmic principle that has since proven its power countless times.

Mirela taught me that a word spoken once is a loud thought, but a word spoken three times is a spell, a force of will sent out into the universe. She also believed that our deeds, both good and ill, return to us threefold.

Over time, I witnessed this truth unfold in my own life. A spontaneous gesture of charity—money given to a beggar on a whim—returned to me threefold. Careless words to a lover—the hurt I once inflicted—returned to me with a devastating force three times over.

And in moments of great peril, when I had nothing left but my voice, I would utter a plea for help three times, and help would come. I was delivered to safety through situations that defied all logic. I know with absolute certainty that it was not my wits, charm, or sunny disposition that kept me alive. Looking back, I realize I was not easy to keep safe. My thirst for adventure often overshadowed my wisdom, my curiosity leading me into reckless decisions.

One night, the Law of Three was put to its ultimate test. A raw, brutal fight with my then-husband had just ended, and he had left for work, a night shift that would end at around three in the morning.

I knew the drill. The unwritten script of our lives was etched in my mind. He would spend an hour in the garage, a bottle of whiskey his only companion, and then he would return, filled with a fury that would find its release in violence. I knew this one was going to be especially bad—the blow I was due had been delayed—and I was terrified.

I did not pray back then. Even the idea of hope was foreign, an emotion I had lost. But in that moment of sheer terror, something shifted. For reasons I cannot explain, my mind reached for a name I had only heard in passing. Frankly, I don't know why I thought of this particular name: Archangel Michael. But in the terror of that empty house, I whispered his name three times—a desperate incantation for help and protection.

The response was not a booming voice or a flash of light, but an exquisite peace that settled over me. It was as if I was being held, swaddled in a love so whole it took my breath away. Muscles I didn't even know were tense began to soften. My shallow, panicked breaths deepened into slow, even inhales. My mind, a whirlwind of anxiety-fueled thoughts, went still, and I was simply there, bathed in feelings of safety and love. Even now, writing these words, I am brought to tears of gratitude and awe.

And then, I fell asleep. In the very moment I was supposed to be alert, on guard, and afraid, I slipped into the sweetest, most peaceful slumber of my life.

I woke up hours later, and he was home. But he was not angry. In fact, he was gentle and almost loving. The rage that had been a certainty hours before was completely gone, replaced by a tranquility very much unlike him.

It was then, in that moment, that I had the certainty, above all doubt, that angels are real. And to this day, when I hear the name Archangel Michael, my heart fills with a warmth and trust that is both humbling and all-consuming. I have called on him many times since, and many times, he has been my salvation. When my time on this earth is done, he is one of the Unseen that I most hope to be able to thank in person.

Mirela's impact on my life was immeasurable. I never got the chance to tell her how her gentle influence had illuminated a direction for me. She passed away a few years after our time together, peacefully, in her sleep. Her sister recounted a story that haunts me, a memory of Mirela speaking in her sleep that night, whispering, "Yes, I will go." I believe it. I believe she chose to leave this world, departing on her own terms, a traveler who got a say in when her journey was done.

It has been thirty years since I last saw her, but her words and guidance are still with me—a constant presence. Her Law of Three philosophy has served as a powerful guide in a world that often feels chaotic and meaningless. Her lessons on building a shield of light were not just an imaginative game for a child, but a foundational training for the astral travels I would one day undertake. I am forever grateful for the privilege of knowing her, a shining light who indicated that the boundaries between this world and the next are not as solid as they seem.

I think of Mirela often, and now, revisiting this chapter of my life, I realize the most valuable lesson she gave me was not the tricks and tips, but the simple knowledge that others were out there—studying, reading, and writing about these things. My world was small, but reading opened the horizon to me. My search was, at last, able to begin, starting with the very core of her philosophy: the power of three.

Mirela's Teachings

In addition to the Law of Three, Mirela shared a lot of wisdom. I feel it would be a disservice if I didn't share it in these pages. The lessons were many, and each was a gift, but I will speak only of those I have carried and applied throughout my own life—the ones I have verified with my own two eyes and my own spirit.

The first thing she taught me was how to see what she called the life-light—the aura. She led me to a small bathroom, pointing to the plain white wall behind me. "To see what is unseen," she explained softly, "it helps to begin with a simple background. The world is loud, and a quiet space helps you focus. Later, it won't matter."

She had me stand before the mirror. "Focus your gaze," she instructed, her voice steady, "on the space right between your eyes. Don't strain. Just rest your eyes there. Hold it for fifteen or twenty seconds, and let everything else in the mirror soften."

I stared, my reflection becoming blurry at the edges. "Soon," she whispered, "you will notice something change in the corners of your vision. A faint light, a soft outline around your shoulders. Don't look at it directly. Just let it be there."

I did, and a shimmering contour appeared in my periphery. "Now," she said, "very gently, relax your eyes and let your gaze drift up toward your forehead. Don't force it. Just allow it to happen."

At that moment, something shifted. The faint, luminous outline blossomed, tracing the shape of my body. It was a shimmering, subtle light, a silent testament to the energy within. Mirela had me practice this daily. My sessions in front of the mirror slowly transformed from a focused ritual into a simple glance. Soon, all I had to do was look, and my aura would manifest.

From there, we moved on to other people's auras. "The steps are the same," she told me, having me practice on her against the white wall. "Once you know what to look for, your eyes will learn to find it anywhere." And she was right. In time, I didn't need the blank background. I began to see the gentle glow around people on the street. Eventually, the colors came, and with them, the auras of animals and the pulsing, vibrant light of plants and trees. This small, secret sight has stayed with me for a lifetime.

Another profound lesson came in the form of protection. Mirela held what she called "group guided meditations," though the circle was small: just my mother, her sister, her mother, and me. Her sessions often focused on what I now understand as astral travel. Each session began in the same way, with the same ritual. "Close your eyes. Relax your body. Now, look inside. Find the light that lives within you. Let it shine, and focus on it until it becomes a sun, brilliant and bright."

As the light grew, she would guide us. "Watch it grow until it surpasses the boundaries of your physical form. Now, visualize a sphere of perfect, clear crystal surrounding you completely. This ball is your armor. It is perfectly transparent, yet ten million times stronger than diamond. It is impenetrable, unbreakable."

I sit here now, typing these memories, and a huge wave of gratitude hits me. After all these years, Mirela's words are still with me. Years later, I would discover these principles woven into physics, mythology, and even neuroscience.

The Law of Three: My Journey to Understanding

For years, Mirela's core beliefs—that we should repeat our intentions three times and that our actions would return to us threefold—had been realities for me, and I felt a responsibility to understand their origins.

My first search for this rule took me straight to the Law of Three (or Threefold Law) of Wiccan, Neo-Pagan, and occult traditions. The principle asserts that any energy, whether positive or negative, that a person projects into the world will be returned to them three times over. This belief is so central to Wicca that it is intricately linked to the Wiccan Rede, which states, "Do what thy wilt, though it harm none." I could see why. Adherents of Wicca exercise extreme caution when casting spells, precisely because of the belief in this threefold return.

The nature of this return is often framed as a profound, simultaneous restoration of the mind, body, and innermost self—a phenomenon I witnessed in my own life.

A positive deed would uplift my thoughts, stir positive emotions, and result in overall well-being. It's a complete, all-encompassing phenomenon. It's an ethical system for a practitioner, and I can see how someone who follows this code would naturally be a cautious and caring individual.

The fact that a belief held by a supposedly disparate group of people so closely mirrored my own experience was my first aha moment. I was in good company.

Finding Patterns in Unexpected Places

My investigation continued to reveal parallels. I found the 369 Manifestation Method, a modern law of attraction technique that uses the numbers three, six, and nine to affirm desires. In this method, the numeral three represents the principles of creativity and manifestation, linking the physical, mental, and metaphysical realms—a familiar pattern.

I found a routine: write or recite affirmations three times in the morning, six times in the afternoon, and nine times in the evening. This practice is rooted in the idea—though perhaps lacking credible proof—that Nikola Tesla believed these numbers held a code of the universe.

Tesla was interested in numerology and the concepts of energy, frequency, and vibration. This modern method suggests that consistent repetition rewires the brain, aligns intentions with the law of attraction, and encourages action toward desired outcomes. It was another clear link between Mirela's instruction to say something three times, this modern technique, and the power of repetition.

But the most surprising revelation came when I began to explore the significance of the number three in biblical and Christian contexts. The number holds symbolic weight here, signifying a sense of perfection, completeness, and a holistic representation of life. For Christians, three expresses a beginning, a middle, and an end, indicating something solid and substantial.

At the heart of Christian theology is the belief in the Holy Trinity—one God existing as three distinct persons: Father, Son, and Holy Spirit. And the symbolism doesn't stop there. Repetition in patterns of three is a prominent literary device in the Bible used to emphasize important themes and messages. The seraphim's thrice-repeated proclamation, "Holy, holy, holy is the LORD of Hosts," emphasizes God's absolute purity. Paul's exhortation to "Rejoice in the Lord always. I will say it again: Rejoice!" highlights the importance of joy. It is the same principle again: repetition, particularly triple repetition, for ultimate reinforcement.

The power of three also permeates key biblical events. The earth was separated from the waters on the third day. There were three patriarchs of Israel: Abraham, Isaac, and Jacob. Jonah spent three days in the belly of the great fish. Jesus' ministry spanned three years, and he was crucified at the third hour. Three crosses stood on Calvary, and Jesus rose from the dead on the third day.

This all reinforced the idea that what I was experiencing was not unique or an isolated belief. Instead, it was a principle woven into the fabric of our foundational mythology and sacred traditions.

The Law of Conservation and Threefold Systems

My exploration into the wisdom of trinities ended, much to my surprise, not in temples or mystical texts, but in the seemingly cold, hard logic of physics.

I found an echo of Mirela's threefold return and the Wiccan Rule of Three in the Law of Conservation.

This fundamental principle of physics states that in any isolated system, a measurable property like mass or energy doesn't simply disappear. Instead, it remains constant over time. That power is never created or destroyed; it merely changes form. Every action has a reaction, and the force you put out into the universe doesn't vanish into a vacuum. It comes back in a different form.[1]

This resonated with me to my core. My observations—what I had witnessed first-hand—aligned with this principle.

If I put positivity and creativity into a project, that energy wouldn't be lost. It would manifest as success, recognition, or perhaps a new, even better opportunity.

If I put out negativity—such as anger, frustration, or deceit—that would also find its way back to me. It was not a direct punishment, but a consequence of the ripple effect I had created. The universe did nothing more than reflect my actions, as the rules of conservation state. It was not a matter of judgment, but a matter of universal reciprocity.

As I dove deeper, I found trinities embedded in the very foundation of our worldview. In physics, our universe is described with three spatial dimensions: length, width, and height. This isn't just an arbitrary number; it's the framework that allows for our perception of depth, volume, and the intricate, interconnected systems we see all around us.

In chemistry, the basic unit of all matter, the atom, is composed of three constituent particles: protons, neutrons, and electrons. These three particles, through their arrangement and interaction, determine the properties of every element in the known universe. It's a beautifully uncomplicated, elegant system that creates infinite complexity. This foundational trio is the basis of everything, from the air we breathe to the stars in the night sky.

---

1. Fritjof Capra, *The Tao of Physics: An Exploration of the Parallels Between Modern Physics and Eastern Mysticism* (Boston: Shambhala, 1975).

Even in the most essential processes of life itself, the number three is central. In biology, the genetic code is read in codons, which are sequences of three nucleotides. This triplet code determines the amino acids that build proteins, essentially acting as the building blocks of life. My own genetic makeup, the blueprint of my being, is built on a foundation of threes, as the language of life is spoken in triplets.

The more I searched, the more I saw that what Mirela had shown me was not some quirk. It was a pattern woven into the very structure of existence, from the largest cosmic structures to the smallest building blocks of life.

The Language of the Universe

My discovery of the trinity in science felt like pulling on a single thread, only to find it was woven into a vast, ancient tapestry. If the number three was embedded so deeply in the fabric of reality, what about other numbers? It was a question that led me from the certainties of the lab to the more mystical corridors of history, where numbers were seen not as mere counters, but as the very language of the universe.

The first stop on this journey had to be with the ancient Greeks, specifically Pythagoras and his followers. For them, the universe was not just described by numbers; it was numbers.[2] They believed that everything, from the orbits of the planets to the notes in a musical scale, had a numerical essence. Numbers held a secret vibration, a divine logic. This wasn't just mathematics; it was a spiritual path. They saw the number ten, the tetractys, as a sacred symbol containing the blueprint for all creation. This ancient reverence for numbers as something more than symbolic echoed in cultures across the globe.

In Abrahamic religions, numbers form a foundation of sacred structure. I saw the power of seven in the days of creation; the twelve tribes of Israel and the twelve apostles of Christ; and the forty days and nights of deluge and wandering. In esoteric traditions like Jewish Kabbalah, I found Gematria, a mystical practice where each Hebrew letter is assigned a

---

2. Matthew Goodwin, *Numerology: The Complete Guide* (San Francisco: Weiser Books, 1994).

numerical value, turning sacred texts into a complex web of mathematical and spiritual meaning. The words of God, it was believed, were also a divine equation.

This ancient practice has found a new voice in the modern world through numerology and the more recent phenomenon of "angel numbers." I learned of people calculating their "life path number" from their birth date to understand their core purpose, seeing it as a vibrational signature for their soul. And I read countless stories of people seeing repeating sequences—111, 444, 555—on clocks, license plates, and receipts, interpreting them as winks from the universe, messages of guidance or reassurance.

Of course, I had to ask: Is there any scientific basis for this? The answer, predictably, is no. Mainstream science views numerology as a pseudoscience, a classic example of the human brain's tendency to find patterns where none exist—a phenomenon known as confirmation bias. And yet, dismissing the experience felt incomplete.

The Swiss psychologist Carl Jung offered a more compassionate bridge with his concept of "synchronicity"—meaningful coincidences that are not causally linked, but connected by the meaning we find in them.[3]

For me, the truth lay somewhere in that bridge. The question wasn't whether a number itself held magical power, but whether numbers could act as a conduit for meaning. Perhaps these recurring numbers are simply a way for our own deeper consciousness—our unseen self—to get our attention, using the most universal and clear symbols we have. They are a knock on the door of our awareness. They are a signpost, not necessarily from an angel or a deity, but from the part of ourselves that is already connected to a larger pattern—a part that is trying to remind us to pay attention. The universe, it seems, doesn't always speak in words. Sometimes, it just counts.

Quantum Superposition and Observation

The parallel between the esoteric and the rational intensified even more when I began to explore quantum physics. The world of quantum mechanics seems foreign and

---

3. Carl Jung, *Synchronicity: An Acausal Connecting Principle* (Princeton, NJ: Princeton University Press, 1973).

counter-intuitive, at least to me, but it provided a surprisingly philosophical, albeit less direct, parallel to Mirela's teachings.

The principle of quantum superposition states that a quantum system exists in a combination of all possible states at the same time. This is the famous thought experiment of Schrödinger's cat—in a box, the cat is both alive and dead until the moment we open the box to observe it. An electron, for example, can be in all possible spin states until it is measured. The act of observation forces the system to "collapse" into a single, definite state.[4]

This concept, for me, served as a perfect analogy for Mirela's "Unseen" and the influence of intention. Before you speak your intention, the future exists as a swirling, hazy superposition of countless possibilities. It's a quantum field of potential, where every outcome—good, bad, or indifferent—coexists.

The practice of stating your intention, especially when done with focus and repetition, is like a manner of observation. It's a movement of consciousness that, according to this analogy, collapses that wave of possibilities into a particular, willed manifestation. It's the difference between something being a theoretical possibility and becoming a concrete actuality. Intention becomes "the observer" that forces the universe to choose a particular path from the infinite number of available ones.

This was more than just a mental game; it was like a cosmic law. When Mirela told me to repeat my intentions three times, her teaching was more than just a ritual. She was teaching me a principle of cosmic observation.

The more one focuses on a designated outcome, the more they are able to bring that outcome into manifestation. It's like each repetition intensifies our focus, each word acting like a photon striking a quantum particle, forcing it into a tangible form.

This idea has an interesting echo in the field of cognitive research, where the observer effect is a well-documented quirk of perception. Our brains are not passive recipients of

---

4. Bruce Rosenblum and Fred Kuttner, *Quantum Enigma: Physics Encounters Consciousness* (New York: Oxford University Press, 2006).

stimuli; they are active interpreters. Our beliefs, expectations, and focus literally shape what we perceive.

If I believe that things are getting better, my brain will start looking for evidence of that belief, and I will find it. My consciousness and intention become an active force in shaping my world. The power of a focused mind isn't a metaphor; it's a measurable force of will. It's the difference between a thought being a fleeting possibility and becoming a firm, unshakeable belief. That belief then guides my actions and, in turn, shapes my understanding of the world. The practice of intention is not hoping; it is a creative flow of focused awareness that initiates the process of manifestation.

Brain Science and Repetition

The force of repetition, from biblical chants to Mirela's simple advice, finds its most direct and compelling arguments in modern neuroscience. The 369 Manifestation Method's reliance on repetitive affirmation isn't a magical trick; it has a clear basis in how our brains are wired.

I was surprised to find that this mystical rule wasn't a secret at all. In the world of communication, the Law of Three is a cornerstone of persuasive speech and powerful writing. There is something in the human mind that finds a pattern of three uniquely satisfying; a trio feels complete and balanced, and is far easier for our brains to remember.

This is the hidden rhythm behind some of history's most resonant phrases, from the French Revolution's cry for "Liberty, Equality, Fraternity" to the American promise of "Life, Liberty, and the pursuit of Happiness." It is the invisible blueprint for our most enduring stories, which are almost always built on a three-act structure of beginning, middle, and end.

Mirela hadn't just taught me a spiritual law; she had armed me with one of the most powerful tools of human connection. To repeat something three times is to give it a cadence, an emotional weight that lodges it not just in the mind, but in the soul.

The phrase, "neurons that fire together, wire together,"[5] perfectly summarizes the principle of Hebb's Law. When you repeat a thought, an action, or a belief, you strengthen the neural pathways associated with it. This process is called neuroplasticity, and it's a beautiful, elegant description of how we can literally change our minds.

By repeatedly focusing my mind on a desired outcome, I was not just daydreaming; I was physically rewiring my brain. The affirmations weren't simply words; they were commands for my neurons. This process made it easier for my brain to recognize opportunities and encouraged me to take actions that aligned with my intentions. It was like I was training a muscle. The more I practiced, the stronger the connection became and the more automatic the process of manifestation grew.

My mind and actions began to work in perfect concert, guided by the intentional pathways I had built.

But it wasn't without effort. Soon, I would learn that victories came after hard work and real focus. It is in the way I looked at my efforts that caused the change. I didn't dread hard work anymore. I didn't mind studying hard anymore. My eyes were on the prize, and, when a positive attitude combines with effort and creativity, things happen.

The consistent repetition of affirmations is a form of training that reinforces new mental patterns over old ones. Our brains are highly efficient. Without conscious input, they fall back on old patterns of scarcity or doubt. The 369 method is an uncomplicated tool to disrupt those old patterns.

By consistently and intentionally reinforcing new beliefs, I was consciously choosing what kind of world my brain would create. The numbers themselves may be symbolic, but the underlying mechanism—that repetition strengthens neural connections and shapes our perception—is a core principle of brain study.

This process also has an effect on our subconscious minds. The subconscious mind is like a vast, fertile garden. It doesn't question or judge; it simply accepts what is planted.

---

5. Norman Doidge, *The Brain That Changes Itself: Stories of Brain Science Pioneers and the Triumphs of Neuroplasticity* (New York: Viking, 2007).

Through consistent repetition, we plant seeds of intention. The conscious mind may get distracted, but the subconscious is always working, always tending to those seeds.

This is why the method works even when you're not thinking about it. The seeds have already been planted, and the subconscious is busy working to bring them to fruition. This explains why moments of clarity or "inspired action" seem to come out of nowhere. They are nothing more than the result of the subconscious mind presenting a solution to the conscious mind.

It's not a superpower, it's the natural, predictable outcome of a disciplined and intentional mindset.

The Map of Mythology

The deeper I went, the more evident it was. This triad extends far from the measurable and into the very essence of human storytelling and belief. Philosophers like Pythagoras considered three to be the perfect number, embodying a beginning, middle, and end. This universal appeal is evident in the myths of nearly every civilization. The notion is more than a cultural artifact; it is a foundational element in human cognition, a primordial pattern that we intuitively understand.

I found this rule of three as a well-established narrative device in countless folktales and literary works. Think of the three wishes granted to a hero, the three little pigs building their houses, or Goldilocks and the three bears. In these tales, the first two attempts often fail, but the third always leads to success or resolution.

This pattern resonates with us because it mirrors our own progression through life. The first attempt is often a test of the waters, the second builds tension and shows our perseverance, and the third provides closure. This structure is so fundamental that it's the basis of the three-act structure in theater and film. The pattern makes literary pieces memorable, stable, and satisfying.

In Greek mythology, the number three is everywhere.[6] The Olympian brothers—Zeus, Poseidon, and Hades—divided the cosmos and ruled the three realms of sky, waters, and the underworld. The three Fates—Clotho, Lachesis, and Atropos—spun, measured, and cut the threads of human life, embodying the inevitability of destiny. The three Fates are a stark, powerful representation of the unchangeable arc of life.

The Norse had their own version of the Fates in the three Norns—Urd, Verandi, and Skuld—who shape destiny and nurture the world tree, Yggdrasil.

The Celtic traditions, with their Triple Goddesses and Triple Spiral, symbolized the cycle of life, death, and rebirth, and the three domains of land, water, and sky. The Celtic myths even featured the motif of the Threefold Death, where a person died in three different ways as a punishment for a major transgression. This underscored that the trinity was not just a symbol of completeness, but also of ultimate cosmic justice.

The prime number three is highly significant in Hinduism. The Trimurti represents the divine triad of Brahma (the creator), Vishnu (the preserver), and Shiva (the destroyer), all seen as manifestations of the one supreme reality. Rituals often involve circumambulating a holy space or deity three times as a demonstration of respect and devotion.

My quest for understanding became a lesson in the collective human unconscious. It affirmed that these three digits were not just a cultural artifact, but a foundational element in how we perceive and organize the world. It's embedded in universal symbols and human concepts. We use three to describe time—past, present, and future—and to describe human action—thought, word, and deed. It's in our traffic lights (red, yellow, and green) and our primary colors (red, blue, and yellow).

The fact that this pattern appears in such disparate areas of human life—from mythology to modern thought—is proof that it is more than a coincidence. It is a bedrock truth about how the universe, our minds, and our consciousness work. Could this be a map that has been passed down through generations, and am I finally catching a glimpse into how to read it?

---

6. Edith Hamilton, *Mythology: Timeless Tales of Gods and Heroes* (Boston: Little, Brown and Company, 1942).

The Silence of Modernity

Looking back on this story, I see a full-blown mythology lesson, a course in esoteric knowledge taught by the universe itself. But the main takeaway for me isn't the sheer volume of cognitive data; it's the fact that this insight was all around us all along, hidden in plain sight. Our ancestors left us a map, a guide to finding our own power and our own awakening. Yet, it seems our modern world really doesn't care to pay attention to it.

My exploration confirmed my suspicion: The rule of three is a universal principle, a collective inheritance of insight that has been passed down through generations in countless forms. From the cyclical laws of physics and the tripartite structures of matter to the archetypal myths that have shaped our consciousness, the number three is a consistent thread. It speaks of balance, completion, and the dynamic interplay of forces. It's a key to unlocking the meaning of our place in the universe, and yet very few people talk about it.

The silence is what bugs me, if I'm being honest. I have witnessed the power of three in my own life, and I know I'm not alone. And yet, our culture remains apathetic—even hostile—to this kind of knowledge.

We focus on studying relics and pieces of bone from a distant past, but disregard the knowledge and wisdom those artifacts represent. We analyze the artifacts, but we don't dare to ask what our ancestors were trying to tell us.

We've become obsessed with the "how" of things, but we've completely forgotten the "why." We don't seek knowledge in myths anymore, and that's a pity, because some of those myths are hidden guides for us to find our way back to ourselves.

It seems to me that, for the modern system to work, we must be fearful and powerless. A fearful populace is a controllable populace, and a powerless one is easily manipulated. People who are disconnected from their own inner wisdom, who feel adrift and without purpose, are far more likely to chase after the false promises of consumerism and distraction. They're more likely to accept the status quo without question, to become cogs in a machine they don't understand or even like. And people who believe in magic—not the sleight of hand kind, but the inherent, creative power within themselves—are not fearful or powerless.

Our schools don't teach about these connections, preferring to silo knowledge into disconnected subjects. Our religious leaders often seem more interested in collecting money than in teaching us how to come closer to God. They give us doctrine and dogma, but they don't give us tools.

And our society? Our world is so drunk on money and distraction that God could literally manifest right in front of our eyes, and we'd ask Him to scoot over because we can't see the TV.

We've traded sacred knowledge for fleeting entertainment and genuine communion for a curated online persona. We gave away our deep sense of purpose for a stream of information that keeps us busy but never fulfilled.

This disconnect is painful because I can see what we're missing. Imagine what our world would become if we reclaimed this lost understanding. How wonderful would it be to be able to study these things in peace—to devote time to researching the mysteries, gathering the pieces, and solving the puzzle? I imagine a world where schools teach about the parallels between neuroscience and mythology, where mystic leaders guide us toward our own inner strength, and where society values insight over wealth.

My immersion in the Law of Three revealed a truth, not just about the universe, but about us. The inherited wisdom of our ancestors, so meticulously encoded in myth, science, and cosmic principles, was meant to be discovered, not lost.

This knowledge is not an esoteric truth to be hoarded, but a map to be followed, and its greatest revelation is this: We are the mapmakers.

We can begin the journey on our own, today, by simply choosing to look closer, and to listen to the truths that echo inside of us. By listening to that inner voice telling us there's more to this. The breadcrumbs have been left for us. It's a collective trove of shared insight that is ours for the taking. So, ask yourself, what truth is waiting for you to find it? What reality lies hidden in plain sight, waiting for you to see it?

Your life, like a story, is a canvas of thought, word, and deed—a constant creative act. You have the power to shape your reality. The question is not whether the universe is listening; the question is, what are you ready to say three times? What will you create? The work begins the moment you decide to start, but it only succeeds when you choose to trust it—to believe in it the same way you believe that the sun will rise tomorrow morning. And hey, who knows, maybe what they say is true and the third time really is the charm.

Chapter 5: The Sea – A Love Story

Gaia herself will remember you if you were kind. To all. To everything. To nature itself. As long as you love life, all is well. As it should be.

—Messages from the Unseen

At fourteen, I was still a kid, at least on the outside. But within the confines of my mind, a relentless quest for authenticity had already taken root.

It began two years prior—a fragile seed of determination, watered by a world that was quickly, breathtakingly expanding. The internet—a fledgling frontier in those days—became my sanctuary.

It was a digital ocean where I could cast my net and pull up articles on religions, wild conspiracy theories, esoteric journals, and the serene wisdom of Buddhist videos. A new world was unfurling before me, a place of infinite knowledge and endless mysteries.

It took me a long time to learn that not every word you read on a glowing screen is true.

I was fourteen, a skinny vessel of unrealized potential, and I didn't understand much of what I was reading. But what I lacked in comprehension, I made up for with a hunger so consuming it was almost painful. I had the kind of primal certainty that the sun will rise tomorrow, and that there was more to this life than what I saw. I knew my search was not a fool's errand.

A whisper inside me, almost like a hum, suggested that not all of those obscure web pages were speaking a piece of truth, but at least some were—revealing a sliver of an unknown reality. In its early form, this technology made it easier for me to find quotes, texts, and knowledge that would have otherwise been inaccessible to a girl in a small bedroom in post-Communist Romania.

Social media was still just a whisper of what it would one day become. The world had not yet learned to share its every waking moment. I wasn't reading from people, not yet, and I hadn't joined a single online community. I was an observer, a reader of static web pages. It became my favorite ritual. I'd grab a bowl of salty snacks, let the rhythm of my music playlist fill the air, and lose myself in the screen, reading about every topic that fascinated me.

One might assume I was a loner—the kind of kid who found solace only in the glow of a computer screen, antisocial and without a life beyond the digital world. But that would be a complete contradiction of who I was. I was a teenager of contrasts, a paradox in a small body. I excelled in school, had a core group of friends—some of whom are still with me, a half-lifetime later—and navigated the typical storms of teenage moods and social expectations. I was a regular teenager, a part of the pack, a player in the grand game of adolescence. Yet, when the last bell rang, the homework was done, and the day's socializing was over, I would retreat to my room, close the door on the ordinary world, and go searching for the extraordinary. I would find the truth, or a semblance of it, in the flickering light of my monitor.

I imagined myself a secret scholar—regular teenager by day, historical texts aficionado at night. The two sides of me would never blend, never merge. I was two people—the goofy, fun-loving teenager, and the old lady with her old books, foundational texts, and heart full of mysticism. Both at the same time, both in the same body.

One sun-drenched day in the middle of summer, a rare impulse struck my mother and brother, and we decided to go to the beach. My mother was never one for the sand and sun, but if both of her kids wanted to go, her resistance would soften.

My brother, with the disciplined focus of an athlete, would swim great distances as a workout, disappearing into the glassy surface of the water for long stretches. My mother, armed with a book, settled onto the sand, ready for a few precious minutes of peace—or so she thought. But the sea had other plans.

When we arrived, the day was flawless. The sky was an expanse of perfect blue, not a single cloud to chip at its perfection. There was not even the slightest hint of a breeze. The sea itself was a sheet of glass, its surface so still you could hardly detect any motion. It whispered a siren song of safety and peaceful days.

I had come to know, long before, that the sea's serenity was a dangerous illusion. My first encounter with its true nature had happened when I was around six years old, a memory as vague as a dream, yet as real as a scar. I can still feel the primal shock of that massive wave hitting me. It knocked me off my feet with its cold, crushing force, and started to pull me back into its immense depths.

Bless her fierce, protective heart, my mother had managed to grab my little hand. She held on for dear life as the wave twisted and pulled and the sand and shells scraped my skin like a thousand tiny razors. In the end, she was able to drag me back to the safety of the beach. It was enough. It was a brutal lesson that taught me that big bodies of water were not a plaything. They were a living, breathing entity capable of swallowing you whole without a second thought.

Despite that lesson—or perhaps because I had foolishly allowed it to atrophy—the glassy, tranquil surface of the ocean was just too inviting. The day was too beautiful to resist. I had been in the water so many times since that first scare that I had grown complacent, forgetting the memory of how quickly things can change, how a serene façade can hide a violent heart. I told my mom I was going in, and she gave a thoughtful request to "be careful." With that, I waded into the water.

After about fifteen minutes of playing mermaid in the shallows, a subtle shift began. The air, only seconds before still, stirred, and the water around me grew agitated, its placid surface giving way to a troubled churn. Faster than I could react, I was being pulled by an invisible force—a current dragging me toward the abyss.

At some point, somewhere in the roiling water, a hole had formed on the seabed, dug out by these currents, and my feet no longer touched the bottom. I tried to swim, but the current was a relentless, invisible hand, pulling me back with every stroke. Panic seized me, and I screamed for help. The vast, empty horizon answered with silence. I didn't know when the water had become so rough, but others had noticed the same thing, and they had gotten out—everyone but me.

I am not sure how long this struggle lasted. Time melted into a distorted, liquid thing. My muscles, burning and exhausted, began to give way. I was too tired, too weak, and nowhere near a good swimmer. The water kept pulling me, an unyielding torment, and I could not reach the sea floor with my feet to rest. By then, I had swallowed a bitter, nauseating amount of salt water, and I was beginning to choke on it.

It was in that moment, in the suffocating silence of my struggle, that the thought hit me with the cold clarity of a knife: "This is it. This is how I die."

A raw, animal terror surged through me. My logical mind, fighting for every last moment of consciousness, started to plead: "I am only fourteen. This can't be it. Life can't be over!" But soon enough, my pleading proved pointless. I was still drowning. I was dying, and it was over. For a second, I was met with the sharp, brutal reality of it. Then, somehow, the terror began to dissipate. It couldn't be avoided—sooner or later, I was going to die.

And so, I let go.

I was still fully conscious when I turned to look up. The sun, a perfect circle of light, shimmered through the agitated surface of the water. For the first time in the entire experience, a new thought—not of panic, but of immense wonder—settled over me. "This isn't a bad way to go. It's peaceful, I'm weightless, and the sun is shining down on me." I was, almost instantly, engrossed in an encompassing sense of serenity that defied logic. And, in an unexplainable way, I was deeply grateful. It could have been so much worse.

As my last conscious thoughts began to drift away, a new physical awareness broke through the calm. I sensed a firm, insistent pull on my hair. It took me a few seconds to register what was happening, but it looked like I was being rescued.

Suddenly, I was out of the water, my head breaking the surface, and, despite the frantic coughing and choking, I took a full, life-giving breath of air.

Somehow, instinctually, I remembered not to struggle, not to grab on. I relaxed, allowing my savior to maneuver me in a safe way, ensuring neither of us would drown. I was able to open my eyes and see him. He was a young man, probably in his twenties, with shoulder-length, dark, curly hair and olive-colored skin.

"Thank you! You saved my life," I rasped, the words a miracle in my burning throat. All the salt water, the screaming, the coughing—it had made my throat feel like it was covered in barbed wire. He didn't reply. He was busy keeping us both alive. At some point, we reached the shore, and he handed me to someone else, a blur in the gathering crowd. I kept whispering "Thank you" until I collapsed, the emotional dam breaking. All the fear, the panic, and the relief—it found its way out in a torrent of sobs that shook my entire body.

My mom, bless her heart, was as white as paper, her face a mask of terror. Looking back, I realize I was a complicated kid to deal with. I had given this poor woman so many scares. But in that moment, surrounded by the kindness of strangers and the love of my family, I was overwhelmed with a wave of gratitude to be alive—to have my mom, my dad, my brother, and my friends.

We searched for the man who saved me, but he was nowhere to be found. He had vanished, lost in the crowd that had gathered on the beach. We never got to properly thank him. To this day, I pray for his blessings, well-being, and fulfillment. And I pray for the same spirit that moved him to rescue me to ignite in us all.

One other thing, beyond the gratitude for my savior and for life itself, stayed with me: the peace. In that moment between life and death, I had been granted a glimpse into what happens when you die. I got a taste of death and the profound serenity that came with it.

Up to that point, death had been a scary thought—a final goodbye, an entry into the great unknown. I had always regarded it with fear. But now, this recently found feeling of acceptance and serenity made me think that maybe it wasn't so bad after all. It wasn't as terrifying as I believed it to be.

For the second time, the sea had reminded me that it is not a plaything. It will try to take what it pleases, and sometimes, it takes people.

I'd be lying if I said this was my last lesson. We never learn the first time around, do we? I still go into the water, and I still can't swim. And, every now and then, the waves still gently remind me not to treat it as a plaything.

But beyond being a story of me nearly drowning, this was a watershed moment. Being able to feel that calmness in the face of death—a death that was conscious, present, and as real as it can get—gave me a quiet reassurance. Maybe, when my time comes to say goodbye to this world, the same serenity will settle upon me, and I will be able to look at the sun and think, "It's not so bad."

The Clinical Mirror: Searching for Self in the Findings

That sensation of overwhelming peace stayed with me. It was so visceral and real that it was impossible to shake. After my experience, the online search for truth that had defined my life took on a new and more urgent focus. I began to look for answers to a question I'd never thought I'd have to ask: What happens in that moment between life and death, and why is it so pleasant?

I wasn't looking for a dry, scientific argument, but for something that might make sense of what I had gone through. I found myself diving into a new kind of search, one that went from ancient wisdom to modern neuroscience. I began to realize that my brush with the unknown, which until then I had perceived as unique and singular to me, was something others had been through, too. It had a name: a near-death experience.[1]

It turns out that my experience—the serenity, the sense of floating with it all—was a common thing for people who had been pulled back from the brink. The documented findings I found, from doctors, scientists, and even philosophers, seemed to point to a kind of paradox. On one hand, death is supposed to be terrifying. And for some, it is. But a lot of what I read talked about this unshakable sense of calm, or even euphoria, that comes with it.

I found different ways to try and understand it.

After the drowning, my initial online search for truth took on a new, more urgent focus. My search for clarity about the supernatural had transformed. I was now looking for a way to make sense of one of the most significant moments of my young life: that sudden,

---

1. Moody, Raymond A. *Life After Life: The Investigation of a Phenomenon—Survival of Bodily Death*. New York: HarperOne, 2001 (original edition 1975).

inexplicable stillness. Instead, what I found was a field of study that offered a cold, clinical theory for my experience.

One of the first things I came across was the idea that my mind had created a defense mechanism. The investigators I read talked about the response to a life-threatening incident.[2] The initial terror—the sheer panic of drowning—could be supplanted by a pervasive detachment.

They called it depersonalization—the mind's profound ability to separate itself from the body to protect itself from overwhelming pain and terror. My out-of-body experience, that incredible sense of watching my own struggle from a neutral place, may have been no more than my brain's way of coping with a frightening loss of control. In this model, the mind, as a last resort, denies its own vulnerability. It becomes a placid, detached observer, an audience to its own demise, as if to say, "This isn't really happening to me."

This explanation, while logical, was a little cold and clinical. But it made a certain kind of sense—a biological mechanism to survive the trauma. It was as if my mind, in its final, panicked moments, had decided to tell itself a comforting story, to edit the brutal nature of my drowning into a beautiful, serene narrative. The thought was both brilliant and a little heartbreaking. Was it possible that one of the most transcendent moments of my life was nothing more than a cerebral deception?

But that theory had a few holes in it, ones that my relentless curiosity couldn't ignore. How could my mind, when I was struggling so hard to breathe and my muscles were giving out, have the time or cognitive function to construct a whole, peaceful mental landscape? It appeared to require a level of conscious effort that I didn't have. And how did I, like magic, become so perfectly calm after being so terrified? The emotional switch was too fast, too total to be a simple psychological coping mechanism. It was more like a moment of grace.

The biggest challenge to the depersonalization theory, however, came from the narratives of others who had similar experiences. I learned that not all near-death cases are peaceful.

---

2. Greyson, Bruce. *After: A Doctor Explores What Near-Death Experiences Reveal about Life and Beyond*. New York: St. Martin's Press, 2021.

Some people experienced an immense void, a terrifying sense of nonexistence and isolation. Others encountered a kind of hell, a nightmarish landscape of torment and suffering.

These statements directly contradicted the idea of a universal, soothing mental defense. If the brain's task was to soothe the body and safeguard the mind, why did it fail so spectacularly for some? Why did it create a landscape of terror instead of a field of comfort? Perhaps the serenity was not a universal revelation, but a mirror of the tranquility I had been searching for all along. That idea, that the closing moments of consciousness are a reflection of one's own soul, sounded so much more complete than a defense mechanism. It transformed my perception from a random act of biology into a moment of self-realization.

The Mind's Last Trick: A Cold Equation for Bliss

Then there was the scientific side of things, the world of neurology and physiology. It was here that my curiosity unapologetically took off. I went from reading esoteric journals to diving into medical papers, searching for a biological basis for the serenity I had come to know. What I found was both fascinating and unsettling. It turns out that right before death, the brain doesn't just shut down; it can actually become active. This idea sounded like a paradox, a cold, elegant theory for my moment of blissful serenity.

I read about a report where an eighty-seven-year-old patient who was on an EEG monitor died. In his last moments, the monitor registered a sudden, powerful electrical storm—a surge of high-frequency brainwaves known as gamma oscillations.[3] Gamma waves, I discovered, are the kind of brain activity linked to high-cognitive functions—thinking, dreaming, remembering, and conscious awareness. This ultimate, purposeful surge of electricity in a dying brain presented itself as a possible neurophysiological basis for the near-death experience.

The theory was humbling. It was so clean and complete, like a cold equation for a complex set of emotions. The brain, in its closing moments of oxygen deprivation, orchestrates a

---

3. Vicente, Raul, et al. "Enhanced Interplay of Neuronal Coherence and Coupling in the Dying Human Brain." *Frontiers in Aging Neuroscience*, 14 (2022).

concluding life review, a kind of biological goodbye.[4] This theory challenges the idea of a chaotic brain shutdown and instead suggests an organized, ultimate biological response.

Complementing this neurological activity was the neurochemical hypothesis. The peace that came over me may have been a massive flood of specific chemicals, like serotonin. It was a tempting idea, a tidy explanation for the inexplicable.

The theory was so clean, and so perfectly articulate! And yet, I couldn't shake the idea that something was missing. It explained the "what" and the "how," but it couldn't quite capture the fundamental, personal truth of the "why." It was like trying to explain the emotion of love by only talking about chemical reactions in the brain. It left me with a sense of awe, but not of fulfillment.

Beyond the Veil: Where Consciousness Does not End

The moment I breached the surface, gasping for air, was a frantic return to the world. My lungs burned, and a tremor ran through my limbs. But beneath the terror and the struggle was an echo of that sublime peace, a ghost of what I had known. It was so real, so tangible, that it was impossible to dismiss.

The scientists had their explanations: a surge of endorphins, a flood of chemicals released by a brain deprived of oxygen, a last-ditch effort to console a body in its final moments.

A part of me—the part that valued logic and reason—wanted to accept this. It was neat and mechanically sound, and it fit within the known laws of biology. It was a tidy, well-paved road that fit into the world.

But the theory sounded hollow. It was as if I was being an observer, like a watcher in a movie of my own life—not a participant. This rupture in the veil had been more than a pleasant sensation; it was a seismic shift in my perception.

While I appreciated the logic, my heart kept telling me that it was more than that. It didn't account for the detachment, the sense of watching the sun from a perspective that wasn't

4. Noyes, Russell, Jr. "The Second Catastrophe: A Study in the Psychology of Survival." *Psychiatry* 40, no. 1 (1977): 61–68.

bound by my body. It couldn't explain the peace that was so complete, so perfect—like a homecoming.

It was this disconnect that led me to parapsychology, a field that served as a bridge between the metaphysical and the physical. This was not about ghosts or superpowers, but about the rigorous exploration of consciousness outside the confines of the brain. A patient, for example, could describe the tools used during a procedure or a conversation held by medical staff while their body lay lifeless.[5]

I began reading accounts from individuals who, while clinically dead, reported seeing and hearing things from an external vantage point that were later verified to be accurate. These cases were more than isolated incidents; they were like a growing body of evidence, a chorus of voices affirming what I had experienced. For me, these were not just dry case studies; they were glimpses of a shared reality that I had been a part of.

From this viewpoint, my experience was more than simply a cognitive illusion. It was an authentic glimpse into a world that exists outside of the material domain.

This resonated with me. It was like finding the final piece of a puzzle I didn't even know I was working on. The idea of consciousness as a field extending beyond me, that my brain tuned into, transformed my experience.

My feeling of being weightless and watching the sun from the water's surface felt less like a chemical reaction and more like a true, unmediated moment of connection with something bigger. My brain hadn't created the repose; it had merely received it, like a radio receiver tuning in to a new station.

My near-drowning was an opportunity, not an accident—a glimpse into a broader conscious field. The peace was a brief memory of a reality that existed beyond my body, a moment of unbroken communion. It gave my near-drowning a new layer of meaning, a purpose that stretched beyond my own small life and into a question about the nature of existence itself.

---

5. Alvarado, Carlos S. "Trends in the Study of Out-of-Body Experiences: An Overview of the 19th and 20th Centuries." *Journal of Scientific Exploration* 3, no. 1 (1989): 27–42.

The Endless Story: Archetypes of the Final Journey

Of course, there was the "magical" side. This was the part of my online search that I'd been on long before the drowning, and it was the part that seemed most familiar. I learned that almost every culture and religion has a narrative for what happens in that moment. Most don't see death as an end, but a purposeful transition—a culminating rite of passage. These traditions gave me a lens for making sense of and contextualizing my ultimate voyage, and they offered a monumental counterpoint to the explanations of the mind.

I read about the idea of a "peaceful death" in Christianity, where it's not just a happy accident, but an ideal, serene transition from worldly turmoil to the afterlife. I found out about the Art of Dying Well, a guide that prepared believers for a good death by teaching them to overcome fear and despair.

For Christians, the serenity of death is a result of a life of faith, rooted in the promise of salvation. It's a hope that makes one fearless. This resonated with the calm that had washed over me; it was as if my own faith, even in its nascent form, had granted me a moment of grace.

In Hinduism, death isn't an end, but a natural transition—a stepping stone to something greater. The ultimate goal for the individual essence is *moksha*—liberation from the cycle of *samsara*.[6] This liberation culminates in eternal bliss. The profound balance I found within, when viewed through this lens, was a flash of cosmic unity, a reward for my conscious journey.

In Buddhism, I was fascinated by the idea of the *bardo*, a crucial intermediate state between death and rebirth. For a spiritually prepared person, this state is an opportunity to achieve enlightenment and perceive the "clear light of death." But for an unprepared person, it can lead to terrifying hallucinations. This duality—the potential for both peace and torment—resonated with my own exploration into the two sides of near-death events.

---

6. *The Tibetan Book of the Dead: The Great Liberation Through Hearing in the Bardo.* Translated by Francesca Fremantle and Chögyam Trungpa. Boston: Shambhala, 2003.

The final illumination is not a universal truth, but a reflection of one's own inner terrain—a mirror held up to the innermost self.

I was very much fascinated by myths, which provided humanity with a framework for understanding the ultimate journey long before any formal religion. Reading this, a warmth spread through my chest, as if a hand had reached across generations to grasp my own. They, too, were searching for a way to make sense of the closing moments of life.

The Egyptian story of the "Weighing of the Heart"[7] was a parallel to the modern-day life review. In this core rite of passage, the deceased's heart was weighed against the feather of Ma'at, the goddess of truth and cosmic order. A heart lighter than a feather was granted entry into a peaceful afterlife, while a heavy one was devoured.

My odyssey was also mirrored in the Greek myths of the Underworld and a climactic judgment. In these myths, warriors would return from the dead to describe a concluding judgment where the virtuous were rewarded and the wicked were punished.

This inquiry was not only about finding facts; it was about finding my story within a larger, collective human story. All of these tales, whether religious or mythological, mirrored my progression. That belief in an ultimate reckoning was not a new idea, but a human archetype—a story told for thousands of years. It made me feel less alone, connected to a vast narrative that transcended my own small life.

So, what was it? What was the peace? Was it a neurological trick? A psychological defense? A glimpse into the afterlife?

I don't think it was one thing. The beauty of it, for me, is that it was all of it. The biological process gave me the sense of stillness, but the emotional letting go allowed me to accept what was happening. And the mystical and mythological narratives gave my story a deeper meaning that went beyond a simple chemical reaction. My mind, my body, and my soul worked in perfect concert, each providing a piece of the puzzle.

---

7. Taylor, John H. *Death and the Afterlife in Ancient Egypt*. Chicago: University of Chicago Press, 2001.

In that moment between life and death, I wasn't a person drowning. I was part of a much larger story, a player in a cosmic drama. It was as if the serenity I felt was a perfect storm of biology, psychology, and meaning. It was an incredible, terrifying, and beautiful reminder that a person's last encounter is as rich and mysterious as life itself.

Echoes of Now

From the present-day vantage point of a beach in New York, I sit and let the sun warm my face. I'm nearing forty, and I've forgotten the tube of sunscreen at home. A small, nagging part of me, the part that once worried about the boogeyman of time, frets about wrinkles and sunspots.

But the deeper, truer part of me—the one that has grown hungrier and greedier for life with every passing year—wholly revels in the pleasure of having the sun on my skin. There is a raging fire inside me that tells me to go, live, and taste the world. My cushy apartment and my predictable job, once a source of comfort, now feel like just half of the story.

My life looks the same as always on the outside: stable, normal, maybe a bit boring. But my priorities have completely shifted. My hopes no longer center on promotions or security; they whisper of nature, of open spaces, and of transformative moments.

As the wind stirs the air around me, foreign thoughts that feel both ancient and as intrinsic to my being as my own heartbeat whisper to me: "You don't need to protect yourself from me, child. All I am is love."

I look up, my eyes scanning the endlessness of the open sky. The sun shines brilliantly, promising as much life as we wish, and I feel love. I see love in the way the light touches the water, in the gentle rhythm of the waves. I am loved, both by the tangible and the unseen. And for a moment, suspended between the wind and the warmth, all is well.

The scent of the ocean is like a homecoming, a sensory anchor that pulls me back through time. I grew up on a beach a world away on the coast of the Black Sea, which taught me its brutal love not once, but twice. I carry the memory of those moments—the cold shock, the strong pull—as deeply as I carry my gratitude for being alive. I still pray that the man who saved me will always have the best this world has to offer, and more.

I come back to this time, this place, this woman I am now, on this beach fairly close to my home in New York. The beach here smells the same. The ocean sounds the same. Regardless of my almost drowning, I feel at home on the beach, and the solace of it fills me. People are all around me, their laughter and chatter a beautiful, shifting mosaic of sound. I wonder what they are thinking. Are they thinking of freedom? Life? The immensity of the ocean and the beauty of the Earth?

I wonder if they think of the seen and the unseen, of how dreams shape the world, or how life always wins, even when it looks like it's losing. Do they contemplate how, in the grand scheme of things, kindness and love are the only things that matter?

A foreign thought, a whisper in the wind that no one else can hear, makes its way into my conscious monologue.

"Gaia herself will remember you if you were kind. To all. To everything. To nature itself. As long as you love life, all is well. As it should be."

I smile, a few tears tracing a course down my cheeks. I feel blessed. What an amazing gift it is to be able to smell this beach right now! A few seagulls land nearby, their cries a sharp counterpoint to the gentle rhythm of the waves. They are looking for food, and with all the pollution and modernization of our world, food is scarce. I wish I had something to offer them. My boyfriend comes back from the water, his form pulling me from my daydream. We talk for a bit.

The water is too cold for me, but he loves it. The currents are strong, and I am still not a good swimmer, but I promise him I will at least go to the shore to get my feet wet. He is ready to go back in, his spirit brighter than I've seen it in months. Healing is beautiful to witness. He is beautiful to watch. I love him, and I thank God for sending me to him, here in America.

My attention returns to the wind on my skin, and the bliss I feel smelling the ocean. I look at the people around me, and I send a wordless prayer: "May they all feel what I feel. May they have peace. May they have bliss. May they have love. Amen."

Now, back to the greatest of games. I wouldn't miss it. I am grateful.

With a new kind of bravery, one born from acceptance rather than recklessness, I stand up and walk into the water. The waves are bigger here than they were in the Black Sea, but I am at peace. A powerful wave comes and knocks me over. This time, it is my boyfriend, not my mother, who grabs my hand. The water pulls me under, and the shells scratch my skin, as they did all those years ago. The ocean twists and turns me, and I let it.

My boyfriend holds my wrist, a warm, strong anchor, and I know I am safe.

I know this is not a struggle. It is the ocean giving me a hug—a long, scratchy hug, but a hug nonetheless. After one good spin, one last salty caress of my skin, the ocean lets go.

My partner, always caring, makes sure I'm okay. But I am more than okay. I am blessed to be alive. The adrenaline in my veins, the sound of the seagulls, the salt on my lips—I am so grateful for it all. With a big, childlike grin, I head back to the shore, my heart soaring with a gratitude I can't quite contain. The sea, brutal as it may be at times, always lets go of me right before I am actually harmed. What an amazing teacher! What a beautiful love!

The sky is bright when I take off my sunglasses. Too bright. I hear a soft whisper in my mind: "You're doing a great job. Activating your light codes." I don't even know what that means. I know I've read the notion of light codes somewhere, but my conscious mind missed it. My subconscious must have pulled that from somewhere. Its ass, probably. But what if it doesn't matter? What if I don't need to understand absolutely everything? Maybe I only need to love life!

Now, I see clearly. I don't need to understand everything. I don't need a map or a reason for the magic. The ultimate truth is not something to be studied; it is something to be witnessed and lived.

I have come to realize that my quest was never about finding all the information. It was about learning to love life, even in its most overwhelming moments. It was about trusting that, no matter what, I am always held. I am always safe. And with that knowledge, I am ready for the next adventure.

All is well—as it should be.

Chapter 6: Three Minutes of Eternity

All of these patients have experienced a floating out of their physical bodies, associated with a great sense of stillness and wholeness. Most were aware of another person who helped them in their transition to another plane of existence.

—Raymond A. Moody Jr., Life After Life

I grew up feeling larger than life, as if the world was a stream of adventures waiting to be had. It was a canvas of endless possibilities, each day a brilliant new stroke of color. Everything was more fun, more vibrant, and more alive. Given just enough freedom to venture past the schoolyard and into the messy, exciting landscape of my late teens, I discovered the thrilling, confusing world of boys, the chaotic symphony of parties, and the sharp, satisfying wit of a well-placed comeback. I became a smart-ass, a title I wore like a crown.

This persona, however, was a flimsy mask over my inner restlessness. On the surface, I was a diligent student, a high achiever who effortlessly navigated the academic world. I had a vivid social life and many friends, and even started working part-time jobs during the summer. By all measures, I was a success.

But underneath, my personality was, to put it mildly, a trainwreck. I had a stubborn, contrarian nature, always asking the "wrong" questions (and too many of them), always bristling with too many opinions. I would refuse to do things that didn't resonate with me, a trait that served me well in some arenas, but made me an absolute nightmare in others.

This internal chaos begged for a logical framework. My contrarian nature wasn't just about being difficult; it was a desperate attempt to find answers that felt true. My relentless questioning turned outward, launching a frantic search for an instruction manual for a self I couldn't understand.

My quest for logic—this voracious seeking—was not a path to meaning, but a frantic endeavor of data collection. From the age of twelve to seventeen, my mind functioned as a library of half-understood truths. I devoured the Abrahamic religions, trying to untangle their complex threads. I delved into psychology, hoping to find a scientific explanation for the chaotic landscape of my own mind. I lost myself in archaeology and mythology, searching for echoes that might explain my unquiet mind. But each book and theory only deepened the chasm of my confusion.

The Bible, in particular, was a stark disappointment. Its pages were stained with what sounded like an insurmountable amount of hate and contradiction, making it impossible for me to believe. The other Abrahamic faiths were no different, mired in the same rigid, exclusionary ideologies. I looked for a home for my reality in other religions, but their principles never even acknowledged the inexplicable experiences that had quietly shaped my life.

Frustrated and exhausted by the search, I ended up throwing my hands up in surrender. I declared myself an atheist, dismissing everything that defied rational facts as "mumbo jumbo." It was a relief, a release from the weight of a quest for meaning that had yielded nothing but more unsolved puzzles. I channeled my energy into the tangible world of school and my newfound freedoms, and managed to convince myself that this was all there was.

The Veil Thins

Life continued on this new, pragmatic trajectory until a mundane moment shattered my carefully constructed narrative. I was seventeen, showering after a long day, when my fingers brushed against a lump in my right breast. It was substantial—an unwelcome, solid mass where there should have been nothing. A cold dread seeped into my bones, but my mother became my anchor. She wrapped her calm around my fear, explaining that sometimes these things happen, and that "scary" didn't automatically mean "dangerous." Her calm wasn't passive; it was a force of action. She got on the phone, a general marshalling her troops, until she had secured an appointment with a top doctor. She packed our bags and took me to the capital, determined to put me in the best hands money could buy. Soon after, I was scheduled for surgery.

The hospital check-in, the tests, the sterile corridors—it all passed in a blur of disquieting efficiency. Two days later, I found myself lying on a cold, uncomfortable table, a silent witness to the substances dripping into my veins, pulling me down into a velvet ocean of unconsciousness. I allowed myself to slip away, a slow, gentle descent into the darkness of the unknown.

I don't remember waking up so much as simply being awake. One moment, there was a descent; the next, I was awake, not in a hospital bed, but in a sun-drenched meadow. My body, or whatever form I inhabited, was weightless and ethereal. I was lying in grass softer than any earthly velvet, and the air was filled with the perfume of blooming things.

I took in my surroundings, and a core sense of joyful recognition vibrated in every fiber of my being. I was in a place very similar to the garden in my dreams. It was a meadow, but the nature around me looked, sounded, and behaved the same as the garden in my visions.

A quiet question began to bloom in the silence: "Did I die?" The memory of the hospital was still there—the awareness that I had gone into surgery. Waking up in this impossible place didn't make sense, and my death felt like the only logical, if surreal, explanation. The idea settled without panic or regret, feeling more like recognition than revelation. This place was a waking dream, its landscape and light a perfect echo of a memory my subconscious had long held. It was a place I was going to visit again one day.

The colors here were unlike anything I had ever seen on Earth—so vivid it was like they were humming with their own inner light. The weather was perfect, a gentle warmth without a hint of oppressive heat, and the flowers were so full of life they almost throbbed. I was ablaze with wonder and excitement to explore the new terrain. It felt like stepping into a fantasy epic, granted sovereignty to revel in this newfound realm to my heart's content. And, as in early life, I was gliding—not walking, but a graceful, effortless motion, like a swan upon a still lake.

As I glided around in delight, I saw him—my cousin, watching me with a gentle, knowing smile. This was the irrefutable proof, the final piece of the puzzle. He had died three years prior—a sudden, tragic end to his life at twenty-two in a motorcycle accident. He was the key that unlocked this new, impossible reality: "I am, indeed, dead."

It didn't bother me. It was not a moment of panic, but of recognition, like a gentle sunrise illuminating a landscape I somehow already was familiar with. I accepted this information with a matter-of-fact ease, the same way I'd accept a sunny day or a discount on my favorite jeans—not with dread, but with a calm, content, and almost excited acceptance.

I floated toward him, and sudden intuition told me I was wearing a white dress—a plain, flowing garment. My cousin remained silent, his smile the only communication I needed. He walked beside me, his presence a comforting anchor in this breathtakingly beautiful landscape. One thing stood out to me, though: his colors. Everything around me was bright and vivid, filled with colors so vibrant that they seemed to be fueled with a different, more powerful type of life force. He, on the other hand, was discolored. Not like the black and white on the old TVs, but more like his skin and clothes, were muted in color—not as vivid or bright.

He was dressed in a pair of elegant black dress pants and a white t-shirt. I found myself thinking how odd his choice of clothes was. The fancy pants paired with the casual top was so unlike him. But in this place, such details were frivolous.

I somehow was aware that he was on "babysitting duty." My own voice was small and childlike, but a torrent of questions came off my lips: "Are we dead?" "Are you a ghost?" "Where are we?" "Where is everyone else?" There was an avalanche of other questions, but I sadly do not remember them. It doesn't matter, as he patiently ignored them all. He quietly walked beside me, his smile unchanging, ensuring I was not left unsupervised. After what I perceived to be an eternity of my one-sided conversation, he motioned for me to stop and listen. I did.

A Return to the Flesh

A chorus of voices, distant but urgent and filled with panic, tore through the peaceful silence. "Julia! Julia!" The sound was a jarring disruption, an irritating tear in the fabric of this beautiful world. In an instant, I was no longer in the meadow. I was back, not in my body, but hovering in a corner of a hospital room—a disembodied observer. I watched as doctors and nurses swarmed around a body lying on a table—my body, lifeless and still. A sense of profound detachment settled over me.

"So I am really dead, huh?" I thought to myself. But there was no regret, no attachment to the flesh I was watching from above. I wasn't even concerned. In fact, I was trying to figure out why I was even here, when I could be gliding in the beautiful garden. As far as I was concerned, I had done my time on Earth, and now I was free to leave whenever I wished. I did not understand what the purpose of me floating there in a corner was, while a bunch of doctors were trying to revive my corpse. It was almost like a rude imposition on my new and improved condition. My personality stayed the same. Even in death, I was looking for answers. I was here in the hospital room, and maybe there was something to see after all. I was also aware that I was timeless, and, as such, there was no pressure to return to the meadow right away. I had eternity for that. I had time to linger. "I'll probably be able to watch my autopsy and find out why I died. It's not so bad!" I was content, accepting of this new fate. My future was limitless, unburdened by the weight of earthly life.

Then, a single, devastating thought pierced through my contentment: "I will have to watch my mother cry at my grave." The bliss shattered. The weightless serenity was replaced by a surge of unbearable, visceral regret. An avalanche of emotions rushed in: sadness, loss, pain, love, mistakes I'd made that could still be fixed. In that moment, I decided that I would not bear the sight of her grief. In that moment, a quiet but firm decision took hold: "I can't have that. My mother will not bury her child." The thought was almost like a command, a gravitational pull so strong it yanked me from the corner and plunged me back into my body.

Through the darkness behind my closed eyelids, I could hear the chaos—panicked voices, and the frantic, high-pitched, highly irritating wail of a machine indicating that I had flatlined. My mind was screaming at them, "Stop! I'm back! You don't need to do this!" But the body wouldn't listen. It was a meat cage, deaf to my commands. I was an entity locked inside my own flesh and bone, a silent witness to my own resuscitation. I was fully awake, fully aware, and fully dead, all at the same time.

Through this paralysis, I felt their panic—the sharp tones of the doctors, the frantic movement happening around me. Then, the first blow. A massive, invisible force struck my chest, a concussive blast without pain that lifted me off the table. I felt a cold liquid snake into my veins, what I assumed was adrenaline, an icy fire forcing every cell to attention. Then came the second blow, just as violent. I poured all my will into moving a single finger, into cracking open an eyelid, anything to signal I was there. Nothing. The feeling wasn't fear; it was profound, maddening annoyance, the spiritual equivalent of being shoved back into a suit of armor that no longer fit. A third and final concussive force hit me. I was a ghost in the machine, a consciousness trapped in a shell they were battering from the outside. I was back, but I was utterly powerless.

At some point, the soundscape changed. The beeping of the machine changed, and I felt the panic around me subside. I figured it meant my heart was beating. Then, mercifully, everything went blank.

The next thing I remember is the uncomfortable rush of oxygen into my lungs—too fast, too unnatural. I opened my eyes and was met with the sterile, sickly green of the recovery room wall. "Ah, fuck. I'm back in this bitch," I thought. I turned my head to the right and saw my mother, her face a pale mask of relief and exhaustion.

"I thought I lost you," she whispered, choking on her own tears, her voice thick with emotion. "You gave everyone such a scare."

If only she'd known. I regretted scaring her, but I was happy to see the light of relief in her eyes. I had done the right thing, returning. "Do you know what you said?" she asked. My mind offered nothing but the abrupt return. I yanked the irritating oxygen mask from my face, ignoring the nurse's horrified protests. It was the doctor who intervened, telling her that if I wanted to breathe on my own, I should be allowed to try, at least. Once the medical staff had retreated, my mother leaned closer.

"You cried," she said softly. "You told me to kiss you because you came back for me, even though you didn't want to come back."

The words struck a chord inside of me, an echo of a memory I couldn't quite grasp. I didn't remember the words, but I remembered the decision. I remembered the meadow, the light, and my cousin's patient demeanor. I told my mother everything, except the horrifying experience of being trapped in an unresponsive body. I reasoned she'd had enough scary experiences for one day. I told her it was a dream, although I knew better.

A few hours later, she returned to my room, her face a mask of perplexed wonder. She had called my aunt to tell her about my dream of my cousin. Romanian tradition holds that when someone dies, we give alms to the living in their name—food, clothing, and household items. My cousin's clothes in my near-death experience—the elegant black pants and the white t-shirt—were the exact items my aunt had given away as alms for him. I had never seen them before. They were not the kind of clothes he would have worn in life. My aunt took my vision as confirmation that he had received them.

What puzzled me did not stem from the hopeful acceptance of this notion, but rather from the fact that no one appeared to wonder why or how it was possible. The clinical report stated that I had been dead for a little over three minutes. But in those three minutes I had traveled, explored, remembered, and connected dots in my head; had a full blown, albeit one-sided conversation with my cousin (and had time to critique his outfit!); then come back to the room, watched the freak show of my own death, made decisions, and experienced my own body as a cage and not as myself. This should all have been impossible! That's a great deal of brain power for a corpse. Yet no one seemed to question it. No one seemed to try to make sense of it. This simple acceptance gave me pause. My mother looked at me as if I was some miracle, and all I could think was, "Why are you not asking questions about how this can be?"

Waking up in the recovery room wasn't a relief; it was an imprisonment. I was a spirit shoved back into a machine I no longer recognized as my own. The lightness and ease of having no body was a fresh memory, and, by contrast, this flesh felt heavy, sluggish, and profoundly uncomfortable. It was as if I were dragging a heavy, wet sack of meat behind me, a vessel that responded to my commands in frustrating slow motion. Every gesture was a chore. I was acutely, disgustingly aware of its inner workings—the squelch of my organs, the gurgle of digestion, the rhythmic slosh of blood. I gave a command and watched my body respond in slow motion. This body was a biological engine, and, for the first time, I could feel every greasy, gross piston fire.

It took weeks for that sluggish, underwater feeling to fade, and months before the constant, intrusive awareness of being a fleshy, ticking thing finally receded into a semblance of normalcy.

But I never forgot the bliss. The feeling of absolute lightness. The immense peace, the unconditional love, the perfection, and the freedom of the Unseen. It was a vision of home, a place I had recognized from my dreams—a place where flowers radiated with a vibrant, inner light, where the sky is freedom, and all is love.

The memory of that blissful meadow, the clockwork precision of my cousin's presence, and the damning proof of my doctor's records created a contradiction my logical mind simply could not ignore. The quest for truth was no longer a philosophical game; it was an urgent matter of self-preservation.

The Library of Half-Understood Truths, Revisited

I returned to my old habit of frantic data collection, but this time it wasn't a quest for enlightenment. My first priority was to establish that I was not the only person in history this had happened to. I needed a foundation to stand on before I could even touch the terrifying world of modern medical explanations. So, my search began not in a lab, but in a library.

I turned to the oldest myths I could find, figuring that if people had been talking about this for millennia, it couldn't be just my own private insanity. It turned out they had. Plato's *Republic* had a story about a Greek soldier named Er[1] who died and then came back to life to tell what he'd seen.

Reading this, I had the first glimmer of hope. I was a small part of a long, unbroken human chain, not an anomaly. The historical progression from old, anecdotal cases to more structured inquiry reflected a gradual shift from dismissing these happenings as mere anomalies to recognizing them as distinct, observable events.

As I read, these accounts, once dismissed as folklore, resonated like echoes of my own journey. The increasing medical ability to resuscitate individuals from the brink of death

1. Plato, *The Republic*, Book 10.

has naturally resulted in a greater prevalence of reported NDEs, making their study more urgent and feasible. It was as if I was part of a long, unbroken chain of human existence that had been largely ignored. The weight of that thought was crushing. I was not an anomaly, but a part of something universal.

The modern scientific investigation was a slow burn. It began with a woman named Celia Green in 1968[2], who tried to categorize OBEs as a type of "anomalous perceptual phenomenon or hallucination." She was one of the first people to systematically categorize such phenomena, even if her initial interpretation was reductionist. This descriptive work laid a foundation.

A year later, in 1969, psychiatrist Elisabeth Kübler-Ross published *On Death and Dying*.[3] This seminal work brought the testimonies of dying patients into the public eye, giving the medical community a reason to pay attention.

But it wasn't until 1972, when a man named John C. Lilly introduced the term "near-death experience," that this extraordinary albeit bizarre phenomenon finally had a name. Green's taxonomy, Kübler-Ross's work, and Lilly's term all contributed to moving NDEs from the periphery to a more defined subject of inquiry. Green's taxonomy provided a conceptual structure, Kübler-Ross's work legitimized studying the dying process, and Lilly's term provided a concise, unifying label. This historical trajectory underscored the academic community's initial struggle to categorize and validate highly subjective experiences, highlighting the tension between anecdotal evidence and empirical methods.

I sat in my room, staring at the words on the page, and was encompassed in a wave of relief so strong it made me weak. It was as if someone had handed me a key to a door I had been trying to open my entire life. I wasn't just the girl who'd died on a cold table; I was a statistic, a data point in a vast and mysterious chamber of human experience. And this made it real, because statistics were real. They were observable and quantifiable, and this gave them the legitimacy I was hoping for.

---

2. Celia Green, *Out-of-the-body Experiences* (London: Hamish Hamilton, 1968).

3. Elisabeth Kübler-Ross, *On Death and Dying: What the Dying Have to Teach Us About Living* (New York: Macmillan, 1969).

The Common Thread

As I continued my exploration, I was struck by the incredible consistency of what people were describing. My rendezvous with the infinite was part of a common, universal pattern, not unique after all. It was a shared phenomenon that transcended culture, age, and religious belief.

The remarkable consistency of these core elements suggested an underlying common mechanism, whether neurological, psychological, or transcendental. This consistency challenged idiosyncratic or hallucinatory explanations, compelling researchers to seek universal biological or mental underpinnings, or to consider interpretations outside of the materialistic.

The things I had seen weren't random figments of my imagination; they were "prototypical elements" that tens of millions of people had also reported. As I read through the list of common features, a powerful and almost dizzying sense of recognition washed over me. My own reality was laid bare on the screen in front of me.

Out-of-Body Experience: This is the awareness of separating from your body and watching the scene unfold from above. I had this sense of detachment while hovering in the corner of the hospital room, my consciousness detached and floating, a silent witness to my own demise. This element was intriguing to researchers because of what they called "veridical perceptions," which are verifiable details that individuals couldn't have possibly known while unconscious. I thought about the patient in the Pim van Lommel investigation who had described watching his own resuscitation, and even seeing the hospital staff remove his dentures. The doctors later confirmed every detail of his story. This was the kind of proof my logical mind had demanded. The silence of the scientific record was broken.

Feelings of Peace and Painlessness: This was my initial sensation in the sun-drenched meadow. The absolute certainty of being dead was not a moment of panic or fear, but of recognition and tranquility. The pain of the physical body, a constant hum of discomfort in life, was gone, superseded by a pervasive positive emotional state.

Tunnel Experience and Bright Light: Testimonies described the impression of passing through a dark, enclosed space towards (or being surrounded by) a brilliant, often loving light. While I hadn't encountered a tunnel, the sun-drenched meadow I'd woken up in was filled with a light so vivid it seemed to hum with its own light.

Interactions with Other Beings: reports from others noted that they had encountered deceased loved ones, spiritual figures, or a "being of light" emanating unconditional love. This resonated with my experience of my cousin, standing there with a gentle smile that held a silent knowing. He held no religious authority, but his silent, comforting calm was the anchor in a world without gravity, and I somehow had the certainty he was there to help.

Altered Time Perception: My one-sided conversation with my cousin had felt like it lasted an eternity. Time, in that place, was meaningless. It was not a measure of moments, but an impression of boundless freedom. The research explained this as a sense of timelessness, where thoughts speed up and a profound understanding of self, others, or the universe suddenly washes over you.

Reluctance to Return: I recognized this in my heart. It was a strong, silent protest, a sentiment of not wanting to return to the body or earthly life. Returning was ultimately a choice, and that choice was made out of a love so strong it transcended death.

I also read about a small percentage of negative or "hellish" NDEs, which involved extreme panic, helplessness, or encounters with demonic creatures. The presence of these episodes, though rare, added a layer of complexity to the phenomenon, proving it was not always a "wish fulfillment" fantasy.

And then I came across the Greyson NDE Scale[4] . This was a sixteen-item questionnaire developed by a psychiatrist named Dr. Bruce Greyson to measure the depth and intensity of an NDE. The development and widespread adoption of this scale was a critical step towards bringing methodical rigor to a subjective landscape of spirit, reflecting the scholarly community's need for quantifiable, reproducible data.

I decided to take the scale myself. I had to know if what had happened to me was real (according to the community that had once dismissed these beliefs). My score, twenty-eight

4. Bruce Greyson, "The Near-Death Experience Scale: Construction, Reliability, and Validity," *Journal of Nervous and Mental Disease* 171, no. 6 (June 1983)

out of thirty-two, was confirmation that what happened, happened. That it wasn't made up. My experience was an anomaly, but it was also a quantifiable data point. This gave me a new way to understand what had happened. It was validation.

The Scientific Reckoning

My journey led me to the work of three men who became my intellectual guides: Raymond Moody, Pim van Lommel, and Sam Parnia. These were the true pioneers of the field, the ones who had dared to pose radical inquiries that most others wouldn't even consider.

The study of NDEs was legitimized by the formation of dedicated academic associations like the International Association for Near-Death Studies (IANDS) and the peer-reviewed *Journal of Near-Death Studies*. These publications moved the subject beyond individual anecdotal collections to a systematic, collaborative study.

I was already familiar with Raymond Moody's book, *Life After Life*. Moody's work, though qualitative, provided the first lens through which to view my account. He was the one who identified fifteen common elements in these accounts. His emphasis on the transformative aftereffects also highlighted the impact of these occurrences, suggesting clinical relevance. I thought about the sheer amount of work he must have done, interviewing people who, like me, were probably afraid of being called crazy.

But it was the work of two other men that most fascinated me.

Dr. Pim van Lommel, a Dutch cardiologist, conducted a prospective investigation in 2001.[5] The conditions were set before the cardiac arrest events, making the data more reliable than retrospective accounts gathered after the fact. Finally, it seemed like the academic community was starting to catch up. Van Lommel's research involved 344 cardiac arrest patients, and his findings were earth-shattering to my logical center.

The study found that the occurrence of an NDE was not associated with the duration of cardiac arrest or how long a patient was unconscious. In fact, NDEs occurred with no

5. Pim van Lommel et al., "Near-death experience in survivors of cardiac arrest: a prospective study in the Netherlands," *The Lancet* 358, no. 9298 (December 2001).

correlation to any of the physiological factors they measured. This directly challenged the idea that NDEs were merely caused by a lack of oxygen to the brain.

The theory that had once been my last line of defense against the inexplicable was now falling apart. Van Lommel concluded that the current materialistic view of the brain-consciousness relationship is too restricted. He proposed the idea of "non-local consciousness"[62]—the concept that our awareness might exist outside of our brains, much like a radio signal exists outside the radio itself. As I read his words, I realized this concept was the silent current running through my entire life, the pattern I have been trying to name in every chapter of this book. The brain wasn't a generator of consciousness; it was a receiver, tuning into a signal originating from a place beyond the physical. As I read his words, it felt like a key turning in a lock I had forgotten existed. This didn't just offer a potential explanation for my NDE; it reached all the way back to the very beginning. Those strange, fragmented pre-birth images I described as my oldest memory—the ones that shouldn't have been possible before my brain was fully formed—suddenly had a theoretical home. If consciousness could be independent from the body, then my earliest memories weren't just fantasy; they were echoes from a state of being that came before.

My research eventually led me to the work of Dr. Sam Parnia, and it felt like a floodlight turning on in a dark room. He led the AWARE studies[6], a project that did something revolutionary: monitor brain activity in patients during CPR, after their hearts had already stopped. What his team found was stunning. For up to an hour after clinical death, they detected the very same electrical brain waves associated with conscious thought, memory, and higher mental functions. It was the academic community's slow, reluctant walk toward a truth I already knew in my bones: Even when the body has shut down, you can still be there, aware.

The numbers were even more validating. Parnia found that nearly half of the survivors had clear memories of events that occurred while they were technically dead. And crucially, he made it clear that these weren't dreams or hallucinations; they were lucid, real perceptions. For me, all the scientific debate about what the data "meant" was just background noise. The real story was that science was finally catching up to an ancient

---

6. Sam Parnia et al., "AWAreness during REsuscitation – II: A multi-center study of consciousness and awareness in cardiac arrest," *Resuscitation* 191 (October 2023).

human experience, providing a possible explanation for how I could have watched my own resuscitation.

The Contradictions and My Unanswered Questions

The deeper I dove into the inquiry, the more I understood how divided the academic community was. For every investigation that pointed toward an independent consciousness, there was a skeptic pointing to flaws in the methodology.

The Slovenian hypercapnia research, for example, suggested that high CO2 levels in the blood might cause NDEs, finding that patients with higher initial partial pressures of CO2 had significantly more NDEs. But Dr. Greyson pointed out that other studies had found the opposite to be true.

The debate, I realized, came down to one central question: Is consciousness generated by the brain, or is it independent of it?

There were physiological theories, which explained NDEs as a byproduct of a dying brain. The anoxia/hypoxia theory, which claimed that a lack of oxygen was the culprit, sounded weak. I discovered that hypoxia usually causes frightening, disorganized hallucinations, not the peaceful, lucid encounters I and so many others had experienced. Plus, my doctor's notes had said my heart had stopped, not that I was suffering from a lack of oxygen. The science also stated that NDEs can occur in situations without anoxia, such as fainting, meditation, or intense stress.

The refutation of the anoxia hypothesis underscored the complexity of NDEs. It also strengthened the argument for more sophisticated physiological models, or even non-physiological explanations, to account for their rich and consistent characteristics.

I also read about the endorphin hypothesis, which suggested that the body releases natural painkillers during stress to cause peaceful feelings. But this theory had no empirical data to back it up, and endorphins are known to scramble the brain's record-keeping, which stood in direct contradiction to the vivid memories of those episodes by me and other people. The explanation was a cold thing, an inadequate label for a personal narrative so warm and meaningful. The academic literature explicitly stated that these speculations are "not supported by any empirical data."[7]

In my case, what was my brain supposedly coping with? I was under general anesthesia, in a deep, peaceful slumber. As far as deaths go, it doesn't get more comfortable than that. There was no pain or trauma to escape from. And if it was a coping mechanism designed to shield me from trauma, it got everything backwards. The NDE itself wasn't scary; it was a blissful moment of pure serenity. It was the return to life that was a brutal, jarring trauma. The "coping" mechanism created trauma instead of preventing it. On top of that, why would a simple defense mechanism know things I couldn't? How did it know to match my cousin's clothes with the alms my aunt offered in his memory? The experience was clear, lucid, and peaceful—the very opposite of the panic and confusion that characterize true depersonalization.

In NDEs, subjects remain very lucid about their identities. Their sense of self is not changed, unlike with depersonalization, where there is often a loss of identity. The model also fails to account for the "hyperalertness" factor, which involves clearly defined, vivid, and accelerated thoughts. It also can't account for the "mystical consciousness" factor, which includes feelings of harmony, unity, and great understanding. These factors are often present in NDEs and are diametrically opposed to depersonalization.

The expectancy hypothesis claimed that I had imagined the occurrence based on what I expected to see. But how would this explain the precise, verifiable details I witnessed? The investigation noted that despite diverse cultural and religious backgrounds, NDEs exhibit consistent core features worldwide, challenging the idea that content is entirely shaped by expectation. The existence of negative NDEs, which are often terrifying and unexpected, also contradicts the idea of a "wish-fulfilling" phenomenon. This theory didn't even come close to explaining what I had gone through.

The materialist view, held by most scientists, claimed that the brain was the sole generator of consciousness. The other view, the one that I now believed in, argued that consciousness was a fundamental force that may exist outside the body. My own experience was a testament to the latter. I wasn't crazy. I had simply gotten a glimpse into...more.

---

7. Greyson, "The Near-Death Experience Scale."

The Unseen and the Unspoken

After I returned, it took days for me to feel comfortable in my own skin again. My body felt fleshy, slow, and a little disgusting. And heavy! It felt like I was pulling this bag of squishy meat after me. The lightness and ease of not having a body was a memory that haunted me. For days, I was freaked out by the feel of my own flesh, as if I had been forced back into a cage that I didn't feel I belonged in.

My mind, once a library of half-understood facts, was now a fractured place, caught between two opposing realities: the world of flesh and blood, and the visceral pull of a place where all was light, laughter, and freedom.

I didn't speak of it afterward. Not really. The fear of being labeled crazy was there, but it was secondary to a much deeper problem: The experience was simply too big for words. How do you explain a place where color hums with its own brilliant light? How do you describe a feeling of love so absolute it makes all earthly affection feel like a shadow? To even try felt like a betrayal of the memory itself.

My logical brain had its folder of research, but my heart held a truth that burned right through it. I had been there. I had walked on grass that felt more real than concrete, worn a simple white dress, and stood with my departed cousin. The bliss of that place—the feeling of absolute lightness and unconditional love—was an afterglow that haunted my return to the heavy, complicated world. It was a place where I didn't have to search for meaning, because I had finally found it. And the meaning was joy and gratitude.

That was the memory that snapped me out of my cynical slumber. It didn't give me answers to prove to anyone else, but it gave me a truth to live by. It showed me that the inevitable is not to be feared. My job wasn't to explain what had happened in those three minutes, it was to honor them with how I lived all the minutes that came after. Life, death, and everything in between—I was finally ready, truly ready, for it all.

Chapter 7: Of Friendships and Rainbows

True friends are always together in spirit.

—L.M. Montgomery, Anne of Green Gables

I was seventeen that summer, recently returned home from the hospital after facing death on the operating table. The near-death experience and the surgery itself had left a physical and spiritual void. Life, once a given, now felt like a borrowed treasure, and I was still adrift in the aftermath, recovering from the profound trauma of dying and coming back.

Through it all, my friend Bogdan was a constant presence. He spent hours on the phone with me while I was in the hospital, his voice a determined anchor against my sadness and boredom. His loyalty was not just a quality; it was a pact.

Bogdan came into my life like a storm, a tempest of sharp wit and boundless arrogance. I was not even sixteen when we met, and my world was already a battleground of adolescent insecurity—a place where every word was a weapon and every glance a challenge. He was no different. Our conversations weren't exchanges; they were skirmishes. A barb from him would be met with a more cutting one from me. We were two stubborn, clever idiots, each believing we held the intellectual high ground.

We circled each other for months, our smiles a rare, accidental sight that would break through the clatter of our one-upmanship. And then, one day, we laughed at the same joke. I said he was adopted from the pet store. It was a truce, a reluctant surrender that blossomed into loyalty.

We still fought, of course—like siblings who know each other's weaknesses and aren't afraid to exploit them. But we were inseparable, two halves of a whole, navigating the chaotic landscape of our late teens. Our bond was a picture painted from mutual secrets and petty favors. I'd cover for his late-night benders; he'd spin a story for my mom so I would be allowed to go out after 9:00 p.m. I'd buy him pizza with my last few coins; he'd charm my teacher into letting me go out during music class. It was a deep-seated loyalty, an unspoken pact that we would always be there for each other, no matter what.

Our friendship was tested, and proven. Within two years, we were inseparable, our mutual loyalty getting us and our friends in all kinds of adolescent trouble.

When I got home from the hospital in August, the lingering sense of otherness from my NDE had settled over me. It was just two weeks later that Bogdan and a group of friends went on a fishing trip. My best friend and I were invited, but an insidious, inexplicable lethargy had settled over me. We stayed behind, a decision that would forever echo with a chilling sense of "what if?"

That night, the phone rang. It was Bogdan, his voice a booming, joyful sound carried on a current of beer-fueled bravado. He was larger than life, a force of nature amplified by the carefree night. "If I die tonight, I'm okay with it," he declared, his words a jarring contrast to his cheerful tone. "I've had so much fun in this life already!"

A cold dread settled in my stomach. The recent brush with my own mortality had stripped away any funny notions about death. I scolded him, my voice tight with a trepidation I couldn't name. It wasn't a dread of death—not really. It was more a hesitancy not to offend life. I told him that while death wasn't something to be hated, life was a gift, a precious and fleeting thing to be cherished for as long as we had it.

He must have noticed the tremor in my voice because his tone softened. "Don't worry, Rary," he said, using my childhood nickname. "Nothing bad will happen to me. I'm almost two meters tall, and I'm made of titanium. If a train hits me, the train will break in half!" He even announced the name of my future dog, a name I had been searching for: "Yullo."

As I hung up the phone, the echo of his laugh faded, but a quiet alarm remained. Why talk of death on a night of fun and bravado? Why would an eighteen-year-old, so full of plans and fire, speak of making peace with his own end? And why a train? For a fleeting second, my mind strayed to a darker possibility, but I dismissed it just as quickly. That was impossible. I knew my friend; he loved life with a fierce, unapologetic passion. He had a full-blown life plan, with three additional backup plans. He was excited for the future, not fearful of it. I told myself it was just the beer talking, a bit of tipsy nonsense amplified by my own jumpiness from my recent brush with death. I was just reading danger where there was none.

And yet, the thought snagged on another memory, a story I'd heard my mother discuss in hushed tones with a neighbor. It was about a middle-aged man who had lived in the same building with us, just a few floors higher. The story went that he came home from work one day, sat in the same armchair he'd sat in every day, and began to read the newspaper, same as every day. Then, he'd calmly looked up at his wife. "Light a candle for me," he'd told her, "so my soul can depart." She did as he asked, bewildered by the strange request. He seemed perfectly fine, healthy even. A few minutes later, he passed away peacefully in his chair.

Looking back now, I can see how his words fit into a pattern far older than the two of us. It's a question that hovers in the quiet rooms of hospices, where caregivers speak of "nearing death awareness"—a state in which the dying seem to gain a special insight, speaking of journeys and seeing loved ones waiting for them. It echoes in history, in the stories of figures like Abraham Lincoln dreaming of his own assassination or Mark Twain predicting his death with the return of Halley's Comet. It lives in the mystical view of "soul contracts," the idea that our final moments are already written into a sacred script. Science, history, and myth all offer pieces of a puzzle.

But, of course, none of these connections were on my mind that night. The stories of neighbors and presidents were dots I would connect half a lifetime later. At that time, I was just a seventeen-year-old girl, and my friend was just a boy who'd had one too many beers. I made a simple choice. I chose to believe he was talking nonsense. And with that settled, I went to sleep and thought nothing more of it.

The next morning, the landline rang. It was a mutual family friend, their voice hesitant. "I wanted to check in, see what you knew about Bogdan." For a second, I felt every cell in my body tense. The conversation from the previous night burned in my head with a new level of alarm. "He's ok," I answered with a fake calm in my voice. "He went fishing with some of our friends in our group, they should be back tonight." An uncomfortable silence followed and then the blow came. "Bogdan died," she said. "In a train accident." The world stopped with a sudden, sickening halt. It couldn't be true. After a few perplexed but polite exchanges with my parents' friend, I hung up and immediately called his number, my thumb trembling as I dialed. I didn't want to ask; I wanted to demand that he pick up, that he confirm he was alive and well. There was no answer.

In panicked disbelief, I called my best friend—or tried to. After the first call I'd made, my cell phone, a cheap, temperamental thing, was dead. Right when I needed it to work. All my contacts were trapped in it. It was a flimsy barrier between me and the truth I was desperate to avoid and find at the same time.

I held the phone in my hands, whispering to the air, to my friend, who I somehow and for whatever reason believed would hear me. "Bogdan, I need to call people to find out about you. I need to inform people of this! Please, help me out here!" It was a plea to the void, a desperate, illogical prayer. To this day, I don't know what made me do that. It was out of character for me back then, despite everything I'd gone through. The skeptic in me did not believe in talking to the dead. I did not believe it was possible.

Like a whisper from beyond, the phone flickered back to life. After the initial shock, I scrambled to copy all the important contacts before it died again, the battery draining in a final, defiant gasp. It was the first sign that something was different, that the veil between worlds had thinned.

I made the calls, piecing together the fragmented story of his last night, then made plans to be there for his family, to offer what little comfort I was able to.

The wake was held at his family's home, the air thick with sorrow and the scent of lilies.

Bogdan's parrot, Chichi, was in his cage on the balcony. He was a Budgerigar, a tiny thing that could fit in the palm of your hand, a flutter of light blue, white, and black feathers. He loved people, and used to sit on Bogdan's shoulder, patiently trying to learn words.

He was a good student, but he needed endless repetition. His entire vocabulary consisted of a few simple words: "baby," "kisses," and "good boy."

We sat on the balcony, a group of shell-shocked teenagers, suffocating in a grief we had no words for. Chichi was on his little perch, just watching the commotion. I remember staring at him and thinking, "You lucky bird. You have no idea of the tragedy unfolding right before your eyes."

But then, as I sat there, Chichi became increasingly agitated. First, he started pacing anxiously up and down his perch. Then, he began ruffling his feathers, his whole body seeming to vibrate. Finally, he started moving erratically inside his cage, fluttering wildly, as if he was desperate to escape.

And then, he spoke. His voice was a clear, disembodied thing: "Julia, speak!"

The words hit me with the force of a physical blow. My first thought was that I'd imagined it. It was impossible. I had never interacted with Chichi more than calling him cute; he couldn't have known my name. No one would have had any reason to teach him my name, let alone that specific, bizarre command. "Am I hallucinating?" I wondered, my mind grasping for a logical foothold. "Is it the grief? The exhaustion?"

It was only when I lifted my eyes that I knew it was real. Everyone else's perplexed, shocked faces were fixed—not on the cage, but on me. My best friend's gaze was a question in itself. At that moment, the attention was unbearable. I had never been a fan of having the room's attention, but now I just wanted to hide. I didn't know what to do. Was I supposed to go for it and make the freak show even freakier, or sit down and pretend I'd heard nothing?

No one said a word, especially not me. I froze. At the time, it felt like the right thing to do. That moment remains my biggest regret. My chance to acknowledge the impossible was right there. My shot at connecting with my friend had been presented to me, with no effort on my part. Everyone else had heard it; I couldn't even be accused of making things up. I should have gone to that cage and spoken to that parrot.

But the same chilling concern won out. The worry that I'd look crazy, that I'd be judged, kept my lips sealed. That silence continued, even later. Once we were alone, my best friend turned to me, her voice barely a whisper. "Did you hear the parrot speak? Did you hear what it said?"

I lied. "No," I said, "I must have not been paying attention." I wanted to hear it from her first. I needed confirmation, one more time, that I wasn't losing my mind.

She looked at me, her eyes still wide. "It said, 'Julia, speak!'" I wasn't crazy. She had heard the same impossible thing. I took this as confirmation that they had all been staring at me because they'd all heard it.

I suppose a part of me always knew this day would come, this day of public reckoning, where I would have to look crazy and tell a story that defied all logic. Perhaps some things simply can't be avoided, only delayed.

After two days of the wake, we were preparing for the funeral. I was exhausted by grief. We all were. I took my best friend and Bogdan's girlfriend back to my place. We needed to rest, to find a moment of solace—to shower and eat something before the last goodbye.

The girls settled in their assigned rooms, and I retreated to my old bedroom. I lay on the bed, closing my eyes. The silence in the room was absolute, yet a sound pierced it: a breath, close to my ear. The sound had no peace to it, but instead was a ragged, hurried gasp, like someone who had been running was sitting right next to me. My eyes flew open, and the sound vanished. I closed them again, and the breath returned, a phantom presence right beside me.

A shiver ran down my spine. I was hearing a sound without an external source, a sound only I could perceive. My mind offered me explanations. It suggested auditory hallucinations from exhaustion and emotional turmoil, or magical thinking due to trauma. These were the usual excuses I'd give myself when something odd happened. But this time, the anxiety wouldn't subside. I knew, with a certainty that chilled me to the bone, that it was real. I got up and turned on the TV—a desperate attempt to drown out the alarm caused by the spectral sound.

The funeral was tragic, a somber procession under a gray sky. It was raining, and in my sadness, I thought that it was fitting. The sky was reflecting the tragedy unfolding in our midst. But then, as if on cue, the sun broke through the clouds and a magnificent rainbow arched across the sky. In Romanian superstition, a rainbow after a death is a sign that the departed is at peace. It was a small, beautiful solace, a moment of light in the overwhelming loss.

After the funeral, a pervasive guilt took root in my heart. My thoughts spiraled into a dark, metaphysical bargain. Had I cheated death just weeks before, only for it to claim Bogdan in my place? Was this some kind of karmic payback? This profound fear that I had failed him simply by surviving was compounded by a sharper, more immediate guilt: I was failing him now, in the aftermath.

The parrot, Chichi, had called out to me—begged me to speak. And I hadn't. I hadn't even reacted. I'd just frozen. The same old concern for the mask, that crippling fear of being judged, had won.

That paralysis kept me speechless, not only in front of that cage, but even with my own friends. I never told them about the ragged, spectral breathing I'd heard in my bedroom. I kept that to myself, too, burying it under the same suffocating fear for the safety of my mask.

The question became an accusation, aimed at my own reflection: What kind of friend was I, really? This wasn't a fleeting thought. This guilt was a physical thing, a relentless, all-consuming ache that gnawed at me for months.

I was seventeen. I had already faced death twice, and was now acquainted with loss and grief. I had no framework for understanding any of it. A deep depression settled in, a heavy blanket of sorrow that smothered me. I isolated myself, spending hours staring at a book, pretending I was reading.

Between the recent ordeal with surgery and dying on the table, and then losing one of my closest friends shortly after, I was angry. No, that's an understatement. I was full of a burning fury directed at God. I wanted to know. Why had this happened? Why take someone so full of life, someone who had brought so much joy?

Was this punishment for my survival? And if that was the case, what was the point in letting me live? The questions were like hot coals stuck in my throat, with no solutions in sight. I don't know when I became angry, but I did. I wanted an explanation. I challenged Death itself to come and make this make sense. I felt like I was owed an explanation.

In the depths of this bleakness, as I was spiraling further into silence and aloofness, something gave. Maybe it was God, finally hearing my pain. Or maybe it was simply my mother, who saw her daughter disappearing and knew the only antidote.

Regardless of the reasons, I woke up one day to my mom telling me to get dressed because we were going out. I got into the cab with her, lost in my own fog. I absentmindedly heard her tell the driver our destination, but the words didn't register.

It was only when we stopped in front of a pet shop that, for the first time in months, I felt a fraction of a second of grace. I have always been happy around animals. To this day, I love them with a love stronger than what I feel for many people.

Inside, a small, almost-white ball of joy assaulted me with happy licks. At that moment, I laughed. The sound felt foreign in my own throat.

"He's yours," my mother said, her voice soft. "He's coming home with us."

An emotional dam broke. I held him, a tiny ball of fluff and pure, unadulterated joy, and I cried tears of happiness. On the way home, I convinced my mom to get a doctor's note for my high school, a fake illness so I could stay home with the puppy. My mother, always an angel, indulged me.

His name was Yullo, a name given to him by a beloved friend who was now forever gone. From that day forward, between happy tails, potty training, and wet noses on my cheek, Yullo began to pull me back to the land of the living.

For seventeen years, he would be my constant companion, confirming a promise made across the veil of death. It was like the universe had taken a friend but given me another in return, a wellspring of comfort to see me through the pain. Yullo, with his soft nose and gentle paws, brought me back among the living.

To this day, many years after his passing, Yullo is remembered in my family as one of our own. He was a family member in his own right, no less beloved than any of us.

Over the years, I had dreams of Bogdan. Some were filled with a known regret of him wanting to return to the land of the living; others, with a peaceful acceptance of the way things unfolded. Time passed. I lost more people, including my father. I earned more scars and learned more lessons. The sharp pain of a dear friend's absence dulled, becoming a lingering ache rather than a gaping wound. Life, as it always does, went on.

But I never forgot all those small signs—not the phone coming back to life as if by a will of its own, not the agitated bird inexplicably speaking words it couldn't have possibly known, and not the breath in my ear. By now I was fully aware that I had a connection to something else, but it had never been this strong. Never before had it been so easy for me to get glimpses beyond the veil.

Was this new? Did this awareness become amplified after my three minutes in the land of the dead? I never got a logical resolution for these inquiries, and I likely never will. The conclusions weren't (nor do I believe they will ever be) satisfactory to the skeptic in me. They weren't factual enough. They weren't quantifiable. They weren't reproducible in a controlled environment. They were not scientific or provable.

Time passed, and over the years the pain of Bogdan's loss became merely a memory—a small scar, one of many. With time, my stubbornness subsided. I learned to look at things from many angles, not only from the lens that served me and my goals well. I learned to treat incredible topics with openness, even though I was still quiet. I was ready to try things. I'd wanted answers for so long. I'd spent most of my life with my nose in books, but I'd never looked inside. It took me twenty years to learn to do that.

Twenty-two years later, back home for a visit, I decided to try something I had always considered a game: astral travel. It was my curiosity, as always, that pushed me to try things I only half-believed were real. My mindset was simple: What could go wrong? I expected to either fall asleep or get bored. I certainly didn't expect it to work.

The room was warm and safe—my childhood bedroom. With the lights dimmed, I settled into my comfortable bed and played a random guided meditation from YouTube. The guide's voice was soft, almost lulling me into a calmer state of consciousness. Following his instructions, I created my protective ball of light, just as Mirela had taught me. Then came the instruction to visualize myself sitting up.

But it wasn't a visualization. It was a physical shift. My consciousness lifted its head, and then slowly, gently, I sat up. My physical body didn't follow; it remained lying on the bed with its eyes closed. But, in my mind's eye, I could see my surroundings almost clearly: the bedroom, the door to my balcony, the bright sunlight pouring through the open window. I simply sat there for a moment, an observer in two places at once. Then, I stood.

Instead of walking, I was gliding. It was an effortless, automatic movement, a muscle memory I recognized from my childhood and my NDE. "I used to do this all the time," I thought with a smile. "How could I have forgotten?" As I moved, I realized the guide's voice was fading into the background, no longer important. I glided out of my room and into the living room, emboldened by my recently found confidence. I looked out the window and wondered how far I could go. I sailed past the open window and out into the street.

"Hey, hey, hey!" a known voice called out from behind me.

I recognized it instantly, even after over twenty years of silence. I turned, and there he was. Bogdan. Over the years, the details of his face had been blurred by time, but now I saw him perfectly. He wore the hat he had loved so much, and an orange jacket—an odd choice for summer. He was cheerful, a wide, bright smile on his face. But there was something distinct about his appearance. While the world around us was in full, vibrant color, he seemed slightly muted, his own colors a little faded. At that moment, I was able to remember my NDE. My departed cousin had displayed a very similar discoloration, despite the very vibrant, otherworldly burst of colors in the meadow where we'd been w alking.

I was startled. I hadn't thought of him before this moment. I'd had no intention of seeking him out. It's not every day you get to float out of your body and have a chat with a friend who passed away two decades before. The sheer impossibility of it all left me perplexed. I kept my mouth shut, afraid that uttering a single sound would shatter the delicate reality of the moment. I tried to take off, to fly, to see how far I could go, but his startling appearance had broken the meditative state. In an instant, I was back in my body, the vision gone.

The thought of him, however, lingered. The questions rushed in. Was he stranded here, for twenty years, trying to reach people? Guilt, that old ghost, settled over me again. Why did my negative emotions always win? What was I so scared of, after all?

That moment was the catalyst. I finally had to acknowledge that these experiences were real for me, and it felt as if the time to make sense of them had come.

At the same time, I had realized there was a lot of work to do—mental work, which would end up helping me understand why I was paying attention to the bad more than the good. But that's a story for another time.

I needed to speak to someone, to find a way to make sense of what was happening. With that need for clarity, I sought out the "mumbo-jumbo" talkers I had spent a lifetime avoiding. I meditated, started a regular practice, embraced rituals and nature, and began a venture into a new world. But my focus remained on Bogdan and the question of whether or not he was trapped here.

Months later, I returned home. It was time to find peace. In a strong meditative state, I prayed to the highest light I knew, the most pure and loving. After so many years of silence, I prayed to Jesus Christ. And as I prayed, the realization hit me: It was not Bogdan's peace that needed Christ, it was mine. Without this catastrophic loss—and without the visions and the strange events—I would have not prayed.

A few days ago, driving home from an outing, "Changes" by Tupac came on the radio—Bogdan's favorite song. As the first notes played, I saw him again in my mind's eye, standing in a brilliant light, with the biggest, happiest smile I have ever seen. He took off his hat and bowed—a theatrical gesture, a final curtain call.

Some will call it self-suggestion, a sad attempt to find closure, and it's highly likely that this is exactly what it was. But it worked. I sleep easy now, fully believing that my friend is well, wherever he is.

But I want to briefly pause and reflect on fear and shame, the recurring themes in this story. What do we really agonize over? Death? It is inevitable; we might as well embrace it. Poverty? I've had my own highs and lows with money. I remember when my very productive marketing job all but vanished during a financial crisis. But, much to my surprise, I realized that I wasn't any less happy when the money was gone. In fact, I remember vividly that I used to laugh so much harder when I didn't have a penny.

This was reinforced for me many years later on a work trip to beautiful, magical India. We saw the luxury and felt the intoxicating energy of the place, but we also visited less fortunate areas. It was there I saw people living in literal cardboard boxes, and what struck me was their open hearts and bright smiles. They had nothing, but there wasn't an ounce of malice in them—only a joy completely untethered from material wealth.

What we avoid, then, is not the lack of money itself. Instead, it is the stigma, the judgment, and the shame of being "other."

It was this worry that kept me from speaking to a parrot, from reaching out to a friend in the astral plane, and from doing so many things I wanted to do in this life. I was sick of it. It was at that moment that the decision was made: I'd say what I had to say, do what I needed to do, and let the chips fall where they may.

A Journey into the Unseen

After everything that happened, I finally faced the fact that I couldn't keep running. The phone flickering to life, the parrot at Bogdan's wake, the ragged breathing in my bedroom, and my moment in the astral plane had all led to this realization. But the worry of being judged had been my companion for so long, a silent partner in my decision to stay quiet about the truth I carried. My life, once so logical and straightforward, had been shattered. My mind, so confident in its ability to offer explanations, had fully run out of them. It was a terrifying, humbling realization.

I had to make sense of what was going on, and for that, I needed a new set of answers—ones that went far beyond the everyday. I had to understand why the world had suddenly become so permeable, why the veil between life and death had turned so thin. This search, this intellectual pursuit, was my way of trying to breathe again, of trying to find a way out of the sorrow that was consuming me. It was a desperate attempt to find a logical route through an illogical world.

In my sadness, I sought a different kind of solace—not in memories, but in a broader human experience. I began to read everything I could about death, grief, and the world beyond. The more I read, the more I recognized reflections of my own story in the beliefs of others, and it began to lift the heavy weight of isolation I had been carrying. I was not alone in this grief, nor in the inexplicable events that followed.

This quest exposed me to a library of human history, a deep dive into how people have been grappling with these same questions for millennia.

The idea of talking to the dead isn't new. For as long as humanity has been around, we've faced the same inescapable condition of mortality and loss.

As a species, we have created stories and rituals to navigate the chasm that death creates, and my own narratives served as a modern echo of these long-standing practices.

I was fascinated to learn about the modern "continuing bonds" approach to grief. This psychological perspective views grief not as a process that ends with detachment, but as an ongoing relationship with the deceased.[1] It was validating to know that the kinship I had with the other side was not a sign of failure to move on. Instead, it was a normal, non-pathological part of the grieving process.

It turns out that a significant number of bereaved individuals—up to 50 percent in some older studies—spontaneously have some form of contact. More recent examinations suggest these numbers may even be an underestimate. These states of contact, which include nightly visions, the experience of sounds, sensing the proximity of the deceased, and engaging in conversations with them, are consistent across various demographics.

This taught me that my responses were not bizarre or unique. Instead, they were a common, human response to loss.

I also read about the psychomanteum, a sensory deprivation method developed by philosopher and psychiatrist Raymond Moody to facilitate contact with the deceased.[2]

Research has shown that participants who undergo this technique report significant reductions in feelings of sadness, grief, and regret, and an increase in feelings of appreciation, gratitude, and love. The therapeutic benefits of a connection with the departed are significant, regardless of whether a specific afterlife communication occurs. This ritual serves a vital psychological function, offering comfort and helping to heal the wounds of loss.

My decision to meditate and seek Bogdan out in the Unseen was my own personal psychomanteum, a way to find peace for him and me. This knowledge also helped me

---

1. Klass, Dennis, Phyllis R. Silverman, and Steven L. Nickman, eds. *Continuing Bonds: New Understandings of Grief.* Washington, D.C.: Taylor & Francis, 1996.

2. Moody, Raymond A., and Paul Perry. *The Light Beyond.* New York: Bantam Books, 1988.

understand that a new, more accepting view of these experiences is emerging in the mental health community, moving away from a pathologizing view toward a more accepting and nuanced clinical perspective.

Exploring the Ancient World's View of the Afterlife

As I embarked on my new adventure, I had to at least visit the oldest of sources: mythology. My logical mind had always assumed the line between the living and the dead was a hard, fast barrier. But in the texts of the Greco-Romans, it was more of a permeable curtain.

This was the perfect metaphor for what I had experienced. The veil had become so thin that I could almost reach through it. It was a world where heroes like Odysseus and Aeneas literally journeyed to the Underworld, a plane of existence that was not just a final resting place, but also a dynamic, interactive space. In these traditions, the dead, or "shades," retained a kind of agency and influence over the living.

The purpose of these perilous journeys, known as a Nekyia or Katabasis[3], was to gain vital prophetic knowledge or resolve unfinished earthly business, not to gawk at the afterlife. In these practices, communication was a transaction—an exchange rooted in ritual. The ritual of pouring libations and offering blood gave the shades enough corporeal substance to communicate and give counsel.

I recognized this as a reflection of my own desperate plea to the void. My dysfunctional phone had died, only to flicker back to life long enough for me to get the contacts I needed. In that moment, I, too, had received a kind of counsel, an answer to my plea.

The idea that the dead still have a stake in the world resonated with me as truth. Why wouldn't they, after all? They still have family here. They have loved ones, dear places, and the cherished past. For a while, however long or short, this world was their home. And most of us can sympathize with the longing to visit home.

---

3. Scodel, Ruth. *Introduction to Greek Literature: From Homer to the Hellenistic Period*. New York: Cambridge University Press, 2010.

Hero cults also captivated me. These were mortals who, after death, were believed to acquire superhuman powers that they could use for either benevolent or malevolent purposes. As a result, the living would perform meticulous rituals and offerings to appease these spirits, seeking their support and protection. This established a transactional relationship, highlighting a belief in a reciprocal economy between the living and the dead. The well-being of the living was intrinsically linked to the proper treatment and remembrance of the dead, reflecting a social contract that extended beyond mortal life.

This was a beautiful idea—that our bond to our loved ones does not end, but rather transforms after death.

I also discovered how the ancient Egyptians took this concept even further with their "Letters to the Dead."[4] These weren't grand philosophical treatises; they were practical, intimate, and often quite mundane requests inscribed on bowls and offered at tombs. People would write to their deceased relatives for things like resolving property disputes, seeking protection from enemies, or even reprimanding a ghost for neglecting household affairs. This showed a belief system where social and familial bonds didn't die with the body. The dead remained active participants in the daily lives of the living, and if you neglected them, they were capable of causing "all sorts of mayhem on earth," including haunting or illness.

This highlights a continuous, interdependent relationship, and it resonated with the way I felt after Bogdan's death—a sense of an invisible presence, an unresolved connection that had to be addressed.

Then I found myself in Norse mythology, where Seiðr, or Norse shamanism, offered a different, more powerful lens. Seiðr practitioners weren't just messengers for the dead; they were vessels who entered heightened states to re-chart the course of fate.[5] This metaphor of "weaving new events into being" from the non-physical realm offered a

---

4. Wente, Edward F. "Letters to the Living and the Dead." In *Letters from Ancient Egypt*, edited by Edward F. Wente. Atlanta: Scholars Press, 1990.

5. Price, Neil S. *The Viking Way: Religion and War in Late Iron Age Scandinavia*. Uppsala: Department of Archaeology and Ancient History, Uppsala University, 2002.

powerful cipher for my own agency. The practitioner became an architect of reality, not a victim of circumstance.

This implied that the spirit domain was seen as a dynamic, interactive interface for shaping both individual and communal destiny. In my own way, that was a part of what I was trying to do in my meditation—to not merely receive, but also act.

Abrahamic Traditions: The Line in the Sand

My next stop was the Abrahamic religions: Judaism, Christianity, and Islam. Here, I found a much stricter and more defined boundary between the living and the dead. The general consensus, with some notable exceptions, was that communicating with the dead was a forbidden practice. This was a direct counterpoint to the truths I had held, and I was determined to understand why.

In the Hebrew Bible, consulting the dead is explicitly condemned as detestable to God. The story of King Saul and the Witch of Endor is a famous example of this condemnation.

Desperate for guidance, Saul consults a medium, who then summons the prophet Samuel's shade. The apparition of Samuel's shade is so jarring that the medium herself is terrified, a shock that betrays her lack of control over the profound emergence.[6] The resulting debate has raged for centuries: Was it truly Samuel? A demonic impersonation? Or a unique occurrence? The answer remains elusive, yet the narrative's lesson is clear: Searching for guidance outside a sanctioned path is perilous, leading to dire consequences.

This validated the chokehold that had silenced my voice. The dread of judgment for seeking the unseen was not new; it was a societal and religious edict etched in history. I wanted to know why.

Christianity and Islam have their own similar frameworks. The New Testament explains that perceived "ghosts" are often demons in disguise, who masquerade as angels of light to deceive individuals and lead them away from God. Jesus's own post-resurrection appearance in a body with "flesh and bones" served to distinguish his resurrected body

---

6. Levenson, Jon D. *Resurrection and the Restoration of Israel: The Ultimate Victory of the God of Life*. New Haven: Yale University Press, 2008.

from a disembodied spirit. This reinforces the Christian view that human souls do not roam as disembodied entities.

In Islam, the souls of the dead enter an intermediary state called Barzakh, and cannot return to the earthly realm. Any perceived ghosts or hauntings are attributed to other supernatural entities like jinn, which are distinct from human souls.[7]

This theological distillation redefines the meaning of a "ghost," attributing perceived paranormal manifestations to a different category of entities.

For me, the most interesting exception in Christianity was the doctrine of the intercession of saints in Catholicism and Eastern Orthodoxy. This wasn't a summoning of the dead, but a prayer to saints in heaven, who could then intercede on behalf of the living with God. It was a structured, permissible form of communication that still reinforced God's ultimate authority and Christ's unique mediatorial role. It was a kind of sanctioned, faith-based support, and it made me wonder: Who gets to draw the line between what is considered acceptable and what is not? Who decides what is a true visitation and what is made up or evil? How do these people know? Is there genuine concern for the safety of our souls, or is it no more than another form of gatekeeping for profit?

Who decides whether we're right or wrong, and what gives these people the right to confirm or contest someone else's reality?

The Modern Quest: From Spiritualism to Science

This brought me to the modern world, where the conversation around these phenomena shifted from religion and myth to an attempt at science.

Modern parapsychology, I discovered, was born out of the 19th century Spiritualist movement, which came into being during a time when people began to look for proof of life after death. The Society for Psychical Research was founded in 1882 to investigate claims of after-death communication.

---

7. Smith, Jane I., and Yvonne Y. Haddad. *The Islamic Understanding of Death and Resurrection*. New York: Oxford University Press, 2002.

I found myself distinctly drawn to mediums like Leonora Piper, whose communications were so detailed and accurate that even skeptical researchers like William James of Harvard University were impressed. However, for every convincing case, there were instances of fraud and flawed studies. Sadly, many prominent mediums of the time were discovered to have been engaged in fraud, using props and stage tricks to fool people.

The mainstream school of thought today remains largely unconvinced, calling parapsychology a pseudoscience because of its lack of reproducible evidence. The field is still considered controversial because it lacks an accepted theory, making it difficult to definitively rule out normal explanations or the "super-psi hypothesis" (which posits that information is channeled telepathically from the sitters' minds, not from a discarnate entity).

Psychological and neuroscientific perspectives offered a different kind of theory, one that spoke directly to my mind. This was a difficult but necessary part of my exploration. They argue that perceptions (such as the perception of a nearby being) are not independent entities, but rather intricate processes within our own brains.

The experience of a sensed entity is a transdiagnostic experience. This means it occurs across a wide spectrum of conditions and contexts, including periods of isolation, exposure to extreme elements, sleep paralysis, bereavement, anxiety, or psychosis.

This was relatable for me. My own encounter with the breathing in my bedroom came during a period of intense grief and isolation immediately after Bogdan's death.

The left temporoparietal junction (TPJ)[8] is a key cerebral region located where the temporal and parietal lobes meet. It acts as a central hub, integrating sensory input from our visual, auditory, and touch senses with the limbic system, which governs emotion and memory.

---

8. Blanke, Olaf, and Sandra Arzy. "The Out-of-Body Experience: Disturbance of Body Schema or Higher-Order Self Processing at the Temporoparietal Junction." *The Neurobiology of the Self in Psychiatric Disorders*, edited by A. L. P. M. F. C. K. Vogeley and T. F. R. W. K. Vogeley. Cambridge University Press, 2011.

Because this precise neural nexus connects our sensory observations with our thoughts and memories, researchers have found that, by electrically stimulating it, they can induce the subjective experience of a shadowy figure. This suggests that presence hallucinations may stem from a mismatch between the brain's prediction of an action and what is actually registered by the senses, leading to the sense of an agent separate from the self.

The occurrence of paranormal experiences, including those interpreted as interactions with the deceased, is associated with specific types of neuronal activity within the temporal lobes of the brain. This was the kind of diagnosis I thought I wanted—a way to understand the breath I'd heard in my bedroom. Though the answer was cold and clinical, it was also a revelation.

Finally, this investigation uncovered for me that our brains construct our reality. What we perceive as an entity separate from ourselves may often be an internal process of meaning-making, especially under emotionally charged or ambiguous conditions.

My friend's death and my near-death experience were extreme circumstances. They could have pushed the brain to the brink of how it constructs a unitary identity, triggering hallucinations.

It was an odd comfort to know that my brain's wiring for finding patterns and meaning—a sculptor of perception known as pareidolia and apophenia—could explain how I interpreted indistinct sounds or an empty room as signs from the other side. My beliefs, my emotional state, and my trauma all played a role in how I experienced the world.

Anthropological and Cultural Reflections

My search also led me to anthropology, which provided a crucial lens through which to understand these anomalies, as it highlighted their embedding within human cultures across time and geography. It was a relief to learn that I was not an anomaly; I was part of a universal human tapestry.

From its beginnings in the late 1800s, anthropology observed that people worldwide reported seeing and hearing spirits, and sought to communicate with them. This widespread phenomenon underscored for me that beliefs in spirits and spirit communication aren't mere anomalies; they are central to how many cultures conceptualize their world and navigate life.

I found myself thinking about all the ways people, for centuries, have tried to make sense of the very things happening to me. I found that, across cultures, these unusual experiences served a purpose, often providing a framework for coping with loss and providing meaning.

I was fascinated by how different cultures conceptualize spirits and their communication methods. For instance, in the Haursepuh community, spiritual sight in the sleep state can serve as a medium for communicating with supernatural beings, and the manifestation of demons in the unconscious can signify impending disaster. In modern Sundanese society, supernatural powers can manifest as sound without a corporeal form, affecting a person's mind and potentially leading them to follow ethereal commands.

In the Nigerian Igbo indigenous tradition, interaction with non-physical entities is a pervasive force. This force has been synthesized into manifestations of the Holy Presence for healing and communal uplift within various Christian denominations.

The Gnawa community in Morocco uses women as leaders in healing rituals. These rituals involve trance dances and music to communicate with spirits that possess participants, aiming for healing and ecstasy.

The existence of these diverse practices demonstrated that what I had been going through was part of a larger, global tapestry of human consciousness.

I was very moved by the practice of ancestor veneration, a tradition in many indigenous cultures that stands in sharp contrast to my own upbringing. In these societies, ancestors are not merely deceased relatives, but are considered active members of households and communities, serving as vital sources of guidance and a wellspring of insight.

I read how indigenous authors described ancestors providing life-enhancing stories and engaging in intergenerational dialogues that offer significant guidance to their communities. These dialogues, which can weave through many temporal directions, are a way of witnessing, grieving, and taking action to respond to past injustices. Ceremonies—from rap ciphering and healing circles to drumming and dancing—are employed to invoke the wisdom of the ancestors, propel communal action, and forge culture and knowledge.

This idea of a continuous dialogue—of listening to the wisdom of those who came before us—profoundly resonated with me. It gave me a significant new way to look at my own experience. Bogdan had been, and continued to be, a source of guidance for me, even after his death. The rainbow at his funeral was a small, beautiful fountain of solace that I had understood. His voice on the phone, his spectral presence in my bedroom, and his appearance in the astral plane and in the car were all, in a way, part of an intergenerational dialogue. This was his way of providing me with guidance and comfort, and pushing me to face my fears.

I had been trying to find clarity in books, but the knowledge had been there all along, in the whispers and signs I had been too consumed by doubt to acknowledge.

The anthropological lens validated my experiences by placing them within a universal human context. This indicated to me that the line between the living and the dead, while not always clear, has been a space of dialogue and communion for humanity since the beginning of time.

Answering the Call

So where did all this information leave me? My exploration had started with a terrifying and transcendent moment, and had followed a course that carried me through myths, strict religious doctrines, and cold, hard empirical truths. Each stop had offered a piece of the puzzle, but none of them, on their own, could fully explain the things I had been through.

The myths told me that these accounts are part of the human story. They offered tales of heroes and shamans who navigated the veil between worlds, aspiring for knowledge and guidance.

The religions told me that the line between heaven and Earth is drawn in different ways, and that what is considered a transcendent encounter in one tradition might be condemned as a demonic deception in another.

And the neurological findings confirmed that my brain does exactly what it is wired to do: try to make sense of the incomprehensible. It does this by linking a sensed awareness to distinct temporal lobe activity or a mismatch in my perception of my own body.

My logical mind, once so confident, had to accept that what I perceived as external might very well be an inherent process of meaning-making.

Ultimately, I realized I wouldn't find the truth I was seeking in a book or study. It was in the last place I thought to look: my own heart.

The parrot's call to me at the wake was not a random utterance. It was a challenge, a moment of reckoning. Whether it came from a ghost, a demon, or my own brain's complex machinations was completely irrelevant. The subjective experience and significant impact of perceived interactions with the deceased are undeniable for many people, and their therapeutic utility in helping individuals manage grief is a promising avenue of exploration.

The experience with Bogdan had been the catalyst. It had forced me to sit down and have a chat with myself—to acknowledge that these occurrences were real for me, and that I was driven to make sense of them.

I had been so consumed by guilt and anxiety—guilt that he had died in my place, and that I had been too hesitant to say anything at his wake—that I had been unable to move forward. The worry that his death was payback for my own survival gnawed at me for months.

My negative feelings had locked away my voice—not just regarding the parrot, but also the breathing I'd heard in my bedroom. This fear of judgment—of being labeled an outsider—had become the internal warden of my life, limiting my every venture.

The call came not from a textbook, but from a parrot, a whisper, and a friend's bow as the curtain fell. Sometimes it was not even external—it was merely an inner nudge, a gentle pull forcing me to look into things more deeply. But maybe I had gone about it the wrong way. Maybe it was about accepting the "what," not understanding the "how."

I'm no longer waiting for somebody else to validate what I know in my heart to be true. I'm ready to step out from behind this mask that has grown uncomfortable, and to tell my story. Maybe sometimes bravery is not about not being afraid. Maybe it is about doing what we need to do, despite how afraid we are.

Modern Connections with the Departed

My astral encounter was a shout from the universe, when I had previously only been listening for whispers. It was the moment that shifted me from being a passive recipient of strange events to an active seeker of answers. My journey mirrored a path walked by countless others in the modern world—a quest to understand if we can truly connect with those who have passed on.

Today, that idea isn't hidden in dusty séance parlors. It's a mainstream phenomenon, led by popular television mediums like Tyler Henry and Theresa Caputo, who bring messages of comfort to millions.[9] Vast online communities gather on social media and grief support forums, creating a global network where people share their own inexplicable experiences and find validation that they aren't alone. Of course, the logical mind (my own included) is quick to point to skeptical explanations: psychological techniques like "cold reading" (where general statements are made to seem specific) or the simple human tendency to find patterns and meaning where there are none.

But what these skeptics often overlook is the profound and personal nature of the signs people receive. They aren't always grand pronouncements from a medium; sometimes they are small, intimate moments that feel like a personal language. These signs, I've learned, often fall into distinct categories—categories I recognized from my own experience with Bogdan.

First, there are the electrical signs—lights flickering, televisions turning on, or a phone that flickers back to life in response to a desperate plea.

There are also symbolic messengers, where the natural world seems to carry a message. At Bogdan's wake, it was the parrot speaking my name—an impossible event that stunned everyone into silence. During that same wake, my best friend was sitting on the steps outside when a stray dog approached her. She told me later, her eyes wide with disbelief, that the dog was crying real tears, its body shaking with human-like sobs. She was certain

---

9. Bown, Fiona. *The Medium Is the Message: Contemporary Mediumship in Popular Culture*. London: Routledge, 2021.

it was a reflection of the overwhelming grief surrounding us, a sign from the universe itself.

And then there is meaningful music. For me, it was hearing Tupac's "Changes"—Bogdan's favorite song—on the radio years later, and seeing a clear vision of him in my mind's eye, tipping his hat with a happy smile. For others, it's the one song that defines their relationship with a parent or partner playing at the exact moment they need comfort the most.

These experiences—the phone, the parrot, the breathing in my room, the song on the radio—weren't just random anomalies. They were a consistent, quiet language. The challenge, I was beginning to understand, wasn't about forcing contact, but learning how to listen.

For those who wish to open themselves to this connection, the practices are gentle and rooted in intention. It can be as simple as lighting a candle next to a photograph and speaking to a loved one, sharing your day and letting them know you're open to a sign. It can be a quiet meditation, where you hold the feeling of them in your heart and ask for a symbol of their peace. Or it can be writing letters to them in a journal, a therapeutic act that often opens a channel for unexpected insights to flow onto the page.

Ultimately, opening your awareness requires the same thing my astral travel did: a momentary suspension of disbelief. I had to set aside my skepticism to allow the experience to unfold. My encounter with Bogdan was a loud, undeniable event that shattered my defenses, but it also tuned my ears to hear the softer whispers that followed. It's about trusting that flutter of emotion, those sudden goosebumps, or that gut feeling that you are not alone. It's about accepting that the most profound connections often defy logical explanation, and having the courage to listen anyway.

Chapter 8: Of Dreams and Dreamers

Six weeks after his death my father appeared to me in a dream... It was an unforgettable experience, and it forced me for the first time to think about life after death.

—Carl Jung

My mind, a place I once considered a well-organized library, is, in reality, a chaotic attic filled with dusty curiosities. Years of studying psychology gave me a catalog to file away my fleeting night visions, teaching me to look for the predictable patterns of memory and emotion. I've grown skilled at it, a nosy detective in the landscape of my own subconscious.

My favorite game with myself, to this day, is to identify the memories my subconscious pulls from to create my dreams. It's a fun game, and it helps me learn more about my own mind. But there are whispers in that attic that refuse to be categorized.

The fact that I am fully aware that I am dreaming—what many call "lucid dreaming"—is also worth noting. I don't have a special method for this; it's not a skill I've ever practiced or tried to hone. For me, it either happens automatically, or it simply doesn't. This state of awareness, this lucidity, seems to be the key that separates a simple dream from something else entirely.

There are night visions that feel less like a set of data and more like a direct transmission from another world. They leave an emotional fingerprint I can't scrub clean, an emotional echo so potent it bleeds into my waking hours. And sometimes, they are more than a trace of the past—they are a glimpse of what's to come. This is the story of those nighttime revelations, the ones that science can't explain. They led me to a truth I'd been searching for my entire life: I am not alone in this.

The Dream of the Priest-King

My first "strange" dream came to me when I was six years old, but its memory is as clear as if it happened yesterday. It was another summer spent at my grandma's house, which was always a delight. I can still remember falling asleep: the open window, the smell of a summer night, and the sound of the crickets outside. I remember closing my eyes and falling into darkness. For a second, I was unsure if I should be alarmed. But then, like a whisper from beyond, awareness dawned that I was asleep, and that this was a vision from my sleeping mind.

A heavy, oppressive shadow fell over my grandmother's house. It wasn't the kind of shade that brings the promise of restful sleep; it was the kind that holds its breath, thick and still like a void. The shadows melted into the corners, leaving no safe space for a child's imagination to rest. It was as if I shrank into a small, insignificant dot hiding in a corner of an endless ocean of black.

It was in this sea of shadows that the dream began—not with a sudden flash of light, but with a subtle, gradual shift in the air, as if the atoms around me had decided to rearrange themselves.

Then, a single figure appeared before me, standing in what looked like the solitary beam of a projector. It was alive, pulsating with a glowing energy that was both visible and palpable. The figure had shoulder-length black hair, a beard, and a mustache. It was male, and his voice was male, too. His face was expressionless; I can't say whether he was scary or inviting. He appeared rather uninterested, in fact. The one thing I couldn't define was his age. He didn't look old, but he certainly didn't feel young.

He wore the robes of a priest or a king, heavy garments adorned with intricate patterns that appeared to move and shift in the pale, ethereal light. They weren't just embroidered; they were alive, pulsating with a silent but visible energy. It was almost fluid. A tall hat that reminded me of a pope sat upon his head, adding to his formidable bearing and making him appear to touch the very ceiling of my world.

His voice was booming and deep—intimidating, yes, but not in a way that caused fear. It was the intimidating presence of a giant protector, an awesome power that I instinctively knew was on my side. In his presence, I felt completely safe, almost untouchable.

The message created a tremor, but it wasn't a tremble of fear; it was a vibration that traveled through me, a language of pure resonance. It spoke of profound, ancient bonds—of family, love, and a deep togetherness. It was a message of oneness, of things coming together.

These were vast, abstract concepts. For a six-year-old, "ancient bonds" and "oneness" meant very little. What I did understand, what I felt in my bones, was the part that mattered: I was not alone, and I was safe. There was this big guy, and he was in my corner!

The words were in Romanian, but he vocalized very slowly, accentuating each syllable as if he strained to articulate a tongue unfamiliar to him. Regardless, the message reached me, as confusing as it was, and I keep the words as a precious secret.

At six, the message itself signified nothing to my young mind. It was a message of love, but to a small child, these things are confusing at best and uninteresting at worst. I had parents that loved me; I was covered. As far as I was concerned, the love was appreciated but unnecessary.

Despite being a kid, I somehow had an instinctual sense of certainty that this dream was special, that it was unlike all others that I remembered. What my young mind latched onto, what made it so special, wasn't the message, but the power behind it.

That power was everything. Still and immense, it rested in the center of the room, radiating a profound and heavy stillness. The power was that stillness, offering a sense of absolute calm. It was a force of nature, a dormant volcano, and I was a child, a small pebble on the side of a mountain.

I understood what it meant to be face-to-face with an authority figure. My movements grew cautious and my voice soft, as if even a misplaced syllable could summon a lecture. There was no malevolence in him, no threat, only an ancient, still, and watchful grace.

The message was one of love and reassurance, and despite the intimidating form before me, a profound sense of peace washed over me.

It was a serenity that made me feel so complete. I was safe, a small bird under the wing of a great eagle. The dream ended as soon as the message was delivered, the apparition simply dissolving into the light from which he came. But the resonance lingered, a whispered echo in my heart.

The vision became a kind of touchstone for me. When I was lost or alone, I would close my eyes and remember. I'd return to that moment of absolute safety. It was the first time I mused that dreams could be more than a jumble of stuff. Of all the night visions I've had, few have left such a clear mark on me. I remember every detail, no matter how short or confusing.

Little did I know that this was not just a message; it was an introduction. It was the first chapter in a book I had no idea I was writing.

I would meet this presence again, in many forms, and not always in my sleep. But that would come much later. It was a signpost on a path I didn't even know I was on, and a first clue that the world was far bigger, stranger, and more beautiful than I had been taught. It was a gift from the universe, a promise that I was not alone.

The Dream of The Luminous Garden

My next unforgettable dream came to me when I was ten or eleven. It was so vivid and real it was as if I had simply woken up in a new place. The transition was seamless, a gentle slipping from one world into another.

As I opened my eyes, I found myself lying on cool grass. I blinked, realizing I was dreaming; I could remember falling asleep in my bed. The texture of the blades of grass was a surprising tickle against my skin. I sat up, taking in the scene before me. A beautiful, sunlit city sprawled out below. The air was warm and filled with the scent of a gentle summer breeze, rustling the leaves of the trees that stood like sentinels.

The light was a brilliant, almost blinding gold, saturating the world with a sense of pure, benevolent energy. To my right, there was a massive, white statue of Jesus, His arms outstretched as if greeting the sun. I had seen images of that statue in a Michael Jackson video, and in my dream, a clear, unshakable feeling of recognition washed over me. I was in Rio de Janeiro.

Why was I dreaming of a city halfway around the world, a place I had only ever seen on a screen? My young mind immediately tried to rationalize the inexplicable, trying to fit this square peg into the round hole of my waking-world logic.

As I stood there, an undeniable pull began to tug at me, drawing me somewhere else. There was no visible path, no way down from the ledge I was on, but the impression of urgency was growing.

I turned around, and there, in the middle of a green field with no walls, no roads, and no rational purpose, was a door. It was just a door, standing alone in a wilderness of green, its wood a reddish-brown tint, its brass handle gleaming in the sun. I walked through it, not with hesitation, but with a sense of excited curiosity, as if I had been called. On the other side, I found a garden of vibrant, luminous colors.

The flowers looked as if they were cut from gems or crystals, their petals humming with a powerful sense of life that I could feel surging through my veins. The colors were not found in any crayon box; they were a living, breathing tapestry of light and shade that radiated pure emotion.

The rush of joy and fervor of the moment were so profound they made me dizzy. Yet what truly seized me was a visceral, absolute recognition. I remembered this place. I have been here before. It felt like a first home, as familiar as my own skin—a truth I had always carried.

I didn't walk; I glided through the garden, the ground seeming to fall away beneath me as I moved, a weightless sensation of pure freedom. The colors were a dizzying tapestry of light and life, and the air hummed with music I could clearly hear, despite not being able to identify its origin.

The perfect calm was so intense that it was like an end to all searching. Then, as if with a single thought, I landed on a beach. My feet were in the cool water, the sand soft beneath my soles. The ocean was a clear, impossible blue. I saw a shark or a dolphin in the distance, but it didn't matter.

The intensity of the state of harmony and freedom was so powerful it woke me up, and those incredible emotions stayed with me for the rest of the day, a beautiful afterglow that I could still feel on my skin. I rushed to my mom, spilling the story out in a breathless tumble of words.

She listened with that feigned importance parents give their kids, a small, polite smile on her face.

"And I felt...I don't know, I felt free!" I finished, searching her eyes for a sign that she understood.

She just patted my head, her smile unwavering. "Well, that's a nice story," she said. "But it was nothing but a dream. It doesn't have to mean anything."

I nodded and smiled, but only partially accepted her answer. I chose to keep the magic in my heart, a secret treasure that no one could take from me. I was used to this by now. I understood that seeking magic wasn't a productive use of my time, according to the grown-ups.

I have never forgotten that place or those feelings. How could I, when I got to see the beautiful garden again? I saw it during my brush with death at seventeen, and again, much later in my mid-thirties, during an involuntary OBE.

What happened that night was a turning point. It was no coincidence that my passion for psychology was ignited. I wanted to understand if dreams were just things our brains made up, or if there was more. I wanted to know if that beautiful, impossible place was real, or if my mind had simply conjured it from nothing.

It was years before I found a potential explanation in the scientific community. It's a phenomenon called lucid dreaming, a state of consciousness where the sleeper achieves awareness of their dream state. It's not a supernatural gift, it's a skill that can be cultivated.

Neuroscientists like Stephen LaBerge have used EOG signals to objectively validate this state, observing that lucid dreams occur during REM sleep, but with a unique hybrid brain activity that mirrors both sleep and wakefulness.[1] Researchers have even found that people who lucid dream have a greater volume of gray matter in their frontopolar cortex, a region associated with self-awareness.

The idea that my brain's own wiring might be the mechanism for these phenomena was a revelation. It didn't diminish the power of the dreams; it gave me a new vocabulary to describe them. It uncovered for me that the mind isn't a passive screen, but an active participant, capable of a heightened state of metacognition.

The dream of the luminous garden gave me a lifelong quest: to reconcile the two worlds I had always known—the one of cold, hard facts, and the one of vibrant, undeniable feeling. It was a voyage that would lead me down unexpected paths.

The Dream of the Devil

Mainstream empirical knowledge often dismisses premonitory dreams, calling them a result of coincidence and bias. It is easy for them to dismiss what they can't explain, to simply file away the unbelievable under random neural firings. But I had one of those, and it was the first time I was given tangible, waking-world proof that there is more—that the world isn't as solid and predictable as they want us to believe. It was a crack in the foundation, a tear in the veneer of the rational world.

I was eighteen, and in my dream, I was with my best friend and two other friends. We were going to a party at an apartment that looked less like a home and more like an office.

I first found myself in a dark hallway. The only illumination came from a small, green conch shell nightlight, casting a sickly glow near a doorway to our right. The atmosphere was strange, a mix of the dim light from the hall and the harsh fluorescent lighting that spilled out from the room beyond. A tense, palpable silence filled the air.

I passed through the doorway and into the living room. The cold, blue tile floor felt strange under the fluorescent light. On one side of the room sat a modern black leather couch. Above

---

1. Stephen LaBerge, "Lucid Dreaming: Psychophysiological Studies of Consciousness during REM Sleep," in *Sleep and Cognition* (Washington, DC: American Psychological Association, 1990).

it hung a painting that looked completely out of place: an old, serene image of a fisherman in a boat on a lake, captured in a heavy, tarnished bronze frame. The contrast between the sleek couch and the old painting was jarring; they didn't match at all.

On the other side of the couch, a grand, dark table dominated the center of the room, surrounded by empty chairs. It was set for a feast, with ornate wine glasses, their decorated legs gleaming strangely under the light.

And at the head of it was the Devil. He was like a monumental statue in size, big and red with horns that curled like black, twisted snakes. He was a sight that commanded observation. I realized I was invisible in my dream, so I was careful not to utter a peep as I drifted across the room and slid into one of the chairs at the table.

Completely unaware of my presence, the creepy host cordially gestured to the room at large—to us all—directing us to feast and enjoy the party.

I did not touch the food and drinks. The air was thin and dry, and a nameless dread caught in my throat, squeezing it tight. This intuition, even in my dream state, made me refrain from any kind of interaction. I was an unmoving witness to a scene I didn't understand, an invisible guest at a dangerous dinner party. I was the unseen visitor. I found the perspective intriguing.

After that, I woke up. The worry that had been strangely absent in the dream suddenly gripped me. My heart hammered against my ribs, and the cold dread of the dream clung to me like a second skin. I tried to dismiss it as just a dream, but the dream's substance refused to fade. It was too real, too urgent to be a figment of my imagination. It was a warning. I did not go back to sleep that night.

The next morning, I felt sluggish, the dream clinging to me after a night of no sleep. I went through the motions of a normal day—showering, having breakfast—but I couldn't shake the unease. Needing a dose of reality, I called my best friend and invited her over for coffee.

She was there in ten minutes. As always, the easy chatter and giggles of teenage friends were the perfect antidote, and the strange, dark images from the night before began to fade.

That was, until she started telling me about a party we were invited to. It was to celebrate two of our friends getting jobs. My stomach tightened as she said their names—they had both been in my dream.

"They both got hired by a small startup," she continued, "and they're having a party at their new headquarters!"

I held my breath, waiting. Then she said the final, chilling detail: The headquarters were in an apartment.

An eerie feeling hit me as soon as she said the words. My palms grew clammy, and a chill traced its way down my spine.

My first impulse was to say no, flat out. The similarities were already too much, and I didn't know if it was smart to ignore such a blatant warning. But I've never known when to quit, and my curiosity always gets the best of me. I had to see. Was it just a wild coincidence? Or was there real danger? Why not see for myself?

I said nothing about the dream to my friend, and agreed to go that night, claiming we had to celebrate our friends' success. In reality, I was going on a personal mission: I had to see if the rest of it was real, too.

My senses were screaming at me by the time we arrived. I stood before the door, and my stomach dropped. The door and the dark hallway looked exactly like my dream, right down to the small, green conch shell nightlight by the doorframe.

My shock was complete as I walked through the same hallway and entered the living room. The blue tile, the black leather couch, the old painting of the fisherman in its bronze frame—it was all there. I felt a cold dread as I sat at the same grand, dark table, surrounded by the same chairs.

Then, the new boss came out to greet everyone. He sat at the head of the table—in the exact same spot where the Devil had sat in my dream. He was incredibly friendly and in great spirits, welcoming us warmly. With a broad smile, he gestured to the table and invited us all to eat, drink, and be merry. The dissonance was dizzying. Everything on the surface was normal and celebratory, but my internal alarm was screaming.

His smile was too large, his eyes a little too bright. It was too much to dismiss. I figured this was enough. I had seen enough to know that the warning was real. The similarities were too many, and I was not going to sit around and wait to see what the actual danger was. As I had done in my dream, I refused anything to eat or drink, my mouth dry as dust. Within fifteen minutes, I had confessed my dream to my best friend, including all the similarities, and convinced her that we really, REALLY needed to leave.

As we were walking out, Dan, the boss, asked for my number, which I politely declined, making up some excuse. I assumed that "I dreamt you were the Devil" didn't sound like a sane reply, so I offered little room for dialogue. A few months later, we found out Dan was married with a child on the way, a fact he had conveniently failed to mention to anyone. He also scammed my friends, overworking them for months and never paying them.

The dream had been a warning, a cryptic but accurate message from a source beyond the material, known reality: *Dan sucks.* Do I think this guy was the actual Devil? No. But I believe he was trouble, and somehow, something out there wanted me to stay out of it. My mind simply pulled an image that could never be mistaken or confused with something else. The Devil is trouble; Dan is trouble. Keep away.

This was not the first time I had a premonition, but it was the first time the detail had been so terrifyingly precise.

This wasn't a case of a similar feeling or a vaguely familiar room. It was identical. Every light fixture, every single wine glass with its decorated stem, the specific painting of the fisherman in its bronze frame hanging over the black leather couch, the exact same green conch shell nightlight in the dark hall—every last detail in my surroundings was something I had already seen, already lived in that dream.

To this day, I have no idea how that happened. I have no logical explanation for how my dreaming mind could have perfectly replicated a place I had never been, down to the last object.

In that moment, the how didn't matter as much as the what. This was it. I now had real, unshakable, undeniable, waking-world proof that there was more. I felt blessed and grateful, thanking the Unseen—the angels, the spirits, whoever was out there and was giving me a warning. It was the ultimate confirmation that what was happening to me was not just a sequence of random events, but a meaningful dialogue with a world beyond my own.

I later concluded that the experiences we have while we sleep are indeed sometimes more than our brains making things up. In the non-waking state, we sometimes step into something else, and the messages, as cryptic as they may seem, can point at things happening in our objective reality.

86

It was months after the dream of the Devil, and I was still consumed by it. I couldn't stop thinking about how my mind had predicted everything that was going to happen—how I had been able to live it all first in a dream. My mind was wrestling with that impossibility, searching for an answer, and it was in that state of intense questioning that I got the next glimpse.

The dream began not with a story, but with a feeling: the sharp, distinct chill of individual raindrops hitting my skin.

The energy of the place was overwhelming, so intense that it felt more real than the mattress I knew was beneath my sleeping body. I was fully lucid. I knew I was nineteen, and I knew I was dreaming. With the detached certainty of a dreamer, I was aware that I was standing barefoot in my pajamas on a slick, paved road. I think we were in the 1800s.

But what I saw was something else entirely. The streets were grim, shining under a gray, heavy sky. The air smelled of wet soil and countryside, and underneath that was the earthy, animal scent of horses from carriages I could hear clopping nearby. I could feel the grit of the wet cobblestones under my bare feet, ancient and uneven, like the streets of Rome.

A train station loomed nearby, and I glided there. By now I knew the gliding well. My dream-task was clear: I had to find my train. It was going to take me somewhere, but I did not know where. I was scanning the signs, confused, trying to find the right platform.

As I searched, I looked to my right, and my breath caught. I saw me.

It wasn't the nineteen-year-old me, the one I knew I was. This was an older woman, perhaps forty-five. Her face was undeniably mine, but older—etched with a solemn, stoic sorrow. She was draped in a heavy, black Victorian gown, the kind worn for deep mourning. I could see the intricate patterns in the lace draping over her boots. I could see the mud staining the edges of her skirt. She had been walking for quite some distance. She looked tired and weary. I watched her the way one watches a stranger, this echo of both past and future. She was accompanied by another woman in a similar black dress.

At first, this older me didn't seem to notice the barefoot, pajama-clad girl staring at her from across the pavement. But then, her gaze shifted and locked onto mine. We made eye contact.

The shock wasn't just that she saw me; it was that she recognized me. I knew she did, because I saw a glimpse of that recognition in her eyes. This grieving, forty-five-year-old me saw the lucid, nineteen-year-old me. She didn't smile. She simply held my gaze for a long moment—an intense, silent communication. Then, she gave a slow, deliberate nod—an acknowledgment.

She lifted her arm and pointed to a sign I hadn't seen, her gaze still fixed on me. It was simple and stark, bearing only a number: 86.

As the scene began to dissolve, a final thought echoed in my mind, clear as a bell: "This is where you get off."

Between the layers of reality and lucidity, my conscious mind translated the message: I die at 86.

I woke up instantly, the cold of the rain still on my skin. Ever since that night, I have carried this unshakable knowing. It is not a fear, but a fact. So strong is my belief that I am actively planning my finances around it. I suppose we'll have to see if the dream was right or not, but for now, the fact that I have been able to cheat death twice tells me there could be truth to it.

Science, the Mind, and the Unseen

Science, of course, has a delightful, clinical story for everything. In its version, our dreams are simply a collection of images, ideas, and emotions that bubble up involuntarily, mostly during the frantic dance of rapid-eye movement (REM) sleep. The explanation is one of pure mechanics. Deep in the brain, the pons fire off random electrical sparks, like static from an old radio. Meanwhile, the prefrontal cortex—the brain's logical, dispassionate accountant, the part that insists on order and reason—becomes less active.

This, experts say, is why our minds' nightly creations so often feel bizarre, illogical, and unbound by the rules of the waking world. The accountant is taking a nap, leaving the rest of the mind to play without supervision.

I read about the activation-synthesis model, which suggests that our sleep-induced mental activity is our brains' attempt to make sense of random impulses by synthesizing them into a coherent story.[2] The threat simulation theory proposes that this sleep-state simulation is an evolutionary tool, a way for our brains to practice for real-world dangers in a safe environment.[3] The memory consolidation theory, on the other hand, argues that these narratives of the unconscious help us organize and process the contents stored in our minds, strengthening some and getting rid of others. All of these theories are presented as cold, hard, and unassailable truth.

Imagine my disappointment, sitting in that silent classroom and hearing the lecturer drone on about these models. They offered a tidy rationale for a monumental human experience, but they left out the most important part: the emotions. The immense sense of peace, the overwhelming joy, the recognition of a place I had never seen—these things were left on the cutting room floor. They were dismissed as a by-product of a misfiring brain, of a limbic system on overdrive.

Science, in its desire for a neat little box, often dismisses anything it can't measure as nonsense. But the very origin of psychology is rather nonsensical, if we want to get real clinical. Imagine if Freud had never started because the mind was too hard to understand and easier to dismiss as fantasy? This intellectual arrogance was as confining as the religious dogma I was trying to escape. It was as if they were saying, "We don't know, so we're going to pretend it's not real."

---

2. J. Allan Hobson and Robert W. McCarley, "The Brain as a Dream State Generator: An Activation-Synthesis Hypothesis of the Dream Process," *American Journal of Psychiatry* 134, no. 12 (1977).

3. Antti Revonsuo, "The Reinterpretation of Dreams: An Evolutionary Hypothesis of the Function of Dreaming," *Behavioral and Brain Sciences* 23, no. 6 (2000).

Years later, I was relieved to find I wasn't alone in these questions. I discovered a field called neurotheology, where science is finally, cautiously bridging the gap between the laboratory and the mystic. Researchers are daring to ask the big questions, using their modern tools to map the brain as it prays, meditates, and reaches for the divine. They are watching what happens to the mind when it touches the infinite. And in these scans, they are finding physical, measurable proof of what mystics have taught for centuries: that in moments of deep contemplation, the part of the brain that defines "me"—our rigid, individual identity—can go quiet. It simply dissolves, allowing for that profound feeling of "oneness" with the universe.

This new intersection of brain and spirit offered a fascinating, beautiful lens through which to look at my own experiences. While it couldn't explain the impossible—how I saw the green conch shell or the fisherman's painting—it did offer a potential partner in explaining the warning about Dan.

Science has long known that our subconscious minds are brilliant, silent observers. They are expert trackers, picking up thousands of tiny, subtle cues that our busy, conscious minds miss completely—a too-wide smile, a flicker in the eyes, or an "uneasy energy."

So, perhaps my subconscious had gathered the data on Dan, sensing the danger long before I did. But the dream itself? That wasn't just my mind filing data. That was an alarm bell. It was the only language—loud, symbolic, and terrifying—that the Unseen could use to finally make me listen. It was my spirit hijacking my mind to keep me safe.

A Toolkit for Lucidity

After years of grappling with the things that had happened to me, I was fascinated to learn that other people were lucid dreaming, too. While my journey to that place felt spiritual, I discovered that for many, it's a skill—and, like any skill, it can be honed through practice. The scientific community, which had always been so dismissive, had actually developed a toolkit for people like me.

For those seeking to cultivate a similar awareness, a great starting point is the practice of keeping a nocturnal log, as well as performing reality checks. Maintaining this log simply refers to writing down everything you remember about your nightly adventures as soon as you wake up. This helps you improve your ability to remember and, over time, recognize "dream signs"—the bizarre or illogical events that can clue you in that you're dreaming.

Reality checks, on the other hand, are actions you perform multiple times throughout the day to test if you're in a dream, such as trying to push your hand through a wall or looking at a clock to see if the time changes. The key is to question your perceptions each time you do it, so the habit carries over into your sleep.

For more advanced dreamers, there are methods like the Mnemonic Induction of Lucid Dreams (MILD) and Wake Back to Bed (WBTB).

The MILD technique, developed by lucid dreaming pioneer Stephen LaBerge, is a prospective memory practice where you set a clear intention to become lucid before falling asleep.[4] It's less of a single action and more of a focused, multi-step meditation. While you can set your intention at the start of the night, LaBerge found the technique is most effective when you perform it after waking up from a dream in the middle of the night (a method now famously paired with WBTB).

The steps are quite specific. First, when you awaken from a dream, you are supposed to recall it in as much vivid detail as possible. Once the dream is firm in your mind, you identify a "dream sign"—a key image or event from the dream that was bizarre, impossible, or just "off;" something that could flag it as unreal.

Then, as you are lying there, ready to fall back asleep, you begin repeating a simple mantra, a mnemonic, such as, "Next time I'm dreaming, I will remember that I'm dreaming." The most crucial part is combining this phrase with visualization. As you repeat the words, you must vividly imagine yourself back inside the dream you just left. You picture yourself noticing that specific dream sign, and, in that moment, you see yourself realizing, "This is a dream!"

This doesn't guarantee success, but it is a powerful way of training your mind. You aren't forcing lucidity; you are planting a seed of intention, priming your subconscious to become self-aware the next time that strange, familiar signal appears.

---

4. Stephen LaBerge, *Lucid Dreaming: The Power of Being Awake and Aware in Your Dreams* (Los Angeles: Jeremy P. Tarcher, 1985).

The WBTB technique is one of the most reliable methods for inducing a lucid dream. It's less of a mental trick and more of a strategic manipulation of your body's natural sleep architecture.

The classic approach is to set an alarm for about five to six hours after you fall asleep. This is designed to wake you during one of your longest and most vivid periods of REM sleep. Once you're up, the goal isn't to start your day; it's to stay awake for a short, specific period, anywhere from twenty minutes to an hour.

What you do during this time is key. Many practitioners use this quiet, pre-dawn window to engage their analytical minds while their bodies are still heavy with sleep. They might read about lucid dreaming, quietly review their dream journals, or simply meditate on their intention.

Then, you return to bed. Your body is still tired and eager to fall back asleep, but your mind is now alert and "primed" with the clear goal of recognizing the dream state. This is why WBTB is so often paired with the MILD technique—you are now in the perfect state to set your intention.

By slipping back into sleep this way, you are positioning your conscious awareness right at the doorway of the next REM cycle. You're far more likely to enter the dream state with your awareness intact, or "catch" yourself dreaming shortly after you begin.

This is a beautiful example of how the world of objective truths and my experiences don't have to be at odds. They are simply two different languages describing the same thing.

I realized that there was a flaw in my approach: It was built on an unquestioning trust in authority, a blind faith that a person with a fancy title knows more about my soul than I do. We used to listen to the wise ones—the shamans and the Zen masters—and we used to have room for wonder. This is what gave rise to progress. But we stopped being curious, and we have become complacent in the truths that are served to us by figures of authority. Even when things don't sound right, we accept them.

What if some of our dreams are more than our brains making things up? What if they are windows into another dimension? What if you have to stand by your truth long enough, with enough conviction, and sooner or later someone will come out and join voices with you?

Years later, long after I had stopped being a child she needed to protect from "just dreams," my mom and I had a talk. It wasn't planned. It was one of those quiet evenings, woman to woman, where the air feels safe enough for secrets. She must have seen me looking at something far away, because she asked me what was on my mind.

I took a deep breath. "Mom...do you remember that dream I told you about? The one where I felt free, where I was gliding?"

She nodded slowly. "I remember."

"I still go there," I said, the words feeling heavy in the air. "And...there's more."

And just like that, the dam broke. I told her everything. I told her about the premonitory dreams, the "knowing" that would come over me, and the "86" dream. I told her about the Devil in the apartment turned into an impromptu office. I confessed that ever since my brush with death at seventeen, it had all become stronger, this constant pulling toward something I couldn't see. I admitted, my voice dropping, "Sometimes, I can still glide. I can still feel it."

I finished, half-expecting her to give me that old, polite smile and tell me I had a vivid imagination. But she didn't.

She was quiet for a long moment, looking past me, as if seeing something I couldn't. When she finally spoke, her guard was completely down. The pragmatic, sensible mother was gone, and in her place was a woman with her own secrets.

"I have a place, too," she said, her voice soft, longing, like when she used to tell me bedtime stories so I'd stop asking questions and fall asleep.

The words came out of her like a confession. "It's not a garden. It's a house. A house...in another time." Her eyes were unfocused, a soft, private smile on her face. "It's a little house, with a fence made of smooth river stones. The windows are big and heavy, and it has simple, white cotton curtains."

She looked at me, her eyes shining. "It's my home, you understand? I still visit it, in my dreams. I'm familiar with every spoon in the drawer and every needle in the sewing box. It's all mine."

In that moment, the barrier between us dissolved. We weren't just mother and daughter; we were two people who had both glimpsed a world behind the veil, and, for the first time, we could finally admit it to each other.

I asked her, my voice a whisper, "What made you say that it's just a dream?"

She paused and turned to look out the window. "The world is quick to judge people who believe in visions as lunatics. I wanted to protect you from being stigmatized."

She could see it and feel it, too. She understood there was more: feelings you just can't deny, knowings as real as our breath. But she too was afraid of the same thing: ridicule, being shunned, and the labels that would follow. She chose to protect herself and me by saying nothing about these topics. I understood. I had done the same thing all my life. But in that silence, maybe for the first time, I saw the core of the shame that so many of us carry.

Authority in Question

This exploration into my dreams and the reactions of others to them forced me to confront a question that had been simmering beneath the surface of my life for years: who gets to define what is real? As I started to speak more about my story, I was met with uncomfortable but anticipated silence—the kind that signifies a line has been crossed. That silence was born from a cocktail of anxiety and ignorance—a fear of the inexplicable, rooted in a belief in the established truth.

The system—whether it was science with its neatly packaged theories, or the religious establishment with its dogma—was telling me to stay in my lane, keep my mouth shut, and, maybe most notably, not trust my own realities. Instead, it wanted me to trust in the words of men who had never walked in my shoes. I couldn't accept that. I grew up in a culture where authority was absolute. You listened to your parents, your teachers, and your priest without question. But my encounters had shattered that simplistic worldview.

I couldn't help but ask: How is it acceptable to listen to a priest who has only read about things that are not of this world, but not to actually give voice to our own real encounters with it? And what exactly am I supposed to do when the same "authority" tells me that my reality didn't happen, that my memories are made up, and that my feelings are a scam?

Where do I go from there? Who decided that these men are our only gateway to God? Was it them, themselves, who clung to their authority, perhaps for money? God doesn't need money. He doesn't need us to be humble in front of our fellow men. We are supposed to seek God, not the approval of our fellow humans.

The contradiction was a constant, abrasive presence. The very institutions that professed to hold the master keys to the mysteries of the soul were the quickest to condemn those who forged their own. I had to ask myself, what if they were the charlatans? What if they were the peddlers of a business that had been selling us something that cannot be bought?

I had always been taught that true faith was a personal relationship, a connection that didn't require an intermediary. But here was a business model that not only required a middleman, but also told me my direct realities were a lie, a sign of sin, or, worse, mental illness.

The thought that I was supposed to pay for forgiveness or confess my encounters to a man who had never had one was, to me, like a betrayal. I've known as much love, as much meaning, and as much tranquility in a fleeting dream as other people have in a cathedral. So why was my spirit-led journey any less valid if it didn't happen in a church?

Did you know that you can commit any sin, go to a priest, pay a sum, and have your sins forgiven—no lessons needed, no real remorse? This practice, known as indulgences, has been a part of religious history for centuries. It's like a transaction, a business deal, not a journey of transformation. How does that sit with you? It sat with me like a rock in my stomach.

This was more than a hypothetical question for me; it was a personal one. The system had told me to hide, to not trust my own heart, and, for the most part, I had listened. I'd played the role and worn the mask. But my lifelong story, with all its detours and inexplicable signs, was real to me, and no one can fake who they are when their only witness is a mirror—not forever, at least.

It was this pull that wouldn't let me be, and I knew in my bones that no one, no matter their title or their clothes, had the right to tell me what I felt inside. My inner knowing was my most valuable possession.

The Wisdom of the Ancients

My search for knowledge took me far beyond the confines of a modern textbook and into the dusty archives of history and mythology, where what happens in our sleep was not random neural firings, but divine messages. It was a quest that felt less like a detached inquiry and more like coming home.

In the Bible, I found countless examples that resonated with my own case. The story of Joseph interpreting Pharaoh's dreams of seven years of famine and seven years of plenty was not just a tale; it was an act of communication from God that saved a nation.[5] Likewise, an angel appeared to Joseph, the father of Jesus, during a dream, warning him to flee to Egypt to protect his family from King Herod.[6] This wasn't a story to me; it was a precedent.

The foundation of my faith-based upbringing, the Christian scriptures, were full of examples of night visions being used for communication from the ethereal realm. They provided a framework where this world of the metaphysical could intervene in the human one—a doctrine that modern religion, in its attempt to become more palatable to a skeptical world, often seems to shy away from.

In ancient Greek mythology, dreams were seen as messages from the gods, a channel for prophecy and guidance. I read about King Croesus, who dreamed his son would be killed by a spear—a warning that, despite his best efforts to prevent it, came true.

I learned about Hecuba of Troy, who dreamed she gave birth to a burning torch—a horrifying prophecy that her son, Paris, would cause the downfall of Troy.

And perhaps most touchingly, Penelope from *The Odyssey* had a dream of an eagle killing her geese, which she later realized accurately foretold her husband's return and his revenge on her suitors.[7]

---

5. Gen. 41 (NIV).

6. Matt. 2:13 (NIV).

7. Homer, *The Odyssey*, trans. Robert Fagles (New York: Viking, 1996), Book 19.

These weren't just fanciful myths; they were a record of a human belief system that honored the power of the dream. They offered compelling evidence that people have been wrestling with the meaning of these occurrences for millennia. This confirmed what I had already grasped internally: that my nighttime revelations were not an anomaly, but part of a long and rich human history of grappling with the unexplained.

My seeking took me even further back, to the dawn of civilization. I quickly realized that my experiences were not new. Far from it, in fact. Mythology and religion had been recording premonitory dreams since the beginning of written history. I wasn't an anomaly. Instead, I had plenty of company.

Ancient Mesopotamian and Egyptian religion, for instance, regarded these nocturnal occurrences as crucial. Take the Epic of Gilgamesh, one of the oldest legends in the world. Its hero, Gilgamesh, was a powerful, god-like king who ruled his people with an iron fist. The gods, in response, created a rival for him: the wild man, Enkidu, who lived in nature among the animals.

Before these two ever met, Gilgamesh had a powerful dream. He dreamed that a star fell from the heavens, landing at his feet. It was so heavy he could not move it, and yet he was drawn to it, embracing it "as one embraces a wife."[8] He brought this portent to his mother, who explained that it foretold the arrival of a mighty companion, a man who would be his equal and his truest friend.

That companion, of course, was Enkidu. The dream was a premonition, a divine message preparing the king for the arrival of the one person who would challenge him, change him, and alter his destiny forever.

This demonstrated that, from the very beginning, humanity understood that pivotal life events could be foretold through the medium of dreams. In Egypt, Pharaoh Thutmose IV recorded a dream on a stele—a stone monument. The dream promised him the throne if he cleared the Sphinx. His recording of it was a clear demonstration that the Egyptians took these messages so seriously they would commit them to stone for all eternity.

---

8. *The Epic of Gilgamesh*, trans. Andrew George (London: Penguin Classics, 2003).

The Atrahasis Epic, a foundational Mesopotamian myth of creation and a great cataclysm, tells of a character who receives a warning to build an ark to survive a coming flood. In Norse mythology, Baldur's disturbing prophetic visions of his own death come true despite his mother's attempts to protect him, showing a fatalistic belief in the authority of a divine message.

These myths, from different cultures and different times, all pointed to the same conclusion: Nighttime apparitions were a bridge between worlds, a vital communication channel from the gods, the spirits, or fate itself.

The Modern Scientific Rejection

Despite our history, modern thought tells me that this is all a big, fat coincidence—that despite countless reports of these occurrences, throughout history and to this day, everything was coincidental. It was nothing but confirmation bias. The answer was a tired wave of the hand, a lazy and dismissive gesture that refused to engage with a question humanity has wrestled with since the beginning of time. It was as if their words were a silent declaration: "We don't know, so we're going to pretend it's not real."

After going over history and mythology, I arrived at the modern world, filled with a renewed sense of purpose. I was certain that science would have some insights. I expected a field of study dedicated to the mysteries of the mind and dreams. But, much to my dismay, there was no such thing. What I found instead was a small, brave group of researchers relegated to the fringes, working in the field of parapsychology.

The name itself seemed like an exile, a word designed to separate the legitimate from the unbelievable. The broader community views this evidence with a skepticism that borders on outright contempt, dismissing it as a result of mental biases, flawed methodology, and simple coincidence. But I dove into their work.

I was fascinated to discover the work of J. W. Dunne, an aeronautics engineer who, in the early 20th century, found himself in the same position I was in. He wasn't a mystic; he was a scientist and a soldier, a man of logic.

In his landmark 1927 book *An Experiment with Time*, he detailed his own methodical, self-run study.[9] He kept a meticulous journal by his bed, scrupulously recording his dreams the moment he woke, before his conscious mind could be polluted by the day's news or outside information. He then went back and rigorously compared these entries to later events, and he was astonished at what he found.

His journals were littered with clear, undeniable fragments of the future. He documented dreaming of newspaper headlines, specific conversations, and minor personal accidents days before they actually occurred.

To explain his data, he proposed a radical idea, one he called "Serialism." He argued that all moments in time—past, present, and future—exist simultaneously as a "block universe." Our waking consciousness, he theorized, is simply a lantern moving along this block in a single, straight line, creating the illusion of linear progression. In sleep, however, our perception becomes unfettered, able to drift and access information from any point along the timeline, just as easily as we might recall a memory from the past.

The concept that the past, present, and future are all happening at once didn't just feel plausible to me—it felt as intuitive as breathing. It was a beautiful, elegant theory that thoroughly explained how I could have seen the living room of a scammer—every last detail—the night before I ever set foot in it. In my dream, I had simply and unknowingly glanced at a page a few chapters ahead.

My search also led me to the work of the Society for Psychical Research (SPR), and I was stunned to find I was walking a path that was already well-worn. Founded in London in 1882, the society wasn't a fringe group of ghost-hunters. Instead, its members included some of the most brilliant and skeptical minds of the day—philosophers, physicists, and scholars like the psychologist William James. They were the first to apply a rigorous, academic lens to phenomena that polite society ignored, dedicating themselves to the serious, scientific study of telepathy, premonition, and other "unseen" human abilities.

That same spirit of inquiry was later brought into the laboratory by J. B. Rhine, a man now known as the "father of modern parapsychology." Rhine did something revolution-

---

9. J. W. Dunne, *An Experiment with Time* (London: A. & C. Black, 1927).

ary: He established a formal parapsychology lab at Duke University, attempting to take these fleeting, personal experiences and pin them down with statistics.[10]

I read about his now-famous experiments with Zener cards—simple white cards bearing one of five symbols: a star, a circle, a cross, a square, or wavy lines. He would have subjects try to guess the symbol on a hidden card, thousands and thousands of times, in a controlled setting, meticulously tracking their results to see if they could defy the laws of logic. It was Rhine who gave a clinical, legitimate name to these "knowings"—extrasensory perception, or ESP.

Discovering the work of the SPR and Rhine was a profound comfort. It showed me that, for over a century, brilliant, skeptical, and serious people had looked at the world, felt that same pull I did, and dedicated their entire lives to proving it wasn't all "just a dream."

More recently, I stumbled upon a modern-day scientific firestorm ignited by a single, well-respected social psychologist named Daryl Bem. In 2011, he published a paper called "Feeling the Future," not in some obscure paranormal journal, but in one of the most prestigious, mainstream publications in his field.[11]

Bem's approach was as simple as it was radical. He took well-established, textbook psychological effects and simply reversed them in time. In one experiment, he had students try to guess which of two curtains on a computer screen hid an erotic image. He found that, over thousands of trials, students scored slightly but statistically better than pure chance—53.1 percent instead of 50 percent. The shocking part was that the computer didn't randomly place the image behind the curtain until after the student had already made their choice.

In another, he had students memorize a list of words. After they were tested on their recall, he had them practice a random selection of those same words. Incredibly, his data showed that the future practice session improved their scores on the test they had already taken.

---

10. J. B. Rhine, *Extra-Sensory Perception* (Boston: Bruce Humphries, 1934).

11. Daryl J. Bem, "Feeling the Future: Experimental Evidence for Anomalous Retroactive Influences on Cognition and Affect," *Journal of Personality and Social Psychology* 100, no. 3 (2011).

Bem was, in effect, claiming to have found statistical, laboratory proof of precognition. The paper's publication by a top journal sent a shockwave through the scientific community. But all these "discoveries" are not accepted by the mainstream.

The backlash was immediate and intense. Researchers around the world tried to replicate his findings and, overwhelmingly, they failed. Instead of convincing scientists to believe in "psi," Bem's paper did the opposite: It helped spark what's now called the "replication crisis" in psychology. Critics argued his results weren't proof of the future leaking into the present, but rather proof that the field's accepted statistical methods were flawed.

For me, the firestorm itself was just as revealing. It showed a mainstream science so rattled by a set of data that it was forced to question its own rules, rather than accept a conclusion that, for people like me, felt entirely possible.

Mainstream study, represented by researchers like Dr. Michael Schredl, offers logical explanations, tying up the loose ends of human experience.[12] They cite cognitive biases like confirmation bias and selective memory as the reasons people believe their nightly visions come true. They argue that we remember the one subconscious narrative that seems to align with a real-world occurrence while forgetting the thousands that don't. It's a comforting lie they tell themselves.

The implicit processing hypothesis suggests that a prophetic dream is our subconscious processing subtle information our conscious mind has missed. This sounds like a cop-out.

It sounds less like an explanation and more like a collective sigh of intellectual defeat. The fact that they can't agree on something doesn't make it non-existent; it simply means it's still being explored.

Regardless of the broad scientific view, people keep reporting these cases. A quick search helped me find a few examples of people who, like me, believed that these manifestations of the sleeping mind were more than things our brains made up during REM.

---

12. Michael Schredl, *Researching Dreams: The Fundamentals* (Cham: Palgrave Macmillan, 2018).

The Aberfan Disaster (1966): This is one of the most famous cases of a collective premonition. A landslide of coal waste buried a school in the village of Aberfan, Wales. Following the disaster, psychiatrist John Barker and journalist John Fairley established a "Premonitions Bureau" and collected more than seventy reports of dreams and premonitions related to the event.[13] A notable case is that of a ten-year-old girl named Eryl Mai Jones, who told her mother two days before the disaster that she was at peace with dying, and that she had dreamed of her school being "covered in something black."[14]

J.W. Dunne's *An Experiment with Time*: In the early 20th century, British engineer and philosopher J.W. Dunne meticulously documented his own precognitive episodes, concluding that a significant portion of them contained elements of his future life. His book, *An Experiment with Time* (1927), detailed his methodology and findings. He claimed to have foreseen in his sleep a volcanic eruption that killed 4,000 people before the Mount Pelée eruption in 1902 (which ended up killing over 29,000). Dunne's work is foundational in the field of precognitive mental phenomena, and is often cited in academic and parapsychological study.

The Mark Twain Case: Mark Twain (Samuel Clemens) famously documented a dream he had of his brother Henry's death. In the dream, he saw his brother's corpse laid out in a metal casket, wearing one of his own suits, with a bouquet of white flowers with a single red rose on his chest.

A few days later, Henry was killed in a steamboat explosion. Mark Twain was shocked to find his brother's body laid out exactly as he had dreamed, even down to the unique flower arrangement.[15]

---

13. J. C. Barker, "Premonitions of the Aberfan Disaster," *Journal of the Society for Psychical Research* 44, no. 734 (1967).

14. Sam Knight, *The Premonitions Bureau: A True Account of Death and Foresight* (New York: Penguin Press, 2022).

15. Mark Twain, *Autobiography of Mark Twain, Volume 1*, ed. Harriet Elinor Smith (Berkeley: University of California Press, 2010).

They call it coincidence, but I call it a miracle. They call it selective memory, but I call it a warning. We were looking at the same thing, but we were speaking two entirely different languages. The difference is that my language has a heart, and theirs has a calculator.

I have come to realize that, for them, it's safer to dismiss a profound moment than to challenge a deeply held belief system. For me, the opposite is true: It is more terrifying to live a lie than to embrace an inconvenient truth.

A Bigger Picture

The problem, as I've come to understand it, is not with science or religion themselves. The problem is with the people who practice them—who build walls and draw lines in the sand, claiming to have a monopoly on truth.

Mainstream scientific research, in its noble quest for objective knowledge, often fails to see the most crucial piece of the puzzle: the individual. Our lives, our experiences, and our way of interpreting the world are all different, a fact that is self-evident yet so often ignored. We are impacted by our upbringing, our culture, and a thousand small social factors that weave the fabric of our lives—all of them man-made constructs.

And yet, we believe in this man-made construct—a system of borders, currencies, and hierarchies. We turn our backs on the natural world that has been here all along. When did we forget that we are a part of nature, attuned to its whispers and rhythms, regardless of our fancy job titles, academic degrees, or the size of our bank statements?

This is where the grand deception begins. We are taught to place our faith in institutions, books, and experts who have only read about the world, never genuinely lived it. They sit in their ivory towers, surrounded by charts and graphs, and tell us that our realities, the things we know in our bones to be true, are all a lie—a consequence of a broken mind. They dismiss our dreams, our visions, and our intuitions as little more than a glitch in the system.

I find solace in those who, like me, had had a moment of reckoning. There are scientists—hardcore ones, in fact—who, after a single experience, changed their tune.

I read about Francis S. Collins, the director of the Human Genome Project, who began as an ardent atheist. He was a man of cold, hard facts, a man who perceived life as nothing more than a series of chemical reactions. But he came to believe in God after realizing science couldn't speak on suffering, love, or our longing for transcendence.[16] His vast intellect had reached its limit, and he had the humility to admit it.

I found a kindred spirit in Antony Flew, a famous atheist philosopher who changed his mind after being convinced by the staggering complexity of DNA that a super intelligence must have been involved.[17] He was swayed by evidence, not by emotion or faith.

And I was moved by the story of Alfred Russel Wallace, who co-developed the theory of evolution alongside Charles Darwin. A man of reason if there ever was one, Wallace later became a spiritualist after his own encounters led him to believe in an unseen universe.[18]

The lesson is a clear beacon of light in the fog of confusion: Just because a person in a big hat or with a fancy title says something, it doesn't mean they're always right. Their knowledge, however vast, is still limited by their own reality.

In my opinion, the issue is not with rational inquiry or religion, but with the people who have co-opted them, who have turned them into rigid systems of control. I can appreciate the progress of intellectual rigor and the lessons of religion. Anything that teaches us to do good and to be better is welcome, after all. The problem starts when we convince ourselves that we are the sole authority on what is real and what is not, when we build an echo chamber where only the approved voices are acknowledged. We tell ourselves that if enough of us state the same thing, it must be the one and only undisputed reality. And the anomalies? The stories that defy easy reasoning? The feelings that a textbook can't quantify? We are quiet about them. We lock them away in a drawer and hope they will disappear, because there aren't enough of us standing together, raising our hands, and saying, "Me too."

---

16. Francis S. Collins, *The Language of God: A Scientist Presents Evidence for Belief* (New York: Free Press, 2006).

17. Antony Flew, *There Is a God: How the World's Most Notorious Atheist Changed His Mind* (New York: HarperOne, 2007).

18. Alfred Russel Wallace, *Miracles and Modern Spiritualism* (London: James Burns, 1875).

The system, it seems, has become a fierce guardian of the well-traveled road. It prefers a deep, comfortable rut—a groove so worn by conformity that it becomes difficult to even see the edges, let alone climb out. We are encouraged to dismiss anything that diverges from this one, accepted way.

But just because a path is overgrown and less traveled doesn't mean it doesn't exist.

What if it simply means that not enough people are talking about it? What if not enough travelers have been brave enough to stand in the full light of day and declare, "My truth is different, but it is no less real."

My journey has culminated in a simple, yet noteworthy conclusion: The deepest wisdom isn't found in a book, classroom, or cathedral. It's found in the undeniable moments of our own lives. It's found in a dream of a luminous garden that feels more real than your own bedroom. It's found in a cryptic warning that saves you from harm. It's found in the brave confession of a mother who held the same private burden for years. This core identity is personal, and it's time for us to start speaking about it.

When we look back at the ancients, what is it that we remember?

We don't remember their day-to-day lives, the fights they had with their wives, or how much their jobs sucked. We remember the extraordinary tales they left behind—their wisdom, their epics, and their secrets.

The Bible never speaks about the quality of the chairs Jesus made as a carpenter. It doesn't detail his profit margins, whether he used imported wood or reconditioned pieces, or how many he sold a month. It speaks of his teachings, his path, and the message of love and unity he tried to share.

Our own legacies are no different. It is our tales that will change the world, not the results of our quarterly performance reviews.

So if you have ever had a vision, a dream, or a "knowing" that you believed was more, now is the time to break your silence. Now is the time to honor it. Write it down. Share it with a friend. Let the world know that you exist, and tell your story—your real story. It matters.

Chapter 9: The Hand in the Dark

You will not die. You will live. As long as you love life, you will live. That's all there is: Love all life, in all its forms. Serve life.

—Messages from the Unseen

Despite everything I knew, my ego—a "doesn't-play-well-with-others" force—refused to cede control. The mask of a cynic had taken hold, a hardened veneer of indifference that I wore like armor. I was determined not to be seen as a lunatic—a label that, in my world, carried a heavy price.

I had the respect of my university peers, people who valued my logical approach and unwavering focus on clean-cut science. I was building a good life, surrounded by an awesome group of friends, always busy and on the go. Between my studies and a full-time job managing a team of promoters, I had so much to lose—or so I thought. I refused to jeopardize this promising beginning with "mumbo-jumbo."

Yet, this façade could not stifle the curiosity that gnawed at me. After being pronounced dead for over three minutes, after the dreams that bled into reality, I was ready to admit to myself that it wasn't reason, but cowardice that kept me from diving deeper. I was an avid seeker in private, devouring books and webpages in the sterile glow of my computer screen, but publicly, my voice remained focused on the provable and the objective.

The most terrifying part was the undeniable fact: I *had* died, I *had* come back, and I *had* seen things that were confirmed by others in the so-called "objective world." The echoes of that death and rebirth were the loudest proof I had, and a part of me was still angry. I was angry because I had lost family and friends; angry because I had almost died; angry because the world no longer made sense; angry because I was "other" from the moment I opened my eyes to the world, and no one understood. It felt like everything was upside down, and the people around me weren't open to talking about the inexplicable.

But regardless of the anger, a resolve had finally settled in my heart. I was ready to see what others who had died and returned had to say. Somewhere on a platform, I found a documentary—a compilation of NDE accounts.

Almost twenty years have passed since that night, but the memory lives on with the clarity of a newly forged moment. Some events are like that, aren't they? They stretch time, stop it, and make everything within them more real than reality itself.

It was night. I was in my bed, fully awake, the small table fan turning in a slow, hypnotic rhythm. My mind would not grant me rest. Though I was only twenty years old, the vivid experience of my death, followed by the loss of my friend and the cascade of spiritual experiences that had peppered my life, left me with more questions than answers. I was exhausted, constantly searching for logical explanations for things that defied logic.

My beloved dog, Yullo, was already a warm, contented lump, curled in a tight ball next to me. I got up, the bed creaking under my weight, and started searching for NDE reports. It was time to see the stories others had to tell. I soon landed on a video. I don't remember what the narrator said, but I returned to bed, pulled the covers up, and started watching.

The man's story differed from my own, yet it resonated with striking similarities. As the video played, a sense of contentment settled over me. I was watching testimonies from people who could understand what had happened to me. That was hope.

In that comfort, a familiar sense of quiet descended, blanketing me in a warmth that started in my chest and spread through my limbs. Then came gratitude, followed by joy and an overwhelming rush of love. For a moment, I thought it was just because my inner world was finally being validated, but I quickly realized that I wasn't really thinking of the video anymore. I was fully engulfed in that feeling. It was not just an emotion; it was an atmosphere. It was the very substance of peace itself, an all-encompassing acceptance that held no conditions and no judgment. This love didn't just fill me; it dissolved me, erasing the boundaries between myself and everything else. It was a perfect, complete wholeness.

How do you even begin to describe a love stronger than what you feel for your own mother? I adore my mother. But this was the source of all love, a feeling that contains all other loves within it. Are there even words for that?

The love and peace grew until my body began to hum. It started as a gentle vibration, but I followed the emotion, allowing it to intensify. Soon, I was vibrating so violently that every cell felt as if it would atomize. My body became a buzzing, humming vessel on the verge of physical disintegration.

It was as if all the energy in my body was colliding with itself, trying to find a way out in a chaotic frequency that was going to make me explode. And yet, underneath that violent physical upheaval, my core feeling was one of profound peace. It was an ecstatic love, a joy so complete that my biological form literally could not contain it.

And then, I saw it.

There was a tunnel—not dark or foreboding, but woven from radiant hues of light. Blue light, to be precise; a color so vivid and dynamic it seemed to vibrate with its own intelligence. From that tunnel, several heads popped out. Four of them? I couldn't make out distinct faces, just humanoid figures, impossibly slender and elongated silhouettes peering from the radiant energy.

And in their center, with a hand extended toward me, was Jesus Christ.

He looked startlingly familiar, almost exactly like the Jesus in a traditional icon: the red robe, the blue sash draped over his shoulder. His palm was open toward me, and I could clearly see the mark from the crucifixion nail.

But in that instant, my rational mind took control, doing exactly what it was trained to do: It began to trace the image, sifting through my memory for a file. It found one. I realized he looked identical to an icon of Christ that had hung in my grandmother's home during my childhood—a stern, gold-leafed image I had stared at every summer night as a child, during dinner prayer.

That specific realization brought a cold rush of doubt. *This isn't real; this is just something my brain is making up, pulling from a deep-seated memory.*

The vibrations were now so intense I feared I might lose consciousness. The sight itself was both beautiful and terrifying, but what truly unsettled me was my dog's reaction.

Yullo, despite me not moving a muscle, woke up instantly. I lay there, eyes wide, fixated on the scene before me, but my loyal Yullo was having none of it. He began to whine, a high-pitched, pleading sound. When I didn't move, he scrambled out of bed, his claws clicking frantically on the wooden floor. He started barking and jumping around, a frantic, insistent plea to get me out of that bed, out of that room. His hackles were raised, his gaze darting between me and the empty space in the room where only I could see the tunnel and the apparitions before me.

It was then I realized he could see—or at least sense—something, too. Something was terrifying him, and I doubted it was unrelated to what was unfolding before me. I had experienced strange things all my life, but this was the first time I was actually seeing something with my very eyes. Another living being was reacting to it, too.

I didn't take Jesus's hand. Instead, I scrambled out of bed and followed my dog into the world of the living. And so, Yullo brought me back to life for the second time.

I felt no fear of Jesus himself. It was my own mind that terrified me. Was I being deceived? Was I going mad?

If I were to take his hand, would I be gone for good? Would I ever be able to come back? Was this a mental illness? Schizophrenia? I had never actually *seen* anything with my own eyes before. Sure, I'd had dreams and feelings and foreign thoughts, but to see a figure standing in the room? And what about that intense sensation, the violent vibrations that overwhelmed me?

In the end, the high vibrations and the breathtaking beauty of the moment subsided, though it took hours for the adrenaline to fade. I sat in the living room with the lights on, drinking water, reminding myself that I was with the living. I was moving, walking, and talking.

The rush of thoughts—my own thoughts—came next: "What kind of asshole sees Jesus and runs?"

Well...this one did.

I am not proud of it, but at that moment, I was sure I was going to die. I figured that, despite my bravado and my past brush with death, I still very much wanted to preserve my life.

My panic shifted from "Was this my only shot at heaven and I blew it?" to "Is Jesus offended because I got scared?" to "Oh boy, I must be batshit crazy."

I wish I could say that a moment of clarity followed, that all was revealed. That did not happen. I was left with even more unanswered questions, on top of all the other unresolved ones I'd had before. Oh, the joy.

Even now, as I write this, I realize how afraid I was; how afraid I still am. And perhaps that's the whole point. What if we come here to face our fears and, eventually, to overcome them? It took me another twenty years to actually get a glimpse of this truth and decide to allow it to happen.

The most important lesson, however, was the message: "Love life! As long as you love life, you will live." I believe that is what that higher power—Christ, in this case—wants for us: to love life in all its forms, especially our own. This is why I'm able to tell myself that Jesus isn't upset with me for my hesitation. It's why I believe my fear wasn't a failure; it was a protective impulse born from the same deep love of life that I was being told to embrace. I simply wanted to preserve my own life. Who could blame me? Being alive is wonderful!

A Waking Spiritual Encounter and the Quest for Answers

Human history is filled with stories of people seeing supernatural beings while they're awake. For millennia, across cultures and continents, these encounters—visions of otherworldly figures, angels, nature spirits, or ancestral beings—have shaped human consciousness. I, myself, had lived through some of these encounters, and for that reason, it was hard to let go of my search.

This new experience compelled me to hunt for answers. My search began where it always did: in the familiar maps of logic, mythology, and religion. I needed to find a name for what had happened, to place it within a known framework.

I sifted through the established definitions, trying to find one that would fit.

Was it a vision? By that, I knew the rational world meant a "perceptual phenomenon," something that might not be physically there. Or was it an apparition—a true manifestation in the room with me, something I could "visually locate?" I wrestled with these terms. I understood the categories, but the very act of trying to label the event felt like a reduction, as if I were trying to fit an ocean into a teacup.

The final possibility—that it was all a hallucination—terrified me. Could my most significant, life-altering moment be dismissed as just a trick of the mind?

I pursued that cold thread of doubt. I had to wrestle with clinical explanations like *pareidolia*—the brain's known compulsion to find recognizable patterns, especially human faces, in random stimuli. Was that all it was? An optical illusion that my mind, in its desperate need for meaning, simply made sense of? This was the ultimate crossroads: Had I experienced a true *theophany*, a sacred manifestation of a deity, or was it all just make-believe?

The quest for definitions showed me something crucial: The event itself is impossible to separate from the way we interpret it. My own assumptions and cultural context—what I already believed—were shaping the occurrence as I tried to recount it. The vague visual of my grandmother's icon, my fear of being mad—they were all part of the filter that colored my perception.

This was a terrifying realization. I had seen something beautiful, a moment of otherworldly love, and my own mind was questioning its validity. The explanations offered a cold assurance, a potential answer that sounded empty, like a betrayal of the truth I had experienced.

My quest became a battle between my heart and my head. My heart told me that the love I was showered with was real, the serenity was undeniable, and the spirit was tangible—that the extremely intense vibration was as real as it gets. And why was my dog reacting to it if it was only in my mind?

My head, however, was filled with a lifetime of conditioning and logic, and the worry of being seen as a lunatic. The more I researched, the more I understood the gap between the *what* and the *how*. Science could explain the mechanics of the experience—the vibration in my body, the vision in my mind—but it could never explain the meaning or the transformative power of that moment.

The Scientific Lens: Was I Going Mad?

My fear of insanity was the primary driver of my research. I wanted to know if there was an answer, a neurological explanation for what I had seen and sensed. I plunged into the field of neurotheology, the discipline that attempts to explain the biological processes behind religious experiences. Researchers use tools like MRI and EEG scans to explore how our brains respond to transcendental beliefs. The idea that an unusual state of consciousness could be explained by brain chemistry both terrified and relieved me.

I read about how the brain changes during these experiences. The "focus" part of the brain (the prefrontal cortex) lights up, while the part that creates our sense of space (the parietal lobe) goes quiet. This "orientation center" is what tells me where my body ends and the rest of the world begins.

The study used a technical mouthful for this: "deafferentation of the posterior superior parietal lobule." In plain English, the brain stops processing sensory input, which allows that rigid boundary of "self" to dissolve.[1]

Dr. Andrew Newberg's research on this "orientation area" resonated instantly.[2] He suggested that when this area is "blocked," the brain simply can't distinguish between "self" and "not-self." That was it. That was the feeling. As that boundary dissolved, a boundless love filled my every fiber, as though my own self was interwoven with everyone and everything. For me, this was more than an intellectual thought; it was a fundamental, bodily experience.

---

1. Andrew Newberg and Eugene D'Aquili, *Why God Won't Go Away: Brain Science and the Biology of Belief* (New York: Ballantine Books, 2001).

2. Newberg and D'Aquili, *Why God Won't Go Away.*

But the validation immediately soured. The science that had explained my experience now threatened to explain it *away*. A single, devastating question landed like a cold shower: Was that boundless love the core of my identity, a truth I carried in my soul? Or was it just a "biological signature"—a temporary brain glitch?

My exploration into the mind-body relationship took me deeper, to the work of Dr. Vilayanur S. Ramachandran. He investigated the neural basis of hyper-religiosity in temporal lobe epilepsy (TLE) patients.[3] Using a galvanic skin response (GSR) to measure emotional arousal, Dr. Ramachandran found that these patients had a heightened emotional response to religious words, while their responses to other topics remained normal. This pointed to a specialized neural circuitry involved in processing theological material.

This was the first hint that my own brain might be wired in a specific way that makes me more susceptible to these phenomena. It was not about being sick, but about a unique configuration of my brain's chemistry.

And then, there was the "God helmet."

When I read about neuroscientist Michael Persinger's experiments[4], a new wave of worry washed over me. He used a device—essentially a modified snowboard helmet rigged with solenoids and wires—to subject the temporal lobes of volunteers to weak magnetic fields. The result? Many subjects claimed to sense a "presence" in the room with them.

If a magnetic field could create the sensation of a nearby being, what did that say about my experience? Did it mean Jesus was an illusion?

This scientific perspective was both terrifying and strangely liberating. It suggested the cause wasn't necessarily something outside of me, but something inside my own brain. The "God helmet" highlighted the brain's capacity to generate spiritual sensations, implying that we have inherent circuits that, when triggered, can create such experiences.

---

3. V.S. Ramachandran and Sandra Blakeslee, *Phantoms in the Brain: Probing the Mysteries of the Human Mind* (New York: William Morrow, 1998).

4. Michael A. Persinger, *Neuropsychological Bases of God Beliefs* (New York: Praeger, 1987).

So, was the brain a barrier to the spiritual, or a bridge? Was my brain simply an instrument through which the unseen could communicate, a sort of receiver tuned to a certain metaphysical frequency?

This entire search finally helped me understand: I didn't have to choose between science and faith. My story was real, and it could be both. I could accept that my brain is wired for these kinds of experiences, while still believing that a higher power used that wiring to communicate with me. The brain might be the canvas, but the ultimate source provides the paint.

The Radio and the Voice

My struggle to square the scientific with the spiritual—the "brain glitch" versus the message from God—led me to the fascinating world of modern-day channeling.

I knew that what had happened to me wasn't channeling. I wasn't sitting in a quiet room, I wasn't in a trance, and I certainly wasn't trying to contact anyone. I was just watching YouTube. And yet, the language these channelers used to describe their process resonated with a startling clarity. They spoke in terms of physics—of frequencies, vibrations, and resonance.

The metaphor they use is simple: a radio.

The radio itself doesn't create the music; it simply "tunes in" to a specific frequency that is already in the air. To get a new station, you have to turn the dial. These channelers describe their process in the exact same way. They aren't "creating" a being; they are intentionally raising their own "vibrational frequency" to match the entity they wish to connect with.

I found this concept everywhere I looked, though the methods varied.

Conscious Channeling: Esther Hicks channels a collective consciousness named "Abraham" while fully awake, describing a "blending" of perspectives.[5] Darryl Anka, who

5. Esther Hicks and Jerry Hicks, *Ask and It Is Given: Learning to Manifest Your Desires* (Carlsbad: Hay House, 2004).

channels an entity named "Bashar," describes himself as a "telepathic translator," with his brain's linguistic center translating a signal into words.[6]

Trance Channeling: J.Z. Knight (channeling "Ramtha") and the late Carla L. Rueckert (channeling "Ra" in *The Law of One*) used a deeper method, setting their own consciousness aside completely to allow the information to come through.[7]

This line of thinking immediately brought up an old, unsettling fear. How was this different from the spirit possession I'd seen in horror movies?

The answer, I discovered, was both simple and profound: consent.

The spiritual texts I found defined possession as a forcible or hostile takeover of a body, always without permission. Channeling, by contrast, is described as a willing and intentional partnership.

This new understanding offered a powerful lens through which to see my own experience. I wasn't a channeler. I hadn't been trying to "turn the dial." But if the brain is a receiver, what if mine, for one spontaneous moment, had accidentally tuned in? What if, without any stimulation, I had gotten a momentary, clear-as-a-bell glimpse of another frequency?

Hallucinations vs. Spiritual Visions

The most difficult part of my self-exploration was grappling with the clinical definition of a hallucination: a sensory perception that happens without an actual stimulus. But what I saw appeared so real and tangible. And Yullo had reacted to it, too.

The truth I finally uncovered confirmed something I'd always suspected: The experience itself and my understanding of it were completely bound together. My fear of madness

---

6. Darryl Anka, *Bashar: Blueprint for Change: A Message from Our Future* (New York: Pocket Books, 1990).

7. J.Z. Knight, *Ramtha: The White Book* (Yelm: JZK Publishing, 1999), 25; Carla L. Rueckert, Don Elkins, and Jim McCarty, *The Ra Contact: Teaching the Law of One*, vol. 1 (Louisville: L/L Research, 1984).

had come from a single, narrow narrative—that if my experience was "just" a biological function, its meaning would dissolve.

But the nuances lie in the context. A voice heard by an individual with schizophrenia might be pathologized, while a similar experience by a mystic might be revered as divine revelation. This implies that the same underlying neurological events can be categorized entirely differently based on cultural and personal frameworks.

Was I finally, truly going mad? The label didn't fit. If this was madness, how could I be so normal in my day-to-day life? Why did it only happen in these specific, isolated moments, like a switch being flipped on and off?

My concern was rooted in the societal stigma around mental illness. But the research taught me that it is possible to live in ambiguity, to accept that an experience can be both scientifically explainable and spiritually significant. The ambiguity isn't a weakness; it's a reflection of the mystery at the heart of human consciousness.

The Religious Lens: A History of Encounters

Beyond the fear of madness, a deeper, colder dread began to settle in. This one wasn't about my sanity; it was about my soul.

The religious programming of my youth, buried for years, came roaring to the surface. *Is this evil? Am I being contacted by something dark pretending to be good? Am I evil?*

But the fear wouldn't stick. It felt hollow. The simple truth was, I never felt evil. The experiences, as strange and overwhelming as they were, had never once felt dangerous. They felt like peace, boundless love, or pure information.

While objective investigation provided a potential "how," Christianity provided the "why." I was relieved to read about the long history of people seeing Jesus, Mary, and other unearthly beings. My revelation wasn't an anomaly; it was part of a tradition that spanned millennia.

I read about the post-resurrection appearances in the New Testament—how Jesus appeared to Doubting Thomas and invited him to touch his wounds to prove he was real.[8] This resonated with me strongly. My mind was like Thomas's—full of skepticism, needing a tangible sign.

I read about Saint Paul's conversion on the road to Damascus.[9] Paul, a man who persecuted Christians, had a dramatic vision of a blinding light and heard Jesus's voice. If a man so hostile to the faith could have such a sudden revelation, my own cynicism could not stand in the way either.

I also found solace in the accounts of mystics like Saint Francis of Assisi, Julian of Norwich, and Teresa of Avila.[10] Their reports, like mine, were often subjective. And yet, they inspired public acts of devotion and the founding of religious orders. The Catholic Church's rigorous process of investigating apparitions—looking for "positive criteria" like credibility and "negative criteria" like mental health issues—struck me as an interesting parallel. The Church was doing on an institutional level what I was trying to do on a personal one: discern the truth.

The Mythological and Folkloric Dimension

My search went even further, beyond my own cultural context. I found that waking encounters are not unique to Christianity; they are a universal human condition found in mythology and folklore all over the world.

The Greeks and Romans believed their gods took human form to interact with mortals. I thought of the story of Semele, who insisted on seeing Zeus's true form and was burned to ash because she couldn't withstand his power.[11]

---

8. John 20:24–29 (NRSV).

9. Acts 9:1–19 (NRSV).

10. Teresa of Avila, *The Interior Castle*, trans. Mirabai Starr (New York: Riverhead Books, 2003).

11. Edith Hamilton, *Mythology: Timeless Tales of Gods and Heroes* (New York: Little, Brown and Company, 1942).

This story made something click for me. It confirmed what I already suspected: My body simply couldn't handle the sheer intensity of what was happening. I had seen the "true" nature of the divine, and it was so overwhelming that my body felt like it was going to explode. It was just like the Greek myths warned: The human and the sacred don't mix easily.

My search also led me to the Norse gods, specifically the story of Odin, who sacrificed himself—hanging from the World Tree for nine nights, wounded by his own spear—to gain the knowledge of the runes for humanity.[12]

This story showed a completely different kind of relationship between the divine and the human. It wasn't about judgment or moral purity; it was about shared struggle, sacrifice, and wisdom. In Norse mythology, humans were not just lowly subjects, but the recipients of powerful gifts.

This idea hit me hard because it directly challenged the unspoken cultural rule that I had to *deserve* my experience. Coming from a background steeped in Christian ideas, I unconsciously believed that a spiritual encounter of this magnitude must be earned. It was a reward for being "good" or "pious." My problem was, I didn't feel any of those things. I just felt...normal.

The Norse myths offered a new model: What if the divine gives a gift, not because the human is worthy, but because the god chose to give it? This thought was a relief. It suggested that maybe I wasn't an imposter. Maybe someone up there just loved me.

A Synthesis of Beliefs

The journey from a reductionist view—believing that what I had gone through was just a hallucination—to a more holistic understanding has been a long one. I now see that the rational mind, religion, and mythology are not necessarily in conflict.

Scientific inquiry offers invaluable insights into the neurological mechanisms that underpin these processes. The fact that our brains have a "default mode network" that can be altered to produce mystical experiences doesn't take away from the transcendent

12. Kevin Crossley-Holland, *The Norse Myths* (New York: Pantheon Books, 1980).

significance of the moment. Instead, it suggests that a higher consciousness can work through the biological pathways that are already there.

The ambiguity of my experience is not a weakness; it is a beautiful dance between the tangible and the ethereal. My search for clarity has not resolved the mystery, but it has given me the tools to live with it. It has given me the courage to write about it, to face my fear of ridicule and mistrust.

So, I write these pages not to claim I'm special, but simply to share my story. In fact, I have come to understand that we all are able to have these experiences, should we embrace a practice with openness.

I've learned that deeply personal experiences like mine are always subjective; you can't untangle the event from the meaning you make of it. The scientific explanations can show what my brain was doing, but they can't prove or disprove the profound meaning I found in it.

Almost twenty years later, during one of my sitting sessions, I was blessed with a feeling of oneness—or Christ consciousness—again. In that state, the foreign thoughts come easier.

This one was rather delightful: "You will not die. You will live. As long as you love life, you will live. That's all there is: love all life, in all its forms. Serve life."

I finally understood what that message truly meant. The Higher Power simply wants us to love Life in all its forms, including our own.

This new understanding cast my old fear in a completely different light. I finally realized why Jesus wouldn't be upset with me for being afraid all those years ago. My panic wasn't a failure or a sin; it came from that very love of life. I was terrified because I wanted to preserve my own self, and I still do. My running from that experience wasn't a rejection of God; it was a choice for life. And I now believe that instinctive choice was perhaps the greatest expression of love of all.

My final realization wasn't just about the experience itself, but about the deep, powerful grip that fear had on me. It came from the awful meaning I was giving the events—the terrifying idea that this was either madness or sin.

This is why I am writing these pages—to face this threat of ridicule and mistrust. This is why I urge you to give a voice to your experience, too. If you have had an experience, let it be known! We need to hear from one another, we need to listen to one another, and we need to exchange notes so that we don't have to be in the dark anymore—so that the next person experiencing things is not hesitant to reach out for an extended hand, whether from a fellow human or something...more.

Chapter 10: Death, Old Buddy, Old Pal

What would the world be without darkness? If it were all just light? Scorched Earth?

—Messages from the Unseen

Not all of my formative experiences happened in the physical world. Some of the most profound were quiet, internal, and deeply personal. I've come to think of them simply as "the visits."

It began with a dream when I was six years old. But the dream was no ordinary dream. A being appeared, not only in my sleep, but in the landscape of my mind. It exuded a stillness as old as time itself—silent, yet radiating unconditional love and a fierce, protective, yet placid nature.

It was like a dormant volcano. I knew, with the primal conviction of a child's intuition, that it could unleash immense damage if it chose to. This knowledge was a shadow, a whisper of its power, but it never tried to hurt or scare me. It never manifested even an ounce of its destructive power around me.

For the longest time, I dismissed it as fantasy, the fanciful invention of a strange child's imagination. It was my imaginary friend, a guardian who watched over me with the patient, unobtrusive care of a parent observing a child at play in a park.

I soon realized the visits weren't random. They had a clear rhythm, arriving almost on a schedule. Every few weeks, I would feel that familiar presence: a hum of energy, a shift in the air. Now that I'm almost forty, I know this presence is my oldest friend. It's one of the very few constants I've had in a life full of change.

As I grew older, our "conversations" deepened. They weren't a verbal exchange in the way we typically think of them. There were no voices or visions. It was more like a game I'd play in my own mind, a fun dialogue with my deepest intuition. It was like I was talking to myself, but a "myself" that felt separate and wise.

This dialogue evolved. I realized I could ask it about things, and the conversations became more complex. I would bring it a question—about school, fear, or life—but it would never give me the solution directly. It played a very specific game. For every question I asked, it would return a question for me. It was a playful exchange of intuitive prompts, designed to lead me to an answer I would find for myself. This wasn't a test or a challenge; it was a partnership, a way of teaching me to listen to my own inner wisdom.

While it never gave me clear answers directly—not until I was ready to find them myself—it always guided me with purpose. Later, in deeper meditative states, an image would simply appear in my mind's eye: a fleeting symbol, a sensation, or sometimes a word. I would then go online and find references to the exact same experience or message I had received. It was a digital breadcrumb trail leading me closer to a fundamental discovery I still couldn't name.

The most significant of these interactions came when this being showed me my own light. I was sad and depressed. Things weren't going the way I wanted them to in my waking life, and this filled me with a deep sadness and disillusionment with the world. There were a few days in a row when I lay in bed, hardly eating anything, defeated and exhausted with life in general. I was not angry nor sad; I was simply done. Tired.

Then the being made itself noticed, trying for several days to coax me into feeling better. Its presence would help for a few minutes at a time, but I was in too dark of a place to hold onto it. I couldn't seem to reach that familiar mental space. It tried the gentle way, the talking way, the playful way, but it did not work. Not this time.

So, instead, it flooded me with an undeniable, positive energy. It was an overwhelming feeling of love, poured into me without reservation. The force of it was so strong it acted like a mirror, forcing me to see my own strength. It was an affirmation of inner resources I didn't know I had—of an energy I possessed but had forgotten how to access.

I was in my late thirties when this happened, and by then the visits were no longer confined to my dreams or fleeting thoughts. If I stood still, I could sense it, a tangible pressure in the air around me. I could feel its touch, as gentle as a breeze on my forehead, as real as a hand on my shoulder.

At this point, I was convinced I was entirely bonkers and had just become an expert at hiding it. Yet, my curiosity won out over my worries. I rationalized it by telling myself I was just playing a game. I was firm on this point: I did not actually believe a separate, individual entity was talking to me. This was all happening inside my own head, an elaborate and fascinating conversation with my own subconscious.

It was a game very similar to the one I'd already been playing for years—the one where I would identify and tag real memories as they surfaced in my dreams. This just felt like a new, more complex version of that internal dialogue. So, I leaned into the game. I started asking questions, probing this "other part" of myself.

I'd ask things like, "Where are you coming from?" "What is your world like?" "What is it like to be you?" I was just playing, but I was also deeply fascinated by the answers that surfaced from within me.

However, I also needed proof—a tangible sign that I wasn't losing my mind. And if I was, I wanted to know, so I could treat it.

During a trip to Romania, I found myself standing outside the office of my former university professor. He was now the director of a mental institution in my city—a man I had once revered as a beacon of reason. I had scheduled an appointment, a pilgrimage of sorts, and prepared to lay out the symptoms that had taken root in my life. I described my waking mental impressions, my inward dialogues, and my awareness that all of this was only in my head.

I didn't ask—I demanded a diagnosis, a neat label to pin on my chaos, and a prescription to make it stop.

He just laughed. It was the same laugh I remembered from my college days—a dry, patronizing chuckle that was designed to dismiss every earnest thing I said.

"Well," he began, leaning back in his chair, "you don't seem ill."

He told me that a rich imagination is not an illness. As long as I felt no negative emotions from my own mental explorations and could clearly distinguish between the objective world and the landscape of my inward life, there was no diagnosis. In polite words, he told me to get a life. As long as my mind was not negatively impacting my day-to-day relationships, work, self-care, and other external things, I was fine. No prescription.

He explained that he dealt with people who genuinely suffered, and that their illnesses didn't look like this. "True mental illness," he said, "reveals itself in the architecture of a person's life—their work, their relationships, the basic act of getting through the day."

Well...I had no issues there. My daily life was a fortress of normalcy. I was a bridge between two worlds, a master of living in two countries at once, and a testament to my own relentless adaptability. I was anchored to a stable, high-paying job, my world was full of rich relationships—a collection of friends, peers, and family members—and even my romantic life was unremarkable in its steadiness. I was taking good care of myself, my home was clean, and my body well cared for. I was lucid, present, and grounded.

According to him, the madness I was so certain of was simply not there. Nothing in my objective reality pointed towards mental illness, and even the fact that I was there in his office, asking for a diagnosis, was a sign that I was self-aware enough to question my own perception.

His advice was a gentle dismissal: to settle down, manage my stress, take some magnesium supplements, and find a hobby or two. And then, he assured me, I would be just fine.

I walked out of his office with a non-diagnosis, more lost than when I had walked in. If I was not mad, then what was I? Instead of being answered, my questions had only multiplied, leaving me to wander through a newly uncertain world.

So, I decided to set a test. The next time the visit occurred, I would issue a direct challenge. My reasoning was simple: If I wasn't completely crazy, then this presence must be objectively real. And if it was real, it had to provide definitive proof.

But what kind of proof would be undeniable? My logic settled on the physical. I had already felt its presence as a tangible sensation—that feeling of a hand on my shoulder. If it could interact with me on that level, then it should be able to leave a visible, physical mark. That would be the only way to know. If this experience wasn't just in my head, it had to provide evidence I could actually see.

With my test now clearly defined, all I could do was wait. I went about my life, but a part of me was on high alert, anticipating the next visit so I could proceed with my investigation. When the next interaction finally began, I was ready. I didn't bother with our usual game of questions. I went straight to my demand. I asked for something absurd, something that could not be explained away by my imagination. I asked for bruises.

"Give me a bruise or two," I silently challenged the "friend" in my head. "Then I'll know for sure that you're real."

The next morning, I woke up groggy, the challenge from the night before almost forgotten. I was on autopilot, just trying to get to the bathroom to brush my teeth. I swung my legs out of bed, and as I stood up, I caught sight of them. I stopped.

On my lower legs were two of the biggest, blackest bruises I had ever seen. They were dark and ugly, as if someone had taken a baseball bat to my shins. My first thought was confusion. I didn't remember hitting anything. Tentatively, I reached down and poked one. Nothing. There was no pain, not even a trace of tenderness, despite their awful appearance.

Then, in that exact instant, the memory of my challenge hit me like a jolt. "Give me a bruise so I can know you're real."

I had been playing. I hadn't actually expected anything to happen, let alone this quickly. I just stood there, staring at my legs, completely in shock. I took pictures, a desperate attempt to capture proof of the impossible—not for others, but for myself. For when doubt would creep in. Even more interesting was the fact that these bruises started healing that same day. By the next day, there was barely any mark left.

That was when I acknowledged it to myself. This being was real. As real as you and I. And it was really good at giving and healing bruises!

After the bruises, it went on its merry way, as it always did. I was certain it would come back; it always does, no matter how difficult I am.

I accepted that it was real, but a new kind of fear loomed: that of sin, of inviting darkness into my life, of making the wrong choices, of upsetting God if I kept entertaining these thoughts.

This cycle of belief and fear was exhausting. I was deeply programmed by societal learning to see the world in black-and-white terms: good and evil. This experience didn't fit, so I constantly worried. What if this was "bad?" What if I was being tricked or misled?

There were times I'd get so scared that I would completely shut it down. I'd deny the connection, refuse to engage, and try to convince myself it wasn't real. My visitor, however, was never bothered by my panic. It seemed to understand my inner conflict, and accepted it all without judgment. It would simply pull back, honoring my need for space.

That unconditional acceptance was the key. It never offered a defense. It never argued or tried to prove it was "good." It just waited, patiently, giving me the space to confront my own programming.

It was in that quiet that I finally reached my own conclusion. I had been wrestling with the idea of "good" and "evil," but the answer was in a teaching I'd known all my life. Christ tells us to love our enemy. He tells us not to judge, but to love that which we fear or hate.

I realized that's what this was. Here was this presence, which my conditioning had labeled a potential enemy, and its only response to my fear and rejection was to be patient and non-judgmental. It was modeling a profound, unconditional love. I finally understood that we are meant to love all of creation, and shadow is part of that creation, just as much as light is.

I remember one conversation when I asked if it was of the dark void. I felt it laugh. It wasn't a sound, but a sudden, energetic signature of pure amusement. The emotional landscape inside me heightened and grew lighter, and I knew this feeling came from it, not from me. This "laugh" was a thought that resonated deep within me.

"What would the world be without darkness?" it replied. "If it were all just light? Scorched Earth?"

That rang true. The "scorched Earth" idea was a perfect metaphor. The Earth needs the night just as much as it needs the day.

This was the next lesson that the being had taught me, though not with words. It showed me—through a silent exchange of thoughts, emotions, sensations, and, very rarely, a visual glimpse—that this balance applied to our inner lives, too. It wasn't about "dark" and "light" as cosmic forces at odds with one another, but about our own emotional range.

The lesson was this: The higher the highs, the lower the lows. The capacity to experience profound bliss, I was shown, is directly linked to the capacity to feel an equally profound despair. One extreme creates the potential for the other. This dance between them isn't a punishment; it's the very mechanism for growth. It is by navigating this full spectrum that we expand, evolve, and become...*more*.

And that, too, made perfect sense. This new perspective cast my own past in a different light. All my pain—my "lows"—suddenly had a purpose. They were never good feelings, but they were powerful teachers. It was only through that pain—through genuinely knowing what it feels like to be uncertain, unsafe, and alone—that I learned empathy. I gained a deep insight into what people need when they are hurt—what to say, and, just as importantly, what not to say. This was the root of a principle I held sacred: how to do no harm.

I finally understood that my path, shadows and all, wasn't a flaw. It was simply the way I was being shaped into the person I always wanted to become.

I understood then. This entity was, for lack of a better word, of the darker kind. It lacked malice, though. It had no desire to do harm. Or, if it did, I have never sensed anything of that sort. For what it's worth, it never did any harm to me. We weren't all that different. And at the same time, I understood that, like everything else, this being was made by God and loved by God, just as I was.

"Why shouldn't God love them?" I found myself asking. They were nothing but kind.

This lens of highs and lows also changed how I saw people—starting with myself. I knew I could be the kindest, most generous, and most loving human being. But I also knew that, when pushed far enough, I could turn vitriolic. I had that light and dark inside me.

Once I saw it in myself, I saw glimpses of it in everyone. People had good and bad sides, good days and bad days. It was just duality, a fact of being human.

This new understanding put my interactions with the being into perspective. It had always been loving, kind, protective, and honest. It never judged my bad side or my fears. This led me to a core belief: In truth, God wants us to love everything.

"We're all of God," it would tell me when I'd question it. Everything has a purpose. Everything is part of Oneness, just as much as we are. We are not above one another, nor are we beneath one another. We all matter.

I couldn't really debate that. What did I know? Nothing. All I had was a collection of volumes talking about these things, but no true knowledge. Just theories.

And so, one night, during one of these visits, I dared to do what I had never dared before. I asked for its name. I hesitated, but I asked anyway. A shiver of uncertainty ran through me. What if there wasn't a name? Or worse, what if it was a name I did not want to hear?

There was a pause. I believe I managed to surprise them. But then, for the very first time, I heard a voice. This was no mere thought in my head; it was a sound, a low, raspy voice from the distant past that spoke directly to my ears.

In slow, fully formed syllables, it said, "Az-Ra-El."

It was the second time I was actually hearing something, and to this day, it is the last time I have ever experienced true auditory sound from my experiences. The sound was stark—the voice was low, guttural, and not human. After the name was spoken, all sound ceased. And to this day, it has not returned.

I didn't know the name, but at least it was a name. I fell asleep. When I woke up, I went to my computer and searched. What I found was interesting. There was indeed a mention of this name. It was the Archangel of Death.

I laughed. It wasn't a small chuckle; it was a deep laugh of profound, cosmic irony.

Of course. Of course it was Death. This was the one concept I had struggled with, fought against, and feared for most of my life. My own death at seventeen. Bogdan's death soon after, which cemented Death as my personal enemy. My father's death,years later. For years, I had directed so much anger at Death itself. I had shouted unanswered questions into the void, challenging it, daring it to make itself seen, demanding that it explains itself.

And here was the punchline: The being I had been yelling at was the same one who had been patiently visiting me, teaching me, and showing me unconditional love my entire life. It had been there all along, patiently absorbing my anger, and I just hadn't known it. To be honest, I found it absolutely hilarious.

But the easy amusement of the encounter itself wouldn't last. Inevitably, once I had time to mull it over, my old anxieties began to surface. The social constructs and dogma I had learned started to clash with the pleasant reality of the experience, making me nervous after the fact. Yet, my visitor was never fazed by this predictable pattern. It was as if it could foresee this internal conflict—this habit of my mind to second-guess and scare itself—and wanted to gently show me that the experience itself held nothing to fear.

Another month passed, and another visit happened. I figured that if it didn't kill me when I was six, or fourteen, or seventeen, or all the other times I was able to sense it around me, it most likely wouldn't kill me now. So, in another gust of curiosity, I asked it what it looked like.

A familiar pattern unfolded. Whenever I landed on a question it was able to actually answer—anything other than a cryptic question in return—this specific pause would occur. It was a profound stillness, a gap in the interaction, as if it was giving my question careful consideration; searching for the right words or concepts my limited human mind could comprehend.

This time was no different. After that deliberate pause, the reply came as a slow, firm thought: "You can't withstand it."

All my life, I had followed my curiosity, and all my life, this being had given me cryptic replies and clues for me to figure out. I refused to let that be the end of it. I had no intention to invite something that could rip me out of my body again or make me feel like I would explode, but I still wanted to know more. I asked it to give me an image I could understand, a face I could look at.

Before my eyes, a vision formed—the face of a human-like being. Not quite human. Its skin was the color of a smoky blue sky, its ears were pointed like an elf's, and it had long, black hair pulled neatly to the back.

The image immediately made me think of Hindu deities. In fact, after going through online searches later, the closest depiction I found to the face in my vision was Lord Shiva, often known as "The Destroyer."

This created a striking paradox. It had a name found in Abrahamic religions, yet it presented an image that strongly resembled a Hindu deity. The attributes of Azrael and the "Destroyer" role of Shiva seemed to have a lot in common, which made me wonder, "Are these deities all the same?" Or, perhaps, was I dealing with a powerful archetype, a universal energy that different cultures had simply interpreted and named in their own ways?

By then, I was aware that these interactions were more than my imagination. I recognized its name, I discerned what it might look like, I was able to identify its energy, its emotional marker, and I was given tangible, objective proof of its realness. And that's when I realized that I didn't know anything.

Something tells me I will never know the real extent of these interactions, not until I cross over and get to see the big reveal. But that is not today.

I still carry fear in me. I still do the push-and-pull. But in one visit, it told me that most people go when they're ready—that, behind the veil, we're not so different. We need one another. Light cannot shine in the absence of shadow, and the void is just nothing in the absence of light.

The philosophy of yin and yang, of balance, of the wholeness of the whole picture, was unfolding in my mind's eye. It was the first time I understood Oneness on an intellectual level: Oneness signified both light and dark, in a seamless, beautiful dance.

This new realization forced me to acknowledge the duality of my own nature. I see both light and dark in every human I meet—and in myself. The world itself runs on a cycle of light and dark. The universe is an intermingling of light and dark, in this infinite, beautiful, cosmic dance.

It's been a lifetime of visits, of questions and veiled truths that I've had to discover for myself. A lifetime of encouragement in sadness and thoughts whispered in my mind. Because of my visitor, I am closer to God than ever before. I follow my intuition more, and the writing of this book is a result of me following the pull of my soul.

This being, may God bless and hold it, was what awakened me. It held my hand, rushed me when I was getting lazy, calmed me when I was getting fearful, and comforted me when I was lonely. It showed me that I belonged, and, when the time was right, it allowed me to see into the dimension beyond our senses, to sense and feel the kinship with everything and with others from their side—spirits of light, spirits of shadows, all the same, just at different places in their journeys.

It was this homecoming that finally initiated my attainment of Oneness, not just my understanding of it on a conceptual level. It was then that I understood that in this ethereal plane there is far less judgment, and that light and shadow are friends—that they are both found in everything, and that these two sides complete the whole.

I am in no way wiser or better, but I see life differently than I used to see it. I see the miracle in everything. Nature is the grandest of clues. The old books, written by the ones who came before us, hit differently now. And all of this freedom—the freedom to speak of the less-traveled roads, to stop and meditate and not be afraid if I sound crazy—all of this couldn't have happened without it.

My guest still comes by, and I now consider him a welcome friend. His presence is always a blessing, and I am always grateful.

Through these experiences, I've come to understand that death is what allows us to truly value life. I realized that life and death can't exist without each other. They are partners in a beautiful dance. This new understanding showed me that I can rest safely in the shadows, just as I can in the light. They are both parts of the same whole; it doesn't have to be one or the other. Life is both.

It makes me want to savor the dance while I'm in it. It allows me to taste life more fully and see the profound beauty in all of it. Light and dark, shadow and sun—I can now love and respect all of it as part of the same miraculous, magical whole.

Azrael: From Avenging Soldier to Compassionate Guide

As I began to peel back the layers of my experience, I found myself researching the figure of Azrael. I had no prior knowledge of this name, but the moment it was spoken in that powerful, raspy voice, I decided I would find out everything I could about the topic.

I was surprised to discover that the name, often translated from Hebrew as "Whom God Helps" or "Angel of God," is a profoundly significant and dualistic representation across Abrahamic and other metaphysical traditions. In Judaism and Islam, Azrael is widely known as the "Angel of Death," an otherworldly being whose primary role is to facilitate the transition of souls from life to death.

I had always thought of death as something to be feared—a finality, a dark and consuming end. I had escaped it twice. Yet, here was the name of my unseen protector, a being who felt as warm as a parent.

The cosmic scale of this being, as described in Islamic belief, was far grander than anything I had imagined.[1] It has 4,000 wings, with one foot in the fourth heaven and the other on the bridge between paradise and hell. Yet, it was the perfect cipher for the formidable, primordial presence I had known since my earliest memory—a being that held the cosmos in its depths and shattered my simple human understanding. This resonated with my visitor's unspoken, firm thought: "You can't withstand it." I learned he was right. I wouldn't be able to comprehend the sight of such a being.

However, the fact that this same deity was also described in New Age beliefs as having the power to heal emotional wounds, offer sacred protection, and reveal hidden truths was like a direct validation of my reality. These descriptions were very similar to my own experience. My unseen friend was most insistent when I was sad, depressed, and lonely.

While some portrayals describe Azrael as an avenging soldier carrying out God's commands, the more common depiction in New Age beliefs is of a compassionate figure who guides souls and comforts the living. This benevolent aspect resonated with the patient presence that had been my life-long visitor.

---

1. Smith, Jane Idleman, and Yvonne Yazbeck Haddad. *The Islamic Understanding of Death and Resurrection*. Oxford: Oxford University Press, 2002.

This complex, dualistic portrayal of Azrael found a striking parallel in my own life. My initial recognition of my visitor's nature—both comforting and intimidating—mirrored the theological dichotomy of Azrael as both a merciful guide and a force of cosmic power.

Discovering that my oldest spiritual friend was the archangel of death instantly created two major problems for me. First, there was the religious guilt. I was immediately worried I was committing some kind of sin. The Church's teachings are not kind to these kinds of personal encounters, and that dogma was deeply ingrained in me. Second, there was the cultural fear. I had to struggle with the world's terrifying idea of the "Angel of Death." This became the central conflict of my life: How could I possibly reconcile my gentle, private experience of this being with its scary, public reputation?

That inner push-and-pull finally calmed down. I stopped seeing things as just "good" or "bad." Instead, I started to understand, on a deep level, that everything was connected. I began to see these interactions not as something to be afraid of, but as a natural part of a much bigger, loving universe.

In the end, I had to accept the simple truth: A being that had been a gentle companion to me for decades was not to be feared, no matter what the world said. My own experience became my new truth. It was my living proof that the fearful, dogmatic stories were wrong, or at least incomplete. My reality showed me a much kinder, gentler side of this powerful being.

The most important lesson was learning to trust my own personal experience over the fearful stories I had been taught. This discovery of Azrael's multifaceted nature was a turning point. It was not just about a name. It was about the realization that negatives and positives could reside in the same being—that shadow was not just an absence of light, but a necessary part of a cosmic dance.

The exploration I conducted was not just a collection of facts; it was a mirror reflecting my own journey, showing me that my experience was no anomaly, but a firmly rooted archetype playing out in my life. It gave me the vocabulary to describe the indescribable and the courage to embrace the parts of myself that had once terrified me. In the end, the most feared name I could have imagined for my friend became the one that set me free.

The Face of the Transformer: The Paradox of Lord Shiva

The face that manifested in my mind's eye—the smoky blue skin and black hair—was not one I recognized from my own religious upbringing. It was an image I associated with Hindu deities, and my research confirmed this intuition. The being in my vision bore a striking resemblance to Lord Shiva, one of the most significant and complex gods in the Hindu pantheon.

While the name Azrael had pointed me toward Abrahamic traditions, the image I was given opened an entirely different door. This being, this friend, was showing me a connection that transcended any single religion.

In Hinduism, Shiva is one of the Trimurti, the trinity of supreme divinity that includes Brahma (the Creator) and Vishnu (the Preserver). Shiva's role is that of the Destroyer. This title is not malevolent; it is essential. He is the cosmic force of transformation, the one who dissolves the universe at the end of each cycle to clear the way for new creation.[2] He is the god of endings that make new beginnings possible.

This resonated immediately with the being I knew—a presence tied to death, yet not frightening. Instead, it was a fundamental part of a larger, loving process.

What I found most compelling was Shiva's profound duality, which mirrored the complex nature of my own visitor. He is a god of absolute paradoxes. He is Mahayogi, the great ascetic who sits in deep meditation on Mount Kailash, detached from the world, covered in sacred ash (*vibhuti*) and oblivious to desire. Simultaneously, he is the ultimate householder—the loving husband of the goddess Parvati and the father of Ganesha and Kartikeya. He embodies both complete spiritual detachment and complete worldly engagement.

In his benevolent form, he is Shankara, the giver of blessings and joy. But he is also Rudra ("the Howler"), his ancient, fierce aspect associated with storms, chaos, and the untamed wilderness. He can also be Bhairava, the terrible annihilator who haunts crema-

---

2. Kramrisch, Stella. *The Presence of Shiva*. Princeton, NJ: Princeton University Press, 1981.

tion grounds. This perfectly matched my own intuition of Azrael: the dormant volcano, a being of fierce, protective, placid nature that could unleash immense damage if it chose to, yet had only ever shown me unconditional love.

The smoky blue skin of my vision is one of Shiva's most famous attributes. According to myth, he drank the Halahala, a terrible poison that emerged from the churning of the cosmic ocean, which threatened to destroy the universe. The poison was so potent it turned his throat and face blue, earning him the name Neelkantha (The Blue-Throated One). In this act, he absorbs the world's darkness and negativity to protect creation—a perfect metaphor for a being that is of the dark, yet not evil.

Beyond the blue skin and matted black hair, Shiva's image is a tapestry of symbols that reinforce his dual nature. He has a third eye on his forehead, representing a higher consciousness. When he opens it, it unleashes a fire that burns away illusion and ego. He wears a cobra around his neck, symbolizing his mastery over death and primal energy. His trident (Trishula) represents the three fundamental powers of creation, preservation, and destruction, and the beat of his small drum (Damaru) is the very rhythm of creation itself.

This entire paradox is captured in his most famous form: Nataraja, the Lord of the Dance. In this depiction, Shiva performs the *Tandava*, the cosmic dance of creation and destruction, all at once. In one hand, he holds the drum of creation; in another, he holds the fire of destruction. A third hand is raised in a gesture of blessing, saying "be not afraid," while his foot stomps on a demon, representing the crushing of ignorance.

Shiva's dance is the universe itself: a constant, dynamic, beautiful cycle of life, death, and rebirth. He is not a grim reaper, but the rhythmic force that ensures the dance continues.

Discovering Shiva felt less like learning about a new god and more like finding a detailed map for a land I already knew. The fact that my visitor, the archangel of death from one tradition, would choose to show me the face of the lord of transformation from another, was a profound lesson. It was the first clue that these powerful concepts—death, change, creation, and destruction—are not separate. They are, perhaps, just different cultural masks for the same, singular, cosmic force.

The Universal Mask: One Archetype, Many Faces

My visitor, who identified with the Abrahamic name Azrael, had shown me the face of the Hindu god Shiva. One is an angel whose duty is to separate soul from body; the other is a supreme god who dissolves the cosmos. On the surface, they are from different worlds, different mythologies, and different spiritual operating systems.

Yet, my own experience presented them as one. Both are "destroyers," but not in a malicious sense. Both are forces of profound, necessary change. Both are ancient, formidable, and, as I had learned, capable of profound, protective love.

I was seeing, firsthand, the function of an archetype. The psychologist Carl Jung proposed that the human psyche contains a "collective unconscious," a shared reservoir of innate, universal images and patterns. These archetypes—like the hero, the mother, the trickster, or the shadow—are the building blocks of our myths, dreams, and religions.[3] They are the primordial forces we give different faces and names to, depending on our culture.

My visitor was a living embodiment of the "transformer" or "benevolent death" archetype. I began to see this same pattern woven throughout global mythology.

In ancient Egypt, the guide of souls was not a terrifying figure, but Anubis, the jackal-headed god. He was a psychopomp, a guardian who protected the dead, weighed their hearts against a feather, and guided them safely into the afterlife. He was a gatekeeper, a judge, and a comforter.

In Greek mythology, Hades was not the devil (a concept that didn't exist in their religion), but the stoic, wealthy ruler of the underworld. He was simply the steward of the realm of the dead, a necessary and unyielding force—but not an evil one. Death itself was personified by Thanatos, who was the twin brother of Hypnos, the god of sleep—suggesting a gentle kinship between the two states.

In Norse mythology, Odin, the All-Father, is also a god of death. He presides over Valhalla, gathering the souls of fallen warriors. But he is also the god of wisdom and ecstatic

---

3. Campbell, Joseph. *The Hero with a Thousand Faces*. Novato, CA: New World Library, 2008.

revelation, a seeker who sacrificed his own eye for deeper knowledge. He, too, contains the paradox of destruction and insight.

What if all these gods, angels, and deities are not separate, competing entities, but rather a spectrum of human interpretations for the same, singular, unimaginable forces? What if Azrael, Shiva, Anubis, and Odin are all cultural "masks" for the same universal archetype—the one that had been visiting me since I was six?

My experience, which had seemed so bizarre and isolating, was actually the most human thing of all: My mind was using the language it had (Azrael) and the images it could find (Shiva) to interface with a truth that is fundamentally beyond all language.

This realization offered a profound sense of peace. My visitor was not "dark" in the sense of being evil. It was "dark" in the way the soil is dark—a place of transformation, mystery, and the potential for new life. It was the other half of the whole. This force was not an enemy of the light; it was its dance partner.

The Dance of Yin and Yang

The momentous realization that the dark is part of creation as much as the light is serves as a central philosophical pillar of my outlook. This understanding moves beyond a simplistic dualism of good versus evil and aligns with a non-dualistic worldview that is central to Eastern philosophies, such as Taoism.

My visitor, the personification of the archetypal night, perfectly encapsulated this relationship. After years of my avoidance, it finally challenged my perspective with that pivotal question: "What would the world be without the shadows? If it were all just light? Scorched Earth?"

I couldn't fight that logic, and I can't express to you the frustration of having a conversation in your head with someone who is smarter than you. The thought resonated with me, of course. It was a soundless question that shattered my preconceived notions.

This interaction served as a direct challenge to my initial dualistic view, prompting a significant inward shift. The push and pull was replaced by an intellectual grasp of Oneness. It was uncomplicated, yet it rewired my entire worldview. If this ancient presence was a creation of God, then how could I, a mere mortal, presume to be suspicious of it or reject it ?

The philosophy of yin and yang posits that the world is composed of interdependent and complementary forces. Yin, the dark side, is associated with cold, passive, and receptive qualities, while yang, the light side, represents warm, active, and assertive qualities. I had been living my life in a constant battle, trying to suppress the yin, to deny the shadow in myself and the world around me.

Yet, as I came to understand, neither force is superior to the other. Instead, they are mutually defining, relying on one another for their existence. This new understanding wasn't just a thought in my head; I felt it physically in my body. It was a deep, emotional shift. It was as if I could "taste life" for the first time in a long time. I started to see the simple, profound gift that life is.

I realized the entire experience had forced me to face parts of myself and the world that I had been taught to reject or fear. This led to some hard questions. Was this agonizing internal fight just me fighting myself all along? Was my own mind using God and dogma as a scare tactic, just to keep me in line with what society expected?

If so, I couldn't blame it. After all, I was the one who had kept my lips sealed for all those years, terrified of being judged and ridiculed; scared of what I might lose if I spoke my truth. Needing more answers, I went back to the books.

The Language of the Unseen: Manifestations and Communication

My mental interaction with my visitor was not a singular event, but a complex, evolving communication that manifested in various forms—from dreams to an audible voice, and even visible marks on my body. Placing these experiences within the broader context of occult and parapsychological phenomena provided a powerful framework for understanding their significance. I came to realize that the universe speaks in many languages, and my visitor was teaching me one of them.

My experience began in a dream, an old story I had long dismissed as the invention of a child's mind. From there, the communication progressed to "thoughts in my head" before culminating in an "audible voice." This progression mirrored the established typologies of visions and locutions in mystical traditions.

For instance, I discovered the work of Saint Augustine of Hippo, who classified manifestations into three types: corporeal (bodily), spiritual (imaginary/mental), and intellectual (intuitional).[4] My initial perceptions, described as visions and mental impressions, aligned with the imaginary type, where impressions are received without the use of the physical senses. I felt validated to learn that in the Christian tradition, such thoughts or locutions are considered a highly significant form of revelatory communication.

The moment I heard a voice with my ears and not just a thought in my head was monumental for me. Such an audible voice is classified as a corporeal locution, a supernatural manifestation to the mortal ears. As I delved into the collective findings, I found a clear distinction between these transcendent phenomena and the auditory hallucinations associated with mental health conditions.

The field of psychiatry indicates that voices present in psychosis are often multiple, abusive, or violent, leading to distress and confusion. In stark contrast, spiritual communications are singular, peaceful, and associated with positive, meaningful outcomes. My interactions with the visitor fit this latter description perfectly. The voice, though low and raspy, was a singular phenomenon that provided a revelation (the name Azrael) and propelled my inner growth.

This, combined with the fact that my fear was conscious and my encounters never caused me pain or anxiety, served to confirm the positive and unifying nature of my experience. These visits were a catalyst for this shift, guiding me from a fragmented worldview to an all-encompassing, non-dualistic understanding of all creation.

It was as if my entire life had been a preparation for this moment, a slow, gentle unfolding of a grand design too big to grasp all at once. This slow, gentle unfolding didn't happen all at once. For years, it was a quiet, ongoing process. The "language" we spoke was a silent dialogue, one that often felt like a secret I held only with myself. The messages showing

---

4. Augustine of Hippo. *The Literal Meaning of Genesis (De Genesi ad litteram).* Translated by John Hammond Taylor. Ancient Christian Writers 41. New York: Newman Press, 1982.

me this grand design were subtle: a fleeting image, a sudden insight, or a flicker in my intuition. I learned to follow this breadcrumb trail, often turning to online searches to find external validation for a truth I could not yet name.

Unexplained Bruises and Marks of Spiritual Contact

The bruises appeared only at my request, as a challenge to my visitor. I woke up with the exact bruises I had requested.

When I first noticed them, I was perplexed. They were big, dark splotches of purple and black, almost staring at me from both of my legs, right under my knees. I could sense my visitor's amused demeanor while I was examining the spots on my calves. The origin of the injury was a mystery, and there was no tenderness to the touch. This was a riddle that defied any logic.

My first instinct was to find a "normal" explanation for it. Was I sick with some unknown illness? Had I injured myself without realizing it? But that logic didn't hold up. The marks had appeared exactly when I asked for them. On top of that, they healed with unnatural speed, fading in a fraction of the time a normal bruise would take. This baffling physical proof was the first real evidence I had of something beyond the ordinary.

This wasn't the scary, sensational paranormal activity you see in movies; this was something different—something real.

In parapsychology, mysterious marks on the body—scratches, cuts, or welts—are frequently attributed to sinister entities. These manifestations are meant to torment, to instill panic and distress in the victim. My experience, however, inverted this typical narrative. The bruises were not a cause of terror, but a means of tangible, undeniable evidence. They were a sign of kinship, not assault. I was never hurt. The marks themselves didn't hurt. In fact, I myself had asked for them as proof.

This aligns with stories from Christian mysticism. While it's important to note that the stigmata are traditionally associated with crucifixion wounds, they have key characteristics in common with my experience, as they are often painless and heal in an unnatural way.

The marks were painless and healed quickly, which made them feel like a physical bridge between my world and the unseen. They weren't a sign of an attack or something to fear. Instead, they felt like a form of tangible communication—a physical message that proved my relationship with this being was real. Once I saw it this way, I stopped worrying. The event wasn't a threat; it was a personal confirmation, a physical sign of a much deeper, ongoing connection.

The Shadow Archetype: A Mirror of the Unacknowledged Self

To fully comprehend the depth of my experience with my visitor, it was essential to contextualize it within established philosophical models of the mind. The process I was going through was not merely a series of events that happened to me, but a process of personal growth.

The visitor was not just an entity separate from me; it was a living mirror reflecting the unacknowledged parts of me. In this reflection, I found a framework in Carl Jung's concept of the shadow archetype.

Jung's analytical psychology posits that the psyche is not a single, unified entity, but composed of various, often competing parts.[5] One of the most significant of these is the shadow archetype. This is the part of our unconscious that houses all the qualities, desires, and instincts that the conscious mind has repressed. It is the repository for everything we find unacceptable, immoral, or unworthy, often due to societal norms, familial expectations, or our own values.

The shadow, which can appear in dreams or spectral manifestations as a dark, wild, or even demonic embodiment, is often initially perceived as entirely negative. We fear it, shun it, and work hard to keep it hidden, pretending it doesn't exist.

However, Jung's insight was that the shadow is not simply a container for our dark side. It is also a reservoir of immense vitality, creativity, and untapped potential. He believed

---

5. Jung, C. G. *The Archetypes and the Collective Unconscious*. Collected Works of C.G. Jung, Vol. 9, Part 1. Translated by R. F. C. Hull. Princeton, NJ: Princeton University Press, 1969.

that the ultimate goal of psychological maturation is not to eliminate the shadow, but to confront and integrate it.

This is a crucial step in the process of individuation, a term Jung used to describe the development toward becoming a complete and cohesive self. Individuation is the process of integrating the conscious and unconscious parts of the psyche to achieve wholeness and a unique identity. It requires a moral effort—the courage to look at the parts of ourselves we have disowned. The more we deny the shadow, the "blacker and denser" it becomes, gaining power over us from a hidden place.[6] By bringing it into the light of consciousness, we can reclaim its energy and transform its negative aspects.

My relationship with Azrael, an entity that embodied both protective love and an unsettling shadow, functions as an external manifestation of this internal shadow archetype. My lifelong engagement with this figure began when I was a child who thought of it as an imaginary friend, and it later evolved into an absolute acceptance of "my oldest friend." This process directly mirrors the evolution of confronting and integrating one's own unconscious self.

I was not just dealing with an outside force; I was engaging with a part of my own psyche that had been projected outward, making the process of integration tangible and visceral. The initial caution I displayed around Azrael's darker aspects was, in fact, my own discomfort with the unacknowledged dark parts of my being. The moment I chose to embrace its complex nature, I was, on a deeper level, accepting the duality within myself.

My ultimate realization that Azrael's shadow was not something to be feared, but rather a necessary part of a cosmic order of light and shadow, was a powerful symbol of personal integration. This was the turning point in the arc of my journey.

By accepting this external entity, I was also implicitly accepting my own inner shadow. I recognized it not as a flaw to be corrected, but as a necessary component of my own being. It was a recognition that the light within me could not exist without a corresponding shadow, and that this duality was not a source of shame, but of power and wholeness.

---

6. Jung, C. G. *Aion: Researches into the Phenomenology of the Self.* Collected Works of C.G. Jung, Vol. 9, Part 2. Princeton, NJ: Princeton University Press, 1959.

This integration of the subjective and objective is the essence of individuation. The transformative process yielded a sense of "wholeness," liberation, and the ability to see life—and myself—differently. Something that came from outside my inner world served as a catalyst for psychological healing and growth. Instead of trying to be a "good" or "light" person by repressing my less-desirable traits, I learned to embrace the full spectrum of my human nature.

This process of integrating the shadow, a journey so vividly represented by my connection with Azrael, freed me from the self-imposed limitations of a fractured self. It allowed me to move forward not as someone trying to be perfect, but as a complete person—a dynamic interplay of all my parts, both seen and hidden from view, acknowledged and unacknowledged. The unknown visitor was not a demon to be exorcized, but a sacred guide leading me back to my own foundational self.

Oneness: A Seamless and Beautiful Dance

My intellectual and emotional breakthrough—the deeply meaningful realization of Oneness—was the culminating point of my entire journey. This concept, which I had only ever encountered in the abstract world of philosophy or the hushed tones of religious lectures, suddenly became a tangible, embodied reality.

In simple terms, Oneness is the direct, lived experience that all beings and phenomena are fundamentally connected. It is the end of the illusion of separation. This isn't just a "hippie" idea or a New Age trend; it is the central, shared truth of mystics and sages across all of human history.

In Hinduism, it is the core of Advaita Vedanta—the understanding that Atman (the individual soul, or self) is not just part of Brahman (the ultimate, divine reality), but identical to it. In Buddhism, the goal of enlightenment is to achieve Nirvana, a state that comes from extinguishing the fires of desire and recognizing the "emptiness" (Śūnyatā) of a separate, permanent self. It is the realization that all things are interconnected.

In Taoism, it is the recognition of the Tao, the single, unified, and natural flow of the universe from which all things arise and to which all things return. Even in mystical branches of Christianity, Judaism (Kabbalah), and Islam (Sufism), the ultimate goal is the dissolution of the self into the divine, a union with God.

Great spiritual teachers and masters, those who had fully realized this state, have tried for millennia to describe this shift in perception. The Sufi mystic and poet Rumi captured it perfectly: "You are not a drop in the ocean. You are the entire ocean in a drop."[7]

This quote, which I had once read as pretty poetry, now struck me as a literal truth. My own experience was not a simple belief; it was a complete reconfiguration of my mind. I came to perceive all of creation as an exquisite and ceaseless interplay of energy—a seamless, beautiful dance of light and shadow, creation and destruction, and all the dualities that define our perceived world.

This realization forced me to confront the duality within myself. My brain, which had previously operated under a rigid, good vs. evil paradigm drummed into me by dogma, began to reconfigure itself. It wasn't an instant "lightning bolt" change, but a slow and profound rewiring.

This intellectual insight was not merely a thought; it was a defining moment that had a cascading effect on how I emotionally and physically interacted with the world. I began to see the world not as an assortment of separate, competing parts, but as a unified, interconnected whole. This wasn't a philosophical exercise; it was a sensory, intuitive experience.

The feeling of separation, of being an isolated individual in an infinite and indifferent universe, began to melt away. In its place came a profound sense of communion and belonging. I was no longer just a spectator; I was an active participant.

My personal, tangible experience—from the gentle, lifelong presence of Azrael to the sudden, physical marks—was my own unique path to this universal realization. It demonstrated to me that Oneness is not just a concept to be studied, but a state of being to be achieved.

This is the ultimate freedom. It is liberation from the fragmented, fearful self. Fear of death, worries about the future, and regrets of the past—all of them lose their power in

---

7. Rumi, Jalal al-Din. *The Rumi Collection*. Edited by Kabir Helminski. Boston: Shambhala, 1998.

the face of this all-encompassing, connected love. Life itself becomes a vibrant, deeply meaningful, and miraculous experience.

Navigating the Line Between Mysticism and Psychosis

As you already know, I constantly questioned myself. I had this one nagging, persistent thought: "I'm convinced I am entirely bonkers and that I just hide it really well."

This kind of self-doubt is a normal and understandable reaction when you experience things that challenge everyday reality. After all, what I was going through—hearing voices, seeing visions, and feeling like I was in a different state of mind—looks a lot like the classic symptoms of a serious mental illness. For a long time, I felt like I was walking a tightrope, completely unsure if I was on a spiritual journey or just losing my mind.

However, modern psychiatric and religious inquiries provide a clear blueprint for distinguishing between a genuine awakening of the soul and a psychotic episode. The key differentiator, as studies have found, is not the content of the phenomenon itself, but rather the effect and outcome of the event.

While psychosis is characterized by distress, confusion, and a loss of social function, transcendental occurrences are more often sought after, and are associated with feelings of solace, hope, and positive life changes. My narrative is a clear example of a positive, transformative process. My initial confusion was a temporary phase, a push-and-pull that resolved into peace and a newfound freedom to express myself.

This is the crucial distinction: The experience led to a closer relationship with God, a stronger intuition, and a more vibrant, meaningful life. The thoughts I was hearing weren't scary; they were guiding me. The visions I saw weren't terrifying; they were comforting. This was the exact opposite of a mental breakdown.

A psychotic break tends to make a person's life fall apart. They might withdraw from friends and family or stop being able to function, and their quality of life might get worse. I never had those problems. My life always was, and still is, as normal as it can be. My path wasn't one of fragmentation or falling apart. It was a spiritual awakening, and it was leading me toward integration—toward becoming more whole.

The Quantum Self: The Brain as a Receiver of Consciousness

All of that being said, my experience remained a mystery to me. Despite everything, I still wanted to know, to understand more. The limitations of classical religious and scientific models of the human experience, in my opinion, were pointing to a need for a more expansive view of consciousness and reality.

For me, this is where speculative theories from quantum physics offer a contemporary, albeit controversial framework for exploring the possibility of interactions and the nature of the unseen.

Traditional thought posits that consciousness is an emergent property of the brain, a product of complex neuronal activity. This view, however, struggles to explain a lifelong, persistent relationship with an entity separate from the self. It would require the brain to be the sole producer of these experiences, yet the brain cannot produce bruises that heal at an anomalous speed.

This is where the notion of the quantum self emerges.[8] Instead of seeing the brain as the creator of consciousness, speculative quantum consciousness theories offer an alternative paradigm. These hypotheses propose that consciousness is not produced by the brain, but is rather a universal property of the universe itself, with the brain acting as a receiver or filter.

My experience can be framed as a compelling, lived example of this non-local relationship. The visits that came by a schedule can be understood as the brain tuning into a persistent, universal frequency or channel, similar to how a radio antenna receives a signal.

This gave me a new way to think about it. It suggested that my consciousness was like a receiver, tuned to a specific "frequency" within a much larger, shared consciousness. The proof that I wasn't just imagining things was discovering that other people had received the exact same messages or had the exact same experiences. This was a powerful confirmation that I wasn't alone; I had tapped into a shared reality.

---

8. Zohar, Danah. *The Quantum Self: Human Nature and Consciousness Defined by the New Physics*. New York: William Morrow, 1990.

This idea of a deep, unseen connection reminded me of a concept from physics: quantum entanglement.[9] As a quick analogy, this is a process where two particles become so deeply linked that what happens to one instantly influences the other, no matter how far apart they are. Einstein famously called this "spooky action at a distance," and it felt like the perfect metaphor for my own life.

I started to wonder: Were my intuitive leaps and the "shared revelations" I found in others a human version of this? Were we all part of a "metaphysical entanglement," capable of sharing information and experiences without ever speaking a word? This idea is further reinforced by Carl Jung's concept of synchronicity, which describes "meaningful coincidences that defy explanation by causality."

The fact that I could find objective verification for a subjective, inner realization—the name "Azrael" and the symbolism of the blue Hindu-like icon—suggests a deeper, unifying force at play. My story is therefore not a solitary happening. Rather, it's a manifestation of an interconnected reality—a cosmic "web" that is only beginning to be explored by both spiritualists and scientists.

Whether my visitor was just an imaginary friend or a being of cosmic dimensions faded into irrelevance over time. The effects of their being in my life were always positive, and for the first time, I found the conviction to admit to this connection.

In a final echo of my journey, it was again a digital community that spoke the truth I had long silenced. One day, a single post on Reddit caught my eye. The original poster was describing their own interactions with a being from the ethereal plane, a story so familiar it was like I was reading a page from my own unwritten diary.

But what truly struck me, what hit me like a revelation, was not the content of their story, but one particular detail. They, too, had asked for their visitor's name, and their visitor had given it in the same slow, clear, and perfectly formed syllables that mine had, as if to ensure there could be no mistake. The name was different, but the way it was spoken was identical. It was a common signature, a language spoken by the spirit realm.

---

9. Radin, Dean. *Entangled Minds: Extrasensory Experiences in a Quantum Reality*. New York: Paraview Pocket Books, 2006.

I found the courage to say, "Me too." I rushed to answer, to share my own story, my own experience. In that reply, I made a statement that, to this day, rings true: "I think of it as my angel, and I truly hope your angel is as amazing as mine."

It was a bridge built from certainty, confirming the fact that I was not alone. There were others, and they had stories that were similar to even my strangest ones. They were just silent.

Chapter 11: When the Skies Open

When you will all be harmless, the skies will open.

—Messages from the Unseen

Sometimes, things happen. All kinds of things that defy reason. But we brush them off as misunderstandings or our minds playing tricks on us—whatever reasons we craft to better secure our masks and personas. But sometimes these things will keep happening until you finally acknowledge them and learn to play with them.

I wish I could say I was one of the people who listened to their inner wisdom, but that's not what happened. I dug my fingers deeper into the known, holding on tight and refusing to acknowledge any of these events. And the experiences kept coming.

Looking back, what else was the universe supposed to do? I still needed to wake up, and I was clearly ignoring the subtle hints. So, it gave me no choice but to listen. It began to speak to me in the one language I couldn't dismiss: the tangible, physical world.

Real things were happening in my waking life—undeniable events that would force me to finally acknowledge the truth. I was being given concrete, real-world evidence that there is *more*—and it was right there. The unexplained began to poke at me, showing up in the most unexpected ways and at the most unexpected times.

The Sighting at the Stadium

The abandoned rugby stadium was our sanctuary. It was a relic, a circular ruin of concrete and rusted metal where the grass grew tall and unruly between the old bleachers. It smelled of dust, urban decay, and rain. For two sixteen-year-old girls trying to avoid getting caught smoking, it was the perfect place. We sat on the dusty bleachers, hidden away from the world.

We were caught in a bubble of easy conversation, the kind that only best friends can have. It was about boys, school, and our hopes—the usual. I don't remember the exact moment our conversation naturally died out, but my attention was snagged by the silence that replaced it.

It wasn't the normal, comfortable, familiar lull in conversation between two friends. It was something else entirely. What struck me as strange was the silence that seemed to fall over the entire stadium.

It was sudden and complete. One moment, the wind was rustling the tall grass. We could hear the distant chirping of birds and all the millions of sounds that create the normal backdrop of life in the city. The next, all of it vanished—not just our voices, but the wind, the birds, the distant traffic...everything. It was as if a heavy blanket had been thrown over the world, muffling every last whisper of life.

The silence was so complete that the only sound left was the frantic beat of my own heart, a drum thumping against my ribs. The air grew still and heavy, carrying with it a faint vibration that I could feel physically. It was as if my body cells were moving in a rhythm I couldn't place.

Then, from between two of the nearest buildings, it came into sight. It didn't soar or swoop. Instead, it simply appeared, steadily and deliberately—this massive, dark, noiseless thing.

At first glance, it was just a blob against the sky, a shapeless, gigantic object made of dark metal. But as it drew closer, the details became clearer, and my mind struggled to make sense of them. It was anything but a blob. It was metallic, but it had no singular, discernible shape. It was full of impossible angles and jagged lines, a chaotic jumble of geometric forms. It was as if it were made of irregularly sized pixels—a big, freaky Lego structure that somehow, against all logic, managed to look like a floating, dark blob.

The color was dark gray, like a wisp of smoke, and though I could see its metallic nature, the metal did not gleam or reflect the dying light. It was dead, flat, and somehow completely chromed. A few red and blue lights pulsed across its surface. They were freakishly small, like tiny pinpricks of color on the hull of a monstrosity. The thing was hovering right in front of our eyes.

It was too close for comfort, far too quiet. It just hung there, suspended in the air. I had never thought myself capable of such visceral, petrifying terror. It seized me completely. It was more intense than when I had almost drowned at fourteen.

A chill unlike anything else shot through my veins, locking my muscles in place and stealing the breath from my lungs. My entire body froze into a statue. I could not move. I could not utter a peep. My mind, usually a chaotic mess of teenage thoughts, was completely blank. It was a terrifying absence of thought.

A more observant person might have tried to snap a photo, to capture this impossible moment, but not us. We were frozen in place, utterly still. My best friend was just as shocked. Her hand was halfway to her mouth, her eyes wide with a terror that mirrored my own. We were two witnesses to the unbelievable, and our only response was petrified shock.

The ominous-looking mammoth began to move again, agonizingly slow. Or maybe it just felt like that. It is possible that my panic simply warped time, making it seem like an eternity. It just floated slowly, completely unconcerned with our presence. As it floated, I somehow managed to push one single thought through the paralyzing terror: "I should take a picture."

But my internal dialogue, the one that had been with me all my life, pushed back. A foreign voice in my head argued, "What if it does not want its picture taken?"

The thought was so clear and immediate that it sounded like a valid reason to do nothing. So I sat there, paralyzed, not a single thought left in my head except for that one piece of advice.

After what seemed like a lifetime, the thing disappeared behind a row of buildings, much to our relief, slowly floating on its way. But once it reached the last two buildings, it never came out from behind them. It just...vanished. It was like it had been swallowed by a portal, or like the reality of the street had simply folded in on itself and consumed it.

The silence lingered, a remaining shadow of its force. It was a full minute after the object was no longer in sight that I managed to break the spell, the silence that still had us both sitting there and staring at the now empty stadium.

"Did you see that?" I uttered, my voice hoarse and trembling. She gave a short nod, a single, clipped "Mhm," her eyes still wide with shock. "Should we just go home?" I asked, and she nodded.

We walked without speaking. The most unnerving part began almost immediately. The closest house on our route home was my brother's, so we went straight there, still shaking. We both told him the story, tumbling over each other's words.

He listened patiently until we were done, and then he laughed. That was it. Just a laugh. He didn't believe us. Or rather, he believed we'd seen something perfectly explainable, but were just two silly girls who had scared ourselves into thinking it was a spaceship.

My brother's laugh was just the beginning. Our parents waved the story off as a teenage prank gone wrong. Our other friends made jokes. The experience that had petrified us, that had changed the way we looked at the world, became nothing more than the basis for ridicule.

This whole idea that having witnesses makes a story credible? It doesn't hold up. Even with witnesses, people will still laugh and call you crazy. To this day, I still do not know what we witnessed.

I have spent countless hours searching for images of UFOs, but none of them resembled the one we encountered. The object should not have been able to fly; something that big should not be able to be that silent. And it defied description, unlike absolutely anything I'd ever seen before, in both fiction and non-fiction. It was a moment of awe, shock, and panic—a glimpse behind the curtain of the world—and it changed me forever.

The Ride to the Beach Resort

It was a summer night in my mid-twenties, and the air was thick with the promise of something wild. Two of my friends and I hopped into a car, eager to leave the sleeping city of Constanta for the electric pulse of Mamaia. Our city, a port town, was sleepy and worn by time. But its neighbor, Mamaia, was a vibrant summer retreat with beaches that hummed with life, a nightlife that was one long, never-ending celebration, and the kind of carefree joy that only a seaside resort can offer.

Our mission was simple: find a cool party, lose ourselves in the music, and forget the mundane for a few hours.

The car hummed, the windows were down, and the warm, salty air blew through my hair. We were passing by a student campus, a cluster of drab concrete buildings isolated in an otherwise empty field, when something odd caught my eye.

It was nothing at first, just a deeper shade of dark against the already black sky. Then, as if someone had flicked a switch, a circular set of lights came to life. They weren't glaring, but a soft, steady light-blue glow that pulsed with a soft energy. The object was large, easily four or five times the size of our car, and it just hung there, suspended in the air.

A familiar chill traced a line up my spine. My body remembered the utterly frozen state from that long-ago day at the stadium. My mouth went dry. "What is that?" I whispered, my voice barely audible above the car engine.

My friends, who had been laughing and scrolling through their phones, looked up, their faces immediately losing their carefree expressions. The circular lights began to move, and the object took off. It didn't soar or slice through the air; it simply hovered in silence.

This silence was different from the one I had encountered as a teenager. That one had been heavy and suffocating; this one was clean and sharp, a complete absence of sound coming from the object itself. But it did not possess the oppressive nature from before, the silence that sucked the noise out of the world around it.

My friend in the passenger seat leaned closer to the window, awe in her eyes. "Did you see that?" she asked, not needing an answer. "It's a UFO, right?"

The question hung in the air with a mix of disbelief and an almost childish excitement. The object was now fully airborne, and as it turned slightly, we were able to see its true form. It was a perfect, matte-black triangle with three large, glowing lights at each corner and a single, smaller light in the middle. It moved with an impossible grace, a geometric shadow gliding over the campus buildings, heading in our direction.

Without a single word, a mutual, unspoken understanding passed between us. My friend in the driver's seat floored the gas. "We're chasing it," she said, a grin of pure adrenaline on her face.

The car lurched forward, and we sped down the empty road, following the silent black triangle. The chase was exhilarating, a mad dash into the unknown. We were no longer on a trip to a club; we were on a mission. The night air whipped past us, filled with the roar of our engine and the pounding of our hearts. It was like a race, but one where we were the only competitors, our car a tiny, frantic speck trying to keep up with the silent, clearly superior craft.

We followed it for what seemed like an eternity, through busy streets and past sleeping neighborhoods, until we reached the end of the road. We were at the edge of the resort, where the land meets the sea. The ship didn't stop. It continued its stealthy, steady flight, moving out over the dark water. We were forced to pull the car over, our headlights illuminating the choppy waves as we watched it continue its impossible journey.

It moved further and further away, until its four lights were just a constellation on the horizon, a phantom that had passed through our lives and vanished into the night.

The conversation in the car ceased again, but this time it wasn't a chilling stillness; it was one of stunned awe. We looked at each other, our faces illuminated by the dashboard lights. The thrill of the chase was gone, replaced by an excited realization. "We really saw that, didn't we?" one of my friends asked. We all nodded, our collective experience a bond that would last forever.

I knew better than to encourage them to tell others about it. I knew the consequences of doing so. Instead, I just chose to keep this shared memory as a hidden treasure. Having witnesses doesn't always matter.

I went back to the research, and I was happy to find references this time. The craft showed in multiple photos across the globe; some say it was a military project, an unacknowledged prototype. This one, unlike the inaudible blob, was a well-known phenomenon. It had appeared in countless photos online, documented by people all over the world. Some claimed it was alien; others insisted it was a classified military craft. Regardless, the flying black triangle is a recurring image in ufology, and I saw it in person.

The Church Bells

I must have been about fifteen. It was late, and I was in my room, wrapped in the storyline of a show I was watching. Outside, the night was still and silent, the kind of quiet you find in a city after everyone has gone to bed. I remember looking at the clock: 11:00 p.m. It hit me that the entire day had simply disappeared, swallowed by a blur of homework and teenage angst.

It was in this peaceful, mundane moment that it happened.

To be clear, in my entire life, I have only truly heard external, physical-sounding noises—one that was not a thought or an internal "knowing"—on two occasions. The second time, as I've already shared, was twenty years later, when I clearly heard the name "Azrael."

This night was the first.

It was in this peaceful, mundane moment that I heard it. It was clear and sharp as a bell, and felt physical. The sound came neither from the television nor my imagination. It was real, sharp, and vivid—and yet only in my head. It was the slow, solemn, sad sound of church bells.

One long, mournful gong. Then another. Then a third and a fourth.

They rang with a heartbreaking finality. The sound was so clear and heavy in the silence of my room that I knew it wasn't just in my head. It felt physically real.

I knew, instinctively, what that sound meant. It was the traditional death knell from the Romanian countryside. In the small villages, this is how the community is told that one of their own has passed away. The church bells ring just like that in the morning—four slow, solemn gongs—announcing to the whole village that Death has visited.

My first thought was a chilling one: "Someone died." The words formed in my head with the same eerie clarity as that of the bells themselves.

A wave of logic washed over me: "It couldn't be real." Why would the bells ring at night, at 11:00 p.m., instead of in the morning? And we didn't live in a small village, but in the city, where this custom was forgotten. I tried to logic my way out of the impossible sound. I told myself the bells weren't real; that only I could hear them.

But that realization was chilling, and it didn't make the sound any less vivid. My mind quickly offered a comfortable excuse: I was just tired, and my brain was playing tricks on me. I turned the volume up on the television, hoping to drown out the haunting memory of the sound. I told myself it was just a coincidence, a tired brain manufacturing a sound it had no business making up.

The next morning, I woke up to a different sound—the murmur of my mother's voice on the phone in the kitchen. Her tone was serious, filled with a mix of shock and sadness that instantly put me on edge.

I walked toward the kitchen, trying to make sense of her distressed words. The news hit me like a brick to the head: My aunt had died. Then, the final, chilling detail: She had passed away at 11:00 p.m. the previous night.

My entire body went cold. The pieces of the puzzle clicked into place with horrifying precision. The time of her death. The impossible bells. My mind reeled. I stood there, rooted to the spot, words trapped in my throat. My mother hung up the phone, her eyes red, and looked at me. She asked me to get dressed, as we were going to show support and pay our respects.

I nodded, turned on my heel, and walked back to my room. I didn't say a word about the bells. I was painfully aware of the fact that, in my family, this kind of talk was not encouraged. In fact, people with narratives like mine—the strange, the unexplained, the "other"—were labeled crazy, superstitious, or something worse. The threat of that label, of being dismissed and misunderstood, was a mighty force. It was a habit I had already learned: to hide, to pretend, to keep my truths to myself.

The label won again. It always won. So I let it go, brushing it off as just another one of those weird coincidences that happened in a world that was already more complicated than I could handle. But I never forgot the sound of those bells, or the chilling certainty that had accompanied them. It was a secret I would carry with me—yet another crack in the wall of my tightly controlled reality.

The Cards

Like most seekers, I've dabbled in just about everything—a little bit of this, a little bit of that. Naturally, divination and the occult were on the list. But I want to be clear: To me, it was all just a game. It was a fun way to bring a little magic into my life, something to do with friends—not a serious spiritual practice.

I had a happy-go-lucky attitude about it. While I understood that divination could be very real in theory—that other people might be able to tap into some hidden power—I was convinced I wasn't one of them. I just didn't think it would actually work for me. In my mind, the probability of me getting a genuine, supernatural result was minimal. I didn't think I had the ability to make it work. I was a teenager, and this all was just fun.

One day, I was at a friend's house, sitting on the floor, doing a reading for someone I cared about deeply. The room was peacefully silent, filled with late afternoon light streaming through the window. I shuffled the deck of cards, the sound of the cardboard rustling a comforting rhythm. I sought nothing in particular, just a general reading about love and life, but the cards had a different story to tell.

The woman kept showing up—an older woman—and with her the undeniable, chilling message of her impending death. It wasn't subtle; it was clear as day. The four sevens of the deck—the cards of sorrow and endings—kept appearing.

They were always followed by the cards of home and destiny, signifying a decisive parting from this world and the end of a long life. The cards laid out a stark, undeniable sentence: Death. The unmistakable split.

A cold knot formed in the pit of my stomach, and my hands trembled. This couldn't be right. It was a game, just a game. I gathered the cards, a shiver running down my spine, and began to reshuffle. I started the reading over from scratch. I tried a different spread, a new pattern, hoping to change the outcome, but it was useless. The same message came through: a relentless, unchangeable truth. The cards kept screaming that this woman, deeply loved in this person's family, was going to pass away.

I tried a third time, then a fourth, and then a fifth, my fingers fumbling with the cards, my heart pounding in my ears. The message remained. No matter how many times I shuffled, no matter what new spreads I laid out, the same four sevens, the same home and destiny cards, kept appearing. The same dark prophecy.

It wasn't a game anymore. It was a horrifying piece of news laid out on the floor in front of me, and a surge of panic washed over me.

My hands started to shake. I quickly gathered the cards and shoved them back into their box, as if I could somehow seal the message inside with them.

I couldn't bring myself to tell my friend what I had seen. How could I be the one to deliver such terrible news? Besides, I reasoned, it was just cards. It was supposed to be for fun. I said nothing. The silence that followed felt heavy and final.

Two days later, my friend called. I could hear the sadness in her voice before she even said a word. She told me that someone dear to her—her aunt—had passed away suddenly. A wave of guilt and sadness crashed over me. The cards had been right, and I had known it was coming. And yet, when it mattered, I had said nothing. I could have given them a chance to say goodbye, to tell the departed that they loved them one more time.

This worry of being labeled as unhinged, of being a harbinger of bad news, was what kept me from voicing my thoughts. I chose to rob them of the possibility to say goodbye in order to protect my image. It was a hard pill to swallow.

"I'm too Big for This Body"

In my mid-thirties, I was a master of the game. The truths that had poked at me since my childhood were now just muffled whispers that I had come to accept as little oddities. I had mastered the part: to be invisible, to be agreeable, and to try my best to fit in.

The role I was playing was easy: If something sounds weird in your head, don't say it out loud. As long as you pretend to be like them, they won't know you're different.

I had gotten good at wearing the mask. I had a respectable job, the praise of my peers, fancy shoes, and a good-looking boyfriend. By all outward appearances, I had it made. I had already decided not to bring any children into the world, which consequently allowed me to enjoy life like a twenty-year-old with money. My days were a mix of fancy cosmetics, international travel, and my true, enduring passion: video games.

It was a regular day. I was sitting on the bed, lost in the digital world of the newest sale on the Xbox store. Everything was normal. I was exactly where I was supposed to be, doing exactly what I was supposed to do.

But as I sat there, something began to build inside me. It was a physical sensation, not a thought or an idea: an intense, rising energy. It felt like light, like a surge of electrical sparks charging my entire being from the inside out.

The energy grew, and it grew fast, an internal pressure that was building at an alarming rate. It coursed through my veins, pulsed behind my eyes, and made my skin feel as though it was humming with electricity. At some point, the pressure was so intense, so all-consuming, that I truly believed I was going to explode. For a short second, I remembered. I was familiar with the feeling. I had experienced it at some point in my twenties, when fear had won and I'd run away after having a vision of Christ. I was not going to do so again. I wasn't going to run. I took deep breaths and allowed it all to unfold.

With this acceptance, a single, foreign thought erupted in my mind—a thought less like an idea and more like a roar: "I am too big for this body!"

The thought was primal, a furious scream of confinement. It was the howl of a lion forced to live its life in a tiny cage, a magnificent being squeezed into a fragile human form.

As this foreign thought unfolded, the energy grew bigger and bigger, becoming almost impossible to contain. My body trembled, and I held the Xbox controller so tightly my knuckles went white. I honestly thought I was going to lose consciousness.

It took me a minute to ground myself, to remind myself of the feel of the mattress, the sound of the TV, and the life I had constructed. I took deep, shuddering breaths, slowly returning to my body.

As I sat there, calming down, another experience rushed in. This one was far more pleasant, yet equally intense. The roar was gone, replaced by a gentle, irresistible pull. I was gliding again. My body was still on the bed, still holding the Xbox controller, but my awareness, my consciousness, had been transported instantly to a place that felt like home.

I recognized the garden. It was the place from a long-forgotten dream, the very landscape I had walked with my departed cousin during my NDE at seventeen. Its reality was startling, more solid than the mattress beneath me.

I glided effortlessly through the space. On my way, I passed a patch of flowers. They were beautifully strange, not just because of their colors, but because of the bursts of light—vibrant reds, electric blues, and bright purples that didn't just sit there. They vibrated with life. As I looked at them, I didn't just admire their beauty; I was able to feel what they did. A resounding, bursting joy coursed through me—a pure, unadulterated happiness of simply existing. I knew intuitively that I was able to feel what they were feeling.

Then I turned to face the sky, and I was met with birds soaring through it. I shared in their feelings. It was freedom—a freedom so complete, so pure that it brought with it an even greater wave of joy. I was untethered, unburdened.

My attention was then drawn to the Earth beneath me. I didn't see it; I felt it—the loving embrace of the planet, the sense of safety and protective kindness that Earth gives us so freely and that we so often ignore. I thought that it was Gaia herself showing me the truths I had been too blind to see. (For those unfamiliar with the term, Gaia is a concept that personifies the Earth as a single, living organism, a cosmic mother.)

I was shown what a little bug would feel, nestled inside the warm, cozy earth—safe, protected, sincerely loved. Their experience was vastly similar to how the universe had felt to me when I was a baby, a visceral truth as old as myself. It was the same peaceful, loving stillness, a knowing that everything was okay.

And then, I took off! I was rising, higher and higher. What fun! What joy! I was engulfed in a long-dormant sense of playfulness. At some point, the world below seemed far away, and I turned to look back. I could see the Earth from a great distance now, a small, vibrant marble in the void, no bigger than a penny. I was in the cosmos, flying.

And that is when I got afraid. The sheer emptiness of space, the vastness of it all, was too much.

The moment I displayed an ounce of fear, I was back in my body, still holding my Xbox controller, as if nothing had happened.

The entire experience couldn't have lasted longer than two or three minutes, but in those moments, I was shown more than I had understood in years of searching.

I felt overwhelming gratitude. I had been shown the game of life itself, and, for the first time, I understood the pieces on the board. In transcendental terms, this is a moment of cosmic consciousness—the profound and sometimes terrifying realization that you are part of a larger, interconnected whole. It's the experience of witnessing your individual self, your consciousness, expand to encompass the entire universe. I was part of it all, I just did not know how to interpret it at the time.

"You Are Running Out of Time"

By now, I was fully aware that something was happening, and that whatever it was, it required my attention. About two weeks after my little trip into the cosmos, I kept sensing the being that had been visiting me my entire life.

Although the being had never caused me harm or done anything to frighten me, I still held some concern, and that was what made me pull back from my interactions with it. It respected my wishes, as always, but said, "You are running out of time."

I expected that it was going to visit me again; it always visited me again, no matter what. But that statement made me worry. "Running out of time for what?" So I immediately started to search and seek more than ever, haunted by the possibility that something bad was going to happen, and that I was going to somehow mess it up because I was running out of time.

About a week later, my visitor was back. "What did you mean, I'm 'running out of time'?" I asked immediately. The answer was just as cryptic as ever: "You need to remember."

After a lifetime of these mental conversations, I was tired of the riddles. I knew I had to pry. This led to a negotiation, right there in my mind.

"Okay, fine," I said. "I'm happy to remember. I want to. I am willing to receive whatever knowledge you have for me, and I'll do whatever is needed, as long as it serves a greater good." Then I laid out my conditions.

"You can't just throw me into the cosmos," I said, thinking back to my last little adventure. "Ripping me out of my body like that is not the way to go. All it does is scare me, and I'm so panicked that I don't understand any of it."

"You have to feed this information to me at a human pace," I continued, "in ways my human mind can actually understand. One by one, easy. I need to be able to handle it without having a complete panic attack. I also need reassurance that God—Source, the Creator, whatever one may call Him—is not going to be upset with me for this."

Once I had that reassurance, it felt like a line had been crossed. This was the point of no return.

Soon enough, I was guided on what to do. That night, I was in bed, and I finally took the leap. I invited "whoever" was there to see through my eyes, to experience the world through me.

That was when it happened! A big elephant, with big tusks and teeth that looked like those of a bunny or a rat—a big elephant-rat with lots of jewelry—was beaming at me. I had been raised Christian, but I was familiar enough with other cultures to know that this elephant was a deity in Hinduism. I remember thinking that my human body was nicer than being an elephant, to which this being in front of me was laughing heartily.

My elephant friend showed me a few quick images. Small ones. They resembled little portraits. Some were human, while others had an alien appearance. "You have been all of them," it told me. It also told me that my mission was just to observe. That was all.

But I believe the most important message sent to me was, "When you will all be harmless, the skies will open." I did not push for more; I understood. We humans can be violent, aggressive, and dangerous. It was a matter of us becoming safe to be around, and not the other way.

Soon after, other beings popped in. I did not see them; I just sensed that they were there. I felt a sense of joy, almost like a celebration. One of the silent thoughts that came to me was, "Welcome to New Earth." That was the sign that I had remembered. I was no longer running out of time.

I remember asking them, "Now what?" They said, "Now you ascend." I was told I could go whenever I wished, but I did not wish to go. I remember asking, "Don't you guys want to see what happens next?" to which I received a wave of feelings of approval.

I have come to understand that this moment of awakening is a powerful metaphysical experience. It is a shift in consciousness, subtle at first, like moving to a higher state of being. These energies were inviting me to leave behind my old, fear-based self and embrace a new, higher perspective.

What's even more interesting was that my visitor was part of that group, too. Yes, a darker being was part of the same group of light beings, and it was a darker being who brought me to the light. This inspired me to look into Oneness, a philosophy that suggests there is no separation between ourselves, others, and God. And from there, everything changed. But at the same time, nothing changed.

Soon enough, the changes became undeniably physical.

My body itself began to shift. It started to actively reject foods that no longer served it, leading to new symptoms and cravings. I eat mostly fruit and raw vegetables now. I'm not a vegetarian—I still love some good fried chicken—but I can only have it in small quantities, and rarely.

This diet change was happening alongside another, more profound physical process. For weeks, I'd been feeling strange, unexplained pressures and pulsing sensations deep in my head—sometimes in the back, sometimes right at my forehead.

That entire process, which eventually led to a moment during meditation where I felt something internally crack open inside my skull (like an eggshell), is a whole story in itself. It's the story of my pineal gland decalcifying and activating, and it's far too detailed to go into here. I will have to save the full story for another time.

The important part is that it *did* open. It left me with a new, permanent awareness—a "sense" that I can still feel pulsing whenever I meditate, like an internal compass helping me connect.

I started getting downloads and putting things together. All my searching couldn't compare with these moments of realization and the clarity that came with it. I'll be the first to acknowledge that I do not know everything; in fact, I know so little that I ask you not to look at me as if I can teach anything to anyone. It's all inside—and the more I go inside, the more I find. The more I find, the more I realize how little I know.

I do not have the whole story. I merely have the first few pages. But this is how I started meditating, and these are all the things that led me to embracing this discipline of spirituality. For some, it may guide you into science; for others, into religion. It's all good, as long as you follow it.

The thing about staying silent is that it feels safe, but that's an illusion. It's the kind of safety that comes from not being found out. But in all honesty, if your song remains unsung, if your tale remains untold, you are invisible—and if you are invisible, you don't acknowledge your own existence. How can you think that you are safe if you can't be who you truly are?

As I write these pages, I am having a massive fight with myself. A war rages in my mind about whether these pages should ever see the light of day. I know that if the people in my life read a fraction of what is in these pages, they will look at me as if I have lost my mind.

Keeping my mouth shut was what gave me this life—the good job, the respectable façade, all the trinkets I've accumulated over the years. I suspect you have similar concerns, and I do not blame you.

I have spent my entire life without a voice, but in that state, I found no safety; I was simply invisible.

Invisibility, I've come to realize, is not the goal. It is an escape. I don't want this life to end without me having a chance to tell my story. The more time that passes, the more I realize that I have to tell the world what actually happened to me. Whether they hear it or not is no longer my concern. I must speak. My voice must be heard by me, first and foremost.

My journey, filled with these wild, inexplicable phenomena—from the UFOs and prescient church bells to Christ in my room and bruises that defied logic—has been a long lesson in validating my own reality. It has taught me that my truths are just as valid as any scientific investigation or religious text.

This is the heart of it all: the freedom that comes from choosing authenticity over social approval. The labels they might throw at me—crazy, lunatic, superstitious—are nothing compared to the self-violence of living a lie. By writing this—by sharing my story—I am no longer afraid of a label. My fear of what others might think has finally lost its power to silence me. In this act of writing, I am reclaiming my voice, not just for the world to hear, but for myself.

Chapter 12: Looking Back

Be Kind. To all. To everything. Be kind to strangers and to those who caused pain. Kindness ripples.

—Messages from The Unseen

Since I can remember, I have had a passion for deeper meanings and the Unseen—for the sacred, for God, the universe, signs, and the occult. My thirst also extended to books about those who came before us, people who shouted truth into the Earth and hoped it would stick.

This innate knowledge that "there's more" has always been with me, and I suspect it has been with many of us. Some of us are given signs, little nudges from the universe, telling us to wake up. We remain without a voice, perhaps uttering a few "me-toos" from the anonymity of our online personas. We smile as if we were in on a secret when we recognize a glimpse of our mutual world spoken aloud. Sometimes someone's story hits home with such force it leaves an echo in our chests, a resonance that vibrates against our ribs. But still, we keep our mouths shut.

Isn't it funny how badly we all want to fit in? We are told from early childhood to be like everyone else—or else. "Do you want to be a pariah? Do you want to die alone? What will the neighbors say?" So we learn to play the role, to stay in our lanes and preserve the magic in our hearts. We notice it all: the lies, the manipulation, the exploitation, the cold mantra of "it's not personal, it's business." Some of us are angry, others sad. And yet, the world never seems to mind, does it? The machine just keeps turning.

This never sat right with me. Even as a child, it all sounded phony, like it wasn't the whole story. The feeling was similar to that knowing you have as a kid that Santa is not real, but you play along with your parents because you'll get toys anyway. Something told me that we were only being shown a small part of a much larger picture. Surely there had to be more to life than this scripted play.

My quest for this "more" began with two of the most accessible systems I could find: religion and education. Ultimately, it didn't really matter which one I embraced. I soon realized they both did the same thing: They told me what to think. Neither offered any original thought, only recycled information from others.

Religion: The Old Soul and the Unseen

My grandma was an extraordinary woman. We spent summers at her modest home in the countryside, where her walls were adorned with woven tapestries and her bedsheets were always spotless white, smelling of sun and wind. She was a down-to-earth woman, and extremely knowledgeable. She had survived World War II, seen regimes change, and lost people she loved, but through it all she chose love and gained wisdom.

Every Sunday, my grandmother would wake us up and herd us to the village church. We'd sit through long, droning sermons, surrounded by the smell of old incense and damp wood, enduring a chorus of bad singing. At the end, we were all expected to kiss the priest's hand, and that ritual always irked me. Yes, even as a six-year-old, I was irked. What can I say? They said I was an old soul. Probably they were just trying to say that I had the demeanor of a cranky old lady.

"Why do I have to kiss his hand? It's hairy! And what if he doesn't wash his hands after peeing?" I asked the question out loud, in the church, in front of everyone, including the poor village priest, who burst into laughter.

After that day, I was no longer required to wake up on Sunday mornings for sermons, but I still had to attend on major holidays. The priest, perhaps out of amusement or mercy, would let me kiss the cross instead. Other people kissed the cross, too, so that was gross as well—thousands of lips on the same metal—but somehow, it still felt like a small victory.

My grandma, however, also had a different kind of faith. She had the knowledge of cures and chants and rituals that were not of the church. She could read fortunes in game cards and in the dark grounds left in coffee cups, and she would do it all openly. I remember watching her gaze into the porcelain cup, tracing the shapes of the sediment, seeing stories of travel, money, or conflict in the sludge. People from the village would come to her. Some had ailments she would treat with herbal remedies, others had worries that needed reassurance, and some simply wanted to know if they would find love soon.

Even as a kid, I perceived a divide between the official religion and the spirit realm. Somehow, in my mind, they did not mix. Although they should have, they didn't. It was always the magic—the cards, the herbs, the intuition—and not the guilt, shame, and feelings of unworthiness that drew me in.

Orthodox Christianity, as it was presented to me, seemed to be built on a foundation of fear, not love. The focus was on our inherent unworthiness, on judgment rather than compassion. Worse, the entire system felt like it was selling access to God—treating the divine as a commodity that could only be reached through their specific rules, rituals, and gatekeepers. This idea that God's grace could be bought, or that I needed an intermediary to translate my prayers, felt fundamentally wrong.

Any genuine, personal connection to the divine, any experience that didn't fit the approved dogma, was immediately labeled as madness, possession, or a lie.

This heavy-handed judgment felt especially hollow when contrasted with the well-known hypocrisy and corruption within the institution itself. It became clear that if I was going to find a God of love, I wouldn't find it within the strict walls of dogma, guilt, and fear. My connection would have to be found outside of all that, free from judgment.

Humanity has built a faith in its own flawed image—a faith that blames God's will for slavery, rape, war, selfishness, and starvation. Despite the fact that we have been killing each other over our faiths for centuries, it was never God's will; it was just us, justifying our behavior.

It took me years, many years, to learn how to find truth in the scriptures, to distinguish what might have been God's word and what was man's attempt to manipulate. I needed to learn what Jesus said, not just what people said about Jesus. This search for truth took me through the Bible, the teachings of Buddha, the Ascended Masters, and more. But that was a long time in the future—a different place and a different version of me.

For now, when the majority of these events were unfolding, I was barely consuming information, trying to make it all make sense in my head. And boy, did I feel like I was being lied to. I did not appreciate it.

What followed was a transcendental and philosophical "salad." Year after year, I grew older and more voracious in my consumption of text: multiple religions, the history of religions, mythology, the Greek gods, the Maya, the Native Americans, paganism. Whatever piece of text fell into my hands, I devoured it.

By the time I was seventeen, I had declared myself an atheist. None of it made sense. Some of it sounded plain evil, and the Pope was getting fatter and richer while the poor were getting sicker and skinnier. I got kicked out of religion class for being too combative with the priest-teacher, calling a bunch of churchgoers morons and the priesthood a bunch of charlatans in ugly dresses and poorly made hats. I was angry, and I wanted to expose the lies. But no one cared to hear me. No one listened.

So I decided I was an atheist—albeit one who was too angry with God to actually be an atheist. Then, one day, a quote from a skinny old man with funny clothing made me want to take a closer look: "Oh, but I like your Christ. It is Christians that I do not like. Christians are so unlike Christ."

Gandhi's toothless smile appears in my mind's eye next to the quote. The truth in what he said was undeniable. I was measuring Christ by the behavior of Christians. What if I was wrong? What if I wasn't supposed to be mad at God and Christ, but at people? I would ultimately find out that my mistake had been to confuse God and Christ with Christianity, churches, and priests. They are absolutely not the same thing.

I focus on Eastern Orthodox Christianity because it was the first religion I was introduced to and raised in it. It feels more honest to reflect on the faith I was exposed to firsthand, rather than to debate faiths to which I had no exposure.

But what if it's all the same? What if God or Allah or Jehovah or Source or whatever other names we choose don't matter, and we've been fighting over nothing? We all describe the same experiences, or very similar ones. We all pray for the same things. We all want love, safety, and peace. Regular people always want these things. And here and there, we ask the heavens for some help. We're not that different from each other, despite our many differences.

The other night, I was watching the Netflix movie *The Two Popes*. This biographical drama imagines intimate conversations between Pope Benedict XVI and Cardinal Jorge Mario Bergoglio. One chilling sequence flashes back to Argentina under military dictatorship, where priests who spoke out were kidnapped or "disappeared." These gruesome images underscore the price some paid for resisting a brutal regime.

Watching that made me wonder what drives humanity to such extremes. Despite our advances—cars, AI, Netflix subscriptions—we remain as violent and greedy as ever. Technology has enhanced our comfort, but it hasn't changed our nature. We still have dictatorships, slavery, and war. Man never ceases to seek and find new ways to destroy his fellow man.

This violence makes sense when you remember that, before civilization and money, we were apex predators. We conquered the animal kingdom and reshaped the planet in our image. The constructs we built—societies, governments, religions, money—are inventions we've collectively agreed on. The natural world is the only reality that predates us, yet we've distanced ourselves from it with screens and food delivery services.

Aren't you bored of scrolling through Netflix, only to find some second-hand show that you absently start watching just to stop after ten minutes? Instead, go outside. Sit in the sun. Breathe. Close your eyes and feel the wind on your skin. That is true joy and contentment. What we really seek is this stillness. When the mind stills, we can listen—and we can hear God. We can hear God in the rustle of leaves and the warmth of sunlight.

So step into nature. Let the sun see you. And if you're a dreamer like me, wave at it when no one's watching. You'll get your vitamin D, and you'll discover something you never thought was there.

It took me years to come to a simple conclusion: It doesn't matter what I call myself—Christian or Buddhist, "spiritual but not religious," or atheist. If I go inside, I will find love, peace, and serenity. I will find comfort when I am sad and safety when I am uncertain.

Angels, God, Ascended Masters—we gave them names, and, in the naming, we made the mistake of thinking our version was the only correct one. We went to war over our choice of names. What if God never wanted us to name Him, exactly for this reason? What if He knew that naming Him would bring division among us? What if all He ever wanted was for us to love life? In my moments of meditation, the message is always a variation of this truth.

There are many ways to say this, but a lot of us have forgotten to love life, with all its gifts and blessings. They get drowned in the loud noise of making money and voting and being angry on social media. But if we stop, if we let the distractions fall to the side, we see the blessings are right there. They have been right there all along. They are in the little things: the feel of the wind on our skin, the warmth of the sun on our cheeks, and the sweet, juicy taste of a piece of fruit.

When was the last time you actually enjoyed the food you ate—genuinely tasted it? If you do not know the answer, please, right now, take a piece of fruit, stop everything you're doing, and just taste it. Don't think, don't look at the time, don't run any checklists in your head. Empty your mind completely. Expect nothing. Pretend you do not even know what that fruit is. Close your eyes and take a bite.

What does the bite feel like? The texture? The juicy sweetness piquing your senses? The pleasure of chewing it? Don't try to define it or name it. Just experience it as if it were completely new to you. Focus on it, and feel the pleasure that piece of fruit brings you. If you focus on your senses with all your awareness, you will see for yourself what a true blessing life is. Somewhere, in this space of complete, immersed presence, you will find God

.

Then stop and think how uncomplicated it all was. It was just a piece of fruit, created by the earth for your enjoyment. It's in this simplicity that you start *being* instead of *doing*. Do you see God now? Do you see all the things that had to happen in order for this piece of fruit to get to you—the biology, the environment, the design of this cycle meant to keep you alive?

Once you start seeing the design itself, you will find the designer giggling at you as if you were playing a cute game of hide and seek.

Education: The System and the Lie

I was a bookworm. I loved studying, I loved learning. I still do. And above everything else, my ego loved having the right answers. I was a straight-A student with an attitude. For some reason, I was always combative. Challenging authority was a hobby of mine, and the more I challenged, the more backlash I got.

Soon enough, I was labeled a "difficult kid." I was a great student, but too combative for my teachers' tastes. Whether I really was difficult or not, I still do not know, but for sure I was an angry kid. And here's the thing with anger: It doesn't always come in the form of shouts and slammed doors; sometimes it comes as silence.

I grew up to be an angry adult—angry at the world, at the lies, and at the social constructs that seemed fueled by exploitation. I was angry at those around me for repeating the same tired nonsense—that my perception of my world was somehow wrong, but theirs was right.

For a while, I thought of my fellow humans as sleepwalkers, calmly following their paths without one asking questions about the system sucking the life out of us all.

My anger was, of course, misplaced. It fed my ego. I had this notion that my anger was a shout for justice, that I could see a reality those around me were blind to. But I was wrong. Many were awake; they just were not speaking up. Could I really blame them for something I, myself, was doing?

In my fight for what I perceived as justice, I honed the skill of choosing the right words to cause pain. And I did cause pain, most often to the people I loved most. It doesn't really matter how right you are, or how entitled you are to feel how you feel. Ultimately, what matters most is how you make people feel.

Education teaches us how to be good little pawns on a chess board we do not see. It tells us we are free to do as we please. If we study hard, we will be given a shiny piece of paper that will make our life like the lives on TV. But they don't tell you that to be a successful CEO, you often have to exploit others. They don't tell you that your lavish future house will come with a mortgage that will shackle you with debt.

Ultimately, they beat down into you the same mantra religion does: don't question, don't think, don't seek. Just be like everyone else.

Going to school is the first step that teaches you to stop living in your own world, at your own pace, and join in with the crowd. Now, this togetherness has its benefits. We cannot live in isolation. It is the lack of questioning that is the problem.

A bunch of people sit at a table and decide what you should be taught. They teach you complicated math that you will forget as soon as you pass the test. They teach you history, which tells you it's okay to kill each other because your ancestors did. "History is written by the victors," they say, and that should terrify us. The victims are never given a voice.

They teach you national pride as if it were real, when in fact it's often just a justification for sending young men to fight and die in wars so a handful of people can gain more money and power.

They teach you to wake up early, rush to eat breakfast, and then go sit in a place where you are told what to be for six to eight hours a day. And they tell you that you are free!

There is not one lesson, not one class, about being kind or loving. There's not a word about expressing ideas, however controversial, in a way that might threaten a system that does not wish to be disturbed.

I'm not saying education is bad. In many cases, it is the beginning of questioning. But our systems are tired. Look at all the highly educated people struggling to make ends meet. Look at how we're only rewarded for our knowledge if it serves society's one god: money.

I wish more children were told how beautiful they are, how marvelous their thirst for life is. I wish they knew how their joy makes the world a better place—how the love they show to tiny animals should guide them for the rest of their life, because kindness is what will turn them into heroes. Children are perfect when they arrive in this world, but then we shove them into classrooms and tell them to stop wondering, stop being in awe, stop being curious! We replace all that with homework and grades. We clip their wings.

There's more wisdom in the purity of a child's wonder than in the bitterness of a politician. Life should come first. Love should come first. We should teach that in schools.

When I finished high school, I decided to study psychology. By this time, I'd had plenty of mystical encounters. I'd faced the mysterious and had premonitions, and two Near-Death Experiences had left me with even more confusion. I stopped questioning the world around me, which all seemed to be in agreement. Instead, I started questioning myself. Was I mad? So I hit the books even harder.

As before, book after book helped me shove more text into my cortex, and yet I was none the wiser. What I knew helped me maintain good grades, but that was just me feeding my ego. The academic material itself was useless to me.

I remember this girl in one of our university classes. She asked a similar question to one of my silent ones: "What about the saints? The prophets? Is there anything on them? On how they could hear God?"

We were seated in the aula magna of the university, a cavernous hall filled with about 350 people. The moment she stopped speaking, a ripple of laughter started from the back and washed over the room. It wasn't a friendly chuckle; it was mocking, sharp, and dismissive.

It broke my heart—for her and for me. The professor showed no more kindness than our fellow students. He gave a retort in the form of, "Well, if they hear voices, they are hallucinating." With that, it was evident to me that it was unwise to raise these questions.

I did not try to learn what I so wanted to learn. Instead, I internalized the idea that the ego mattered more. It was important to fit in so I wouldn't be laughed at, ridiculed, and shunned like that poor girl who had just committed the sin of being braver than I was.

My peers looked up to me, and I could have stepped in and comforted her. It would have given her a bit of light. But I did nothing of the sort. I sat there quietly, watching my peers treating her unjustly. My ego won, as it had always won. I was a coward.

I regret that I never went to her to hug her, encourage her, and thank her for her bravery—that I never told her, "Me too! I too wonder about these things!"

I did none of those things. Instead, I kept my distance like everyone else, because I shrank from the possibility of being labeled as she was. I still think of her now, almost twenty years later. If this book ever finds her, and I pray it does, I want to tell her now: "Me too. I have been wondering about those things my entire life. Thank you for your bravery! You are braver than I am, and I am sorry that, by my inaction, I contributed to your pain."

We must let people ask questions. We cannot evolve if we're kept in boxes, if we're told what to think and believe.

Society: A Rigged Game

The thing with civilization is that it requires a big group of people to agree for it to be sustainable. If you fracture that group into multiple smaller groups, they will tend to disagree. Now, for practical reasons, we see how it is necessary for us to get along. The issue is that once a "generally agreed truth" is selected, all the other truths become moot. We learn to shun, ridicule, and attack everything that threatens the status quo. Before you know it, the generally agreed-upon truth is considered law.

In the late stages, this looks like reduced freedom of speech, institutions deciding which books to ban, and organizations hoarding wealth and knowledge. When push comes to shove, they'll burn a witch or two at the stake. Remember, they even persecuted Galileo.

And for truths that cannot be explained? Well, thank God we don't burn people in the public market anymore. We ridicule them instead. We make fun of them until the offenders are terrified of ever uttering a word again. In a climate like this, how is someone supposed to ask questions?

We have separated from nature, refused to listen to its call, and refused to commune with the very thing that keeps us alive. Because make no mistake—it's not our jobs and social status that keep us alive. Those things can be taken away in an instant. What keeps us alive is this gem of a planet.

What if we all agreed that we don't really know anything—that if we're honest with ourselves, the only objective constant is nature? Everything else is man-made.

What if we stopped judging? What if we all, collectively, agreed that we don't really know what's going on? Wouldn't that be better than trying to acquire more paper, more money, more wealth?

It is not laughing and ridicule that will get us out of this hole. It's the conviction that every human life matters. Every single animal matters. Every blade of grass.

God created this world, not us. It is not ours to twist into our own image. It's not ours to exploit. We are part of nature, and we are just along for the ride. We must preserve life. We must be kind to everything around us.

This is one of the messages I often get during my sessions: "Be Kind. To all. To everything. Be kind to strangers and to those who caused pain. Kindness ripples."

We've damaged our ecosystem for greed, so we can have more billions, more mansions, more stuff. We're all guilty. We're all responsible for fixing it. And in that shared responsibility, are we not one?

To the Skeptics, with Love

These words are for the people who, much like me, are hardly impressed. Fazed by nothing. They are the people who believe in nothing unless they, themselves, can both see it and explain it.

For my whole life, I've been afraid of you—so much so that I've pretended to be one of you, putting on a mask in an attempt to preserve a sense of normalcy. My fear of you came not from your skepticism, but from the aggressive rejection of knowledge that can be so intimidating. Most of us "weirdos" are the first to admit we don't know anything. Our experiences leave us with unresolved puzzles, not with solutions.

Your skepticism is needed and welcome because it allows us to open the stage for debate, for questioning, and for finding potential truths together. It's not the skepticism itself that's harmful. It's the disdain that many of you project onto us—the snark, the superior laughter. This is what we dread.

The world needs your skepticism. I remain intimidated by you, and I would be lying to say otherwise. I'm so intimidated that I'm not even sure if these pages will ever see the light of day. In a world where nobody believes in anything, your approval feels like a highly sought-after badge of honor.

But let's try a quick thought exercise. Imagine, just for a moment, that something truly unexplainable happened to you. What would you do? It's a difficult position to be in, isn't it? Would you feel comfortable announcing it to everyone, or would you be tempted to keep it secret? Is it not the most common human instinct to doubt our own senses before we doubt the "normal" reality that everyone else seems to agree on?

This is where skepticism becomes harmful: It forces people with stories into silence. And in silence, in the absence of debate, there is no progress.

The mask of the skeptic is a useful one. I've worn it my whole life, and it has served me well. But I realized that the "me" who benefited from the life I built was a censored, muted, watered-down version of my true self. The true me, the one with magic in her heart, was always kept silent and hidden.

I realized that silence only helps exploitation thrive, not freedom. Freedom can only be found in the authenticity of who we are. As long as we don't show ourselves to the world as we are, we don't truly exist. We're just a role we play.

So I ask you to please keep an open mind. When you hear us speak, when you see us act weird, just keep an open mind. Question our logic, question our perceptions—we welcome it. We actually want to answer these questions, and want your help in making sense of the things that keep us up at night. But, if you could, please leave the disdain at the door.

I'd like to invite you, dear skeptics, to get to know us a little bit. We're not all that different from you. We have the same pains, the same fears, the same wishes. Ultimately, all people want is peace, safety, and freedom. Everything else is just fluff. So I thank you for your skepticism. Let's work together.

The Quiet Truth

The thing about seeking is that the more you seek, the more lost you feel. For a long time, my search was less like a quest and more like a frenzy of voracious consumption. It was a mad scramble to fill my brain with as much information as possible: books on history, articles on quantum physics, documentaries about consciousness, scriptures from a dozen different faiths. I was a sponge, soaking it all up.

My cortex turned into a tangled mass of competing ideas and theories—a library of cognitive material that just sat there, sending thoughts at a dizzying speed. It was a kind of intellectual pride, a sense of having "mastered" a subject.

But what I came to realize is that what I was doing failed. I was just consuming and containing academic data. The books themselves weren't the answer. They were just fingers pointing at the sun.

The actual self-evident truth came when I finally put the books down—when I stopped trying so hard to find the logic outside myself and decided to just be still.

But how was I to do that? For me, it meant learning to still the torrent of my own mind. As I practiced this, as I allowed my own inner wisdom to surface, the scattered pieces I had been chasing finally began to align. The cacophony of a thousand different theories receded, leaving me with a simple, undeniable clarity.

I began to see the game for what it was—a social construct, a system of control, a role we're all so desperate to play. But I saw it from a different perspective. It was no longer a source of my anger or frustration, but a fascinating, intricate puzzle. The more I stayed open, the more truth I felt I was given, not from books, but through an expanding awareness within me.

My awareness began to see and feel more, to perceive connections that had always been there, but been hidden by the noise. Suddenly, I realized I was not alone. In that silence, I heard and felt a presence, a knowing.

I even started to feel as if I could anticipate events. This wasn't a superpower, and I certainly didn't feel superhuman. It was more like I was watching from a different vantage point, from the center of the storm. To some, this might look like prediction, but I personally think it was just good old plain common sense. At last.

Or maybe it wasn't even about prediction. It was about connection. I was simply becoming more aligned with my own inner world, with nature, and with the quiet flow of the universe itself.

This all led me to a significant lesson, one I found summed up in a single, powerful text: "Be still. And know that I am God."

To me, this means exactly what it says. Still your body, quiet your mind, and listen. It's a practice of surrender, of letting go of the need to have all the answers and trusting that everything you need to know is already within you. Chase nothing, expect nothing, and reject nothing. Just stay open and still.

For whatever reason, it works—for me, at least.

When I sit in meditation, it's only a matter of time before I feel loved. I feel held. All is well, and as it should be. In those moments, I can't help but smile and cry, my heart overflowing with a gratitude so immense it feels almost unbearable.

One message, above all others, seems to be present during my meditative states: "Value Life. Serve it. Embrace it. Love it." It is so clear, so pure. It is a command to love life with all its imperfections.

If we can do this, we won't need to kill one another for land or resources. We won't hurt and starve one another for profit, war, or pleasure. Cruelty ends where love starts. Power, as we have been taught to understand it, becomes unnecessary in the face of love.

And when no one is following a leader, there are no leaders to follow. What better things are there to follow than love and life, anyway? They are inside of each of us.

I hope that by sharing this, it gives you the courage to find and give expression to your own understandings, as well.

Before I Go...

This is my first time trying to write a book, and I am not a writer in the traditional sense. I don't have a practiced hand for spinning great tales, nor a formal education in the craft.

I'm just a person with memories that, in the depths of my heart, demanded to be told. I felt them stirring like a restless current, and I had to set them free. This book is the result of that surrender, a testament to an endeavor that is far from over.

It is a quest that took me forty years to truly start. There will be more to come, because this mission continues to unfold. As new events arise, maybe I will be here to share them.

Since the first word was written, something has shifted within me. I've found a bedrock of inner calm, an anchor I didn't know was missing. I've made changes in my life, found solace in the practice of meditation, and discovered a happiness I had long given up on.

I am now more grateful, more free, than I ever imagined I could be. But in the end, that is only my story. The true purpose of this first volume was to cast a light over my own brand of weirdness, to finally hold it up for the world to see it for what it is.

And here it is—all of it, out in the open, a collection of experiences and moments for everyone to read. I can tell you, now that the deed is done: The sky hasn't fallen. The world still spins on its axis. No disaster has come to pass.

As for you, I see you. I see your wisdom all over the internet, in the safety of private chat rooms, in the anonymous comments section of a meditation app. I hear the soft whisper of "me too" that echoes between us.

My hope in taking this step was never to gain your attention for myself. It was to turn your attention back to your own realities, to the moments you have held in secret. I know there are countless people out there who have had moments, encounters, and events they can't explain.

Perhaps you simply dismissed it as nonsense, like I did for so long. I spent a lifetime doing that, pretending those memories were nothing more than a trick of the mind. It can feel like safety, ignoring our own truth.

But what if you didn't ignore your inner reality anymore? What if, instead of pretending it never happened, you held that moment up for all to see? What if you invited curiosity and skepticism? What if you let truth breathe in the open air?

It is only through honest, vulnerable conversation that a collective understanding can be found. We have to be willing to look at these things, to talk about them, to share them with a community that can help us make sense of them.

My theories might be wrong, and half of them likely are. My own encounters might not be big enough to warrant further investigation. But that doesn't matter, in the grand scheme of things. My biggest question, the one that fills me with a sense of purpose, is this: What if *your* story is the next piece of the puzzle?

For so long, we've been searching for our tribe in the shadows, hoping to find a glimmer of ourselves in the quiet chambers of the internet. But what if the real way to build a community isn't in whispers, but in a collective roar? What if the real way to build a community is to simply leave undeniable, unerasable evidence of our time on Earth?

I urge you now, with every fiber of my being, to create. Write books. Compose songs. Paint the feelings in your heart onto a canvas. Record podcasts. Whatever your medium, whatever your voice, use it. Put your story out there in a way that feels true to you. Because soon, there will be enough of us that we can no longer be laughed into silence. We will no longer be dismissed. We will simply *be*.

I often wonder what might have been different if a child like me had found just a little more openness in my environment. What if I had stumbled upon books or stories that mirrored my own unexplained world? It wouldn't have solved everything, but it would have eased so many worries from my young mind.

Just getting a glimpse into someone else's similar experience would have been a profound comfort. It would have made me feel less lonely and less weird. Perhaps that constant, nagging fear of ridicule would have felt a little less powerful, and I wouldn't have been so afraid to be myself.

Knowing I wasn't alone...that would have been a gift.

If you have faced the unexplained, know that you are not crazy. You are not alone. You are part of a group of people who have been dealing with the same worries, thoughts, and fears. Know that reaching out always brings you closer to others.

The specifics are irrelevant. Through diligent practice, one realizes these experiences are universal, not exclusive. The issue is the rigid conditioning we've received since our earliest years—a deliberate programming against inward focus that keeps most of us divorced from our own capacity. No person should ever have the right to silence his fellow man. We were all created equal, and we are all entitled to our voices. So use your voice. Words have power. Authenticity has power.

I can't tell you how much I look forward to reading your books and poems, marveling at your art, and swaying to the notes of your songs. I speak to you now, my fellow Quiet Ones. This book is nothing less than a love declaration to you all. You're why I wrote it! My inspiration was you. All of you.

It is with immense joy, pride, and gratitude that I now stand up and say out loud, "Yes, me too!" And so I ask you, now that my story is out there, fully and honestly: Why not give your story a voice?

What if, in our collective coming out, we can make a difference in someone else's life? What if we speak from our hearts with such honesty that the next generation won't have to hesitate to share what they know to be true? What if the very secrets we have been clinging to—the ones we have been told to hide—are the same secrets we are meant to unveil, to cast into the light?

What if the next child, teenager, or young adult won't have to worry alone? What if they find a plethora of books, videos, art, and podcasts that discuss the things they are experiencing?

Before you tell me there are already books and podcasts, let me tell you: There aren't enough. Nowhere near enough. In fact, these topics are still discussed with an acknowledgment of stigma, even in these very same podcasts. The stigma is often in the intro. It's as if even the podcaster is trying to protect themselves from looking crazy.

But what if we all spoke, every single one of us? What if we all stood up and said, "Me too?"

Imagine the relief these "strange" kids will feel when they realize they are not alone. That we are here. That we were always here. That others before us were always here. That these unexplainable things, as inexplicable as they are, are common and have happened since the dawn of humanity.

We must be a voice, for their sake, so that, when their time comes to make their voices heard, their voices will not tremble with the same fear that ours did.

Because they will know that they are not alone. They will know that we are here, and that we have always been here.

We were just **quiet all along.**

Bibliography

Abu-Izzeddin, Nejla M. *The Druze: A New Study of Their History, Faith and Society.* Leiden: Brill, 1984.

Alvarado, Carlos S. "Trends in the Study of Out-of-Body Experiences: An Overview of the 19th and 20th Centuries." *Journal of Scientific Exploration* 3, no. 1 (1989): 27–42.

Anka, Darryl. *Bashar: Blueprint for Change: A Message from Our Future.* New York: Pocket Books, 1990.

Augustine of Hippo. *The Literal Meaning of Genesis* (De Genesi ad litteram). Translated by John Hammond Taylor. Ancient Christian Writers 41. New York: Newman Press, 1982.

Bandura, Albert. *Social Learning Theory*. Englewood Cliffs, NJ: Prentice Hall, 1977.

Barker, J. C. "Premonitions of the Aberfan Disaster." *Journal of the Society for Psychical Research* 44, no. 734 (1967): 169–181.

Barker, J. C. *The Premonitions Bureau*. London: The Bodley Head, 1967.

Bem, Daryl J. "Feeling the Future: Experimental Evidence for Anomalous Retroactive Influences on Cognition and Affect." *Journal of Personality and Social Psychology* 100, no. 3 (2011): 407–425.

Birrell, Anne M. *Chinese Mythology: An Introduction*. Baltimore: Johns Hopkins University Press, 1993.

Blanke, Olaf, and Sandra Arzy. "The Out-of-Body Experience: Disturbance of Body Schema or Higher-Order Self Processing at the Temporoparietal Junction." In *The Neu-*

robiology of the Self in Psychiatric Disorders. Cambridge: Cambridge University Press, 2011.

Blanke, Olaf, et al. "Stimulating Illusory Own-Body Perceptions." *Nature* 419 (2002): 269–270.

Bown, Fiona. *The Medium Is the Message: Contemporary Mediumship in Popular Culture*. London: Routledge, 2021.

The Boy Who Lived Before. Documentary. United Kingdom: Channel 5, 2006.

Brown, Roger, and James Kulik. "Flashbulb Memories." *Journal of Experimental Psychology: General* 106, no. 1 (1977): 73–97.

Campbell, Joseph. *The Hero with a Thousand Faces*. Novato, CA: New World Library, 2008.

Collins, Francis S. *The Language of God: A Scientist Presents Evidence for Belief*. New York: Free Press, 2006.

Crossley-Holland, Kevin. *The Norse Myths*. New York: Pantheon Books, 1980.

DeCasper, Anthony J., and Melanie J. Spence. "Prenatal Maternal Speech Influences Newborns' Perception of Speech Sounds." *Infant Behavior and Development* 9, no. 2 (1986): 133–150.

Descartes, René. *Meditations on First Philosophy*. 1641.

Dunne, J. W. *An Experiment with Time*. London: A. & C. Black, 1927.

Einstein, Albert, Boris Podolsky, and Nathan Rosen. "Can Quantum-Mechanical Description of Physical Reality Be Considered Complete?" *Physical Review* 47, no. 10 (1935): 777–80.

Flew, Antony, and Roy Abraham Varghese. *There Is a God: How the World's Most Notorious Atheist Changed His Mind*. New York: HarperOne, 2007.

Green, Celia. *Out-of-the-Body Experiences*. London: Hamish Hamilton, 1968.

Greyson, Bruce. *After: A Doctor Explores What Near-Death Experiences Reveal about Life and Beyond*. New York: St. Martin's Press, 2021.

Greyson, Bruce. "The Near-Death Experience Scale: Construction, Reliability, and Validity." *Journal of Nervous and Mental Disease* 171, no. 6 (1983): 369–375.

Hamilton, Edith. *Mythology: Timeless Tales of Gods and Heroes*. New York: Little, Brown and Company, 1942.

Hayne, Harlene. "Infant Memory Development: Implications for Childhood Amnesia." *Developmental Review* 24, no. 1 (2004): 33–73.

Hepper, Peter G. "Fetal Memory: Does It Exist? What Does It Do?" *Acta Paediatrica* 85 (1996): 16 20.

Hicks, Esther, and Jerry Hicks. *Ask and It Is Given: Learning to Manifest Your Desires*. Carlsbad, CA: Hay House, 2004.

Homer. *The Odyssey*.

Jung, C. G. *Aion: Researches into the Phenomenology of the Self*. Collected Works of C.G. Jung, Vol. 9, Part 2. Translated by R. F. C. Hull. Princeton, NJ: Princeton University Press, 1959.

Jung, C. G. *The Archetypes and the Collective Unconscious*. Collected Works of C.G. Jung, Vol. 9, Part 1. Translated by R. F. C. Hull. Princeton, NJ: Princeton University Press, 1 969.

Jung, C. G. *Memories, Dreams, Reflections*. New York: Vintage Books, 1961.

Kant, Immanuel. *Critique of Pure Reason*. 1781.

Klass, Dennis, Phyllis R. Silverman, and Steven L. Nickman, eds. *Continuing Bonds: New Understandings of Grief*. Washington, D.C.: Taylor & Francis, 1996.

Knight, J. Z. *Ramtha: The White Book*. Yelm, WA: JZK Publishing, 1999.

Kramrisch, Stella. *The Presence of Shiva*. Princeton, NJ: Princeton University Press, 1981.

Kübler-Ross, Elisabeth. *On Death and Dying: What the Dying Have to Teach Us About Living*. New York: Macmillan, 1969.

LaBerge, Stephen. *Exploring the World of Lucid Dreaming*. New York: Ballantine Books, 1990.

Leibniz, Gottfried Wilhelm. *Monadology*. 1714.

Leininger, Bruce, and Andrea Leininger. *Soul Survivor: The Reincarnation of a World War II Fighter Pilot*. New York: Grand Central Publishing, 2009.

Levenson, Jon D. *Resurrection and the Restoration of Israel: The Ultimate Victory of the God of Life*. New Haven: Yale University Press, 2008.

Long, Jeffrey, and Paul Perry. *Evidence of the Afterlife: The Science of Near-Death Experiences*. New York: HarperOne, 2010.

Montessori, Maria. *The Absorbent Mind*. New York: Henry Holt and Co., 1995.

Moody, Raymond A. *Life After Life: The Investigation of a Phenomenon—Survival of Bodily Death*. New York: HarperOne, 2001 (orig. 1975).

Moody, Raymond A., and Paul Perry. *The Light Beyond*. New York: Bantam Books, 1988.

Morse, Melvin, et al. "Near-Death Experiences: A Neurophysiological Explanatory Model." *Journal of Near-Death Studies* 6, no. 2 (1986): 79–90.

Newberg, Andrew, and Eugene D'Aquili. *Why God Won't Go Away: Brain Science and the Biology of Belief.* New York: Ballantine Books, 2001.

Noyes, Russell, Jr. "The Second Catastrophe: A Study in the Psychology of Survival." *Psychiatry* 40, no. 1 (1977): 61–68.

Origen. *On First Principles* (De Principiis). c. 220–230 AD.

Ovid. *Metamorphoses*.

Parnia, Sam, et al. "AWAreness during REsuscitation – II: A multi-center study of consciousness and awareness in cardiac arrest." *Resuscitation* 191 (2023).

Persinger, Michael A. *Neuropsychological Bases of God Beliefs*. New York: Praeger, 1987.

Piaget, Jean. *The Origins of Intelligence in Children*. New York: International Universities Press, 1952.

Piaget, Jean, and Bärbel Inhelder. *The Psychology of the Child*. New York: Basic Books, 1969.

Plato. *Meno*.

Plato. *Phaedo*.

Plato. *The Republic*.

Price, Neil S. *The Viking Way: Religion and War in Late Iron Age Scandinavia*. Uppsala: Uppsala University, 2002.

Radin, Dean. *Entangled Minds: Extrasensory Experiences in a Quantum Reality*. New York: Paraview Pocket Books, 2006.

Rahula, Walpola. *What the Buddha Taught*. New York: Grove Press, 1959.

Ramachandran, V. S., and Sandra Blakeslee. *Phantoms in the Brain: Probing the Mysteries of the Human Mind*. New York: William Morrow, 1998.

Rhine, J. B. *Extra-Sensory Perception*. Boston: Bruce Humphries, 1934.

Rovee-Collier, Carolyn. "The Development of Infant Memory." *Current Directions in Psychological Science* 8, no. 3 (1999): 80–85.

Rueckert, Carla L., Don Elkins, and Jim McCarty. *The Ra Contact: Teaching the Law of One*. Vol. 1. Louisville: L/L Research, 1984.

Rumi, Jalal al-Din. *The Rumi Collection*. Edited by Kabir Helminski. Boston: Shambhala, 1998.

Sabom, Michael. *Light and Death: One Doctor's Fascinating Account of Near-Death Experiences*. Grand Rapids: Zondervan, 1998.

Scholem, Gershom. *Major Trends in Jewish Mysticism*. New York: Schocken Books, 1941.

Scodel, Ruth. *Introduction to Greek Literature: From Homer to the Hellenistic Period*. New York: Cambridge University Press, 2010.

Silverstein, Shel. *Where the Sidewalk Ends*. New York: Harper & Row, 1974.

Smith, Jane I., and Yvonne Y. Haddad. *The Islamic Understanding of Death and Resurrection*. New York: Oxford University Press, 2002.

Stevenson, Ian. *Twenty Cases Suggestive of Reincarnation*. Charlottesville: University Press of Virginia, 1974.

Stevenson, Ian. *Where Reincarnation and Biology Intersect*. Westport, CT: Praeger, 1997.

Taylor, John H. *Death and the Afterlife in Ancient Egypt*. Chicago: University of Chicago Press, 2001.

Teresa of Avila. *The Interior Castle*. Translated by Mirabai Starr. New York: Riverhead Books, 2003.

The Bhagavad Gita.

The Bible.

The Gospel of Matthew.

The Pearl of Great Price.

The Qur'an.

The Tibetan Book of the Dead: The Great Liberation Through Hearing in the Bardo. Translated by Francesca Fremantle and Chögyam Trungpa. Boston: Shambhala, 2003.

The Zohar.

Tucker, Jim B. *Return to Life: Extraordinary Cases of Children Who Remember Past Lives*. New York: St. Martin's Press, 2013.

Van der Kolk, Bessel. *The Body Keeps the Score: Brain, Mind, and Body in the Healing of Trauma*. New York: Viking, 2014.

Van Lommel, Pim, et al. "Near-Death Experience in Survivors of Cardiac Arrest: A Prospective Study in the Netherlands." *The Lancet* 358, no. 9298 (2001): 2039–2045.

Vicente, Raul, et al. "Enhanced Interplay of Neuronal Coherence and Coupling in the Dying Human Brain." *Frontiers in Aging Neuroscience* 14 (2022).

Wallace, Alfred Russel. *Miracles and Modern Spiritualism*. London: James Burns, 1875.

Wente, Edward F. "Letters to the Living and the Dead." In *Letters from Ancient Egypt*. Atlanta: Scholars Press, 1990.

Zohar, Danah. *The Quantum Self: Human Nature and Consciousness Defined by the New Physics*. New York: William Morrow, 1990.

Acknowledgments

First and foremost, to **my mother**: You have been my number one cheerleader throughout my entire life. Thank you for supporting me in even my most unconventional endeavors. I simply would not be the human being I am today if not for you.

To **Erik**, for challenging me to write.

To my **life-long best friend, 1.20 Meters**—thank you for the endless patience you've shown in listening to my crazy stories. Your ear has meant the world to me.

About the Author

Julia Pax holds a master's degree in clinical psychology—a field she originally studied in hopes of finding logical explanations for the unexplainable events in her life. When the textbooks couldn't provide all the answers, she turned her focus to the creative world of marketing. Originally from Romania, she now lives in the United States, where she works as a project manager for a leading marketing agency.

For years, Julia kept her spiritual experiences hidden, fearing the stigma that often surrounds the unseen. She wrote *Quiet All Along* to break that silence, reclaim her authentic voice, and encourage others to explore their own mysteries without fear.

When she isn't seeking proof of the afterlife or managing corporate projects, Julia can be found gaming, painting, sipping tea, or relaxing at the beach. She loves animals, and shares her home with her partner and Guinness, a silver tabby rescue who stole her heart at first sight. She is currently documenting her ongoing journey as a "brand new spiritualist," combining her psychological background with her new reality.

www.ingramcontent.com/pod-product-compliance
Lightning Source LLC
LaVergne TN
LVHW100526110826
845146LV00002B/795

* 9 7 9 8 9 9 4 2 6 0 4 1 8 *